W9-ACB-604

The Challenge of Detracking:
A Collection

Edited by
James Bellanca
and
Elizabeth Swartz

IRI/Skylight Publishing, Inc.
Palatine, Illinois

The Challenge of Detracking: A Collection
First Printing

Published by IRI/Skylight Publishing, Inc.
200 E. Wood Street, Suite 274, Palatine, IL 60067
800-348-4474 or 708-991-6300
FAX 708-991-6420

Creative Director: Robin Fogarty
Editors: Erica Pochis, Liesl Banks-Stiegman, Julia E. Noblitt
Book Designers: Michael Melasi, Bruce Leckie
Type Compositor: Donna Ramirez
Production Coordinators: Amy Behrens, David Stockman

© 1993 IRI/Skylight Publishing, Inc.
All rights reserved.

Library of Congress Catalog Card Number: 93-79951
Printed in the United States of America.
ISBN 0-932935-50-8
0565-12-93

Table of Contents

The Challenge of Detracking: A Collection

When it comes to good and bad school practices, many educators and would-be reformers pray to the god of educational research. In practice, especially when the critical issue is tracking and ability grouping, more often than not, the research is ignored.

Since the start of the twentieth century, more than 700 research studies have examined the practice of slotting students by ability. In the overwhelming majority of those studies, respected educational researchers have documented the negative effects of tracking. Jeannie Oakes and Robert Slavin document the damage that tracking and ability grouping inflict on students. Jomills Henry Braddock highlights the role of tracking in trapping minority and low-income students in low tracks with little hope of escape. While reform lip service lauds educational equity, the realities of tracking practice go unchanged.

Why have only a few schools taken advantage of the research and abolished tracking, leveling, and ability grouping practices documented to be more harmful than helpful?

There are several possible reasons.

1. **The problem is systemic.** At the turn of the century, American schools were restructuring from the agricultural model, represented by the one-room school house, to the factory model of instruction. The factory model was constructed on the assumption that the school's role was to prepare as many students as possible to work in the emerging manufacturing plants of the early

twentieth century. Just as these new factories were designed for the most efficient handling of the most amount of products in the least amount of time, the schools were designed to handle the most number of students in a school year. Curricula were designed to prepare the students to work on the assembly line. For this, knowing how to read, write, and do math was most important. Civics was thrown into the curriculum to reassure politicians that the flood of immigrants who were crowding the new schools would be "good Americans." As the century progressed, the boxes of science, social science, and business education expanded the product line.

> **After the Great Sputnik scare in the late 1950s, pressure increased for schools to do more than offer the basics.**

After the Great Sputnik scare in the late 1950s, pressure increased for schools to do more than offer the basics. College preparation, the gifted child, and advanced placement courses were added as the most efficient means of refining the school products and guaranteeing that American brain power would dominate the global marketplace.

Rather than make essential changes in the factory model, educators elected to run the assembly lines faster and to expand the product line. Just as manufacturers with many product lines adjust the assembly line to slot and store new lines of goods, the schools also adjusted the assembly line to slot and store the different student types.

Different school "factories" experimented with different sorting models. Some opted for the efficiency of straight tracking. Using test scores, they placed all students with the same aggregate test scores in all subject areas into a single group. Once in this group, the students stayed together until they dropped out or graduated. Usually this school factory had three or four tracks or levels. This was tracking in the purest sense.

Other schools opted for more flexibility. Students who tested with uneven scores in different subjects were placed in groups that matched each score. Thus a student who scored high in math was placed in the high group for math and science. If the same student scored low in reading, he was placed in the low group for social studies, language arts, and all other courses. Once in a group, the student might work his way to a higher group if tests or teacher recommendation favored the move. This practice, more flexible than tracking, was called ability grouping.

For many years, the practices of tracking and ability grouping were restricted to high schools. In the 1980s, parallel with a call to return to the basics, the practices trickled down through junior highs, middle schools, and even as far as the primary grades. It is not unusual to see tests in the second and third grades used to sort students into "them that has" and "them that don't."

At first glance, it is easy to defend the tracking practices. Given the assumptions made at the turn of the century about learning and how schools ought best be organized to promote learning, the sorting system makes some sense. Tracking and ability grouping follow as night after day as the best way to go when the school metaphor is the assembly line. The practices are a logical part of a systemic model that views schooling through the lens of the factory.

2. **The problem is value based.** If an educator, parent, or researcher accepts the premises on which the factory model was built, then the sorting practices make sense. These premises value classification, the sorting of objects into categories based on observable and measurable data, as the most efficient way to organize the school. In the case of the school, those students with highest ability, as shown by their strong performance on standardized tests, ought to receive the best opportunities to acquire information. Those who perform poorest get a separate curriculum, slowed and lightened, so they can have an equal chance to succeed.

Because the best students often have a greater capacity to memorize the curricular information as measured by standardized tests, it is believed that they ought not be inhibited in their learning by those with less capacity to store and recall. By grouping students on the basis of measurable ability, fast with fast, slow with slow, and middlers with middlers, assembly line efficiency is supposed to provide the best chance for learning for each student.

When educators, parents, researchers, and educational leaders reject the factory model premise, they start with a different set of school values. They are more likely to believe that schools ought to be an environment that enables each individual to emerge as a unique, fully developed person. Rather than seeing the school as factory, they perceive it as an artist's studio. In this context, the sorting practices of tracking and ability grouping make no sense. Each student is a piece of work to be crafted and shaped. The teacher as artist takes the raw material and develops it to its capacity. Finished works are displayed and hailed for their special forms. Some are simple, others complex. Some students take a short time to emerge to full beauty; others take longer. There is no attempt to make any child fit into pre-formed molds. Instead, the teacher-artisan creates the environment and uses his or her talents to construct each work of art with its own special character.

> Each student is a piece of work to be drafted and shaped. The teacher as artist takes the raw material and develops it to its capacity.

Given the basic and different value beliefs inherent in each of the metaphors, advocates of each argue for different ways to improve schools. The factory group works to refine the efficiency and effectiveness of the assembly line sorting system; the studio group seeks to construct the classroom as a studio in which each work moves toward completion as a unique piece of art.

When the researchers debate the pluses and minuses of each approach, they often assume they are starting from the same beliefs and values. Their disagreements focus on the methods, not the values. As a result they are like two ships passing in the night. As long as the conflict continues at the method level, there is much question as to whether research, as accurate, reliable, or valid as it may be in any given study, can ever resolve the disagreements between the advocates of each approach. There will need to be a change in the understanding of learning and what parents and educators value most in the learning process.

3. **The problem is political.** In every school, there are parents who get involved and parents who avoid contact with schools. For the most part, the active parents are the high-achieving, successful mothers and fathers of the high-achieving, successful students. These parents are the most likely to volunteer as nursery school aides, run PTA bake sales, attend parent nights, call the principal, or fight for their child's placement with the best teacher. A few even win school board offices.

At the other end of the spectrum are the parents who stay away from the school. While their children are the most discussed in faculty conversations, these parents are the most likely to be condemned for failing to raise more responsible, more motivated students. As the discussions go, what more can be expected of students whose parents care so little? (In school parlance, uncaring parents are those who do not get involved as volunteers, attend parent nights, check homework, or answer phone calls.) Putting aside the judgments, the fact remains that those parents who do not get involved are the least likely to voice opinions about curriculum, apply pressure for class placement, complain about poor teaching, or make waves about schedules, book assessments, or bullies on the playground.

When it comes to the tracking issue, politically active parents have the edge. They can ensure that the school starts a gifted program and that their child gets placement in the right sections taught by the best teachers with the best resources. Because these parents have worked inside the school political power base, they are well positioned to ensure that threats to their child's program are fended aside. In the meantime, the less active parents have no say when their low-performing child is assigned the newest teacher's class, is relegated to the back row, sent to the principal for discipline purposes, or is taught the same watered-down math curriculum year after year. "If," starts every political argument, "those parents really cared . . . ."

Listening to the defenders of tracking and ability grouping, the arguments never sound systemic, value based, or political. They sound like, "You don't understand the distinction. We ability group, but we don't track. In ability grouping any student can switch at any time," or "The colleges require it. It is unfair to our students if we try to change the system," or "Competition is what this nation is about," or "Those kids would slow down my child. *My* child, after all, is a motivated learner."

Examine the defenses of tracking and ability grouping.

1. **The Distinction Defense.** In the years I taught in one of the nation's most prestigious public high schools, the principal made the "distinction" speech each September to the new teachers. In that high school, eighth grade standardized test scores were used to place all students into four ability groups or levels. If a student wanted a change, the policy was "show you earned it and ask." In practice, the student needed the signatures of a parent, a teacher, an advisor, and a dean. In any given year, one in five hundred students survived this bureaucratic gamut and made a successful level change. In theory, the policy allowed any student to change. In practice, once painted a color (each level had a color code "to avoid stigmas"), a student rarely changed that color.

Some of the non-movement may have been attributable to the curriculum. In both mathematics and English, the curriculum differentiation between the top and bottom groups was substantial in both quantity and quality. The slow pace and "easier" reading for the low group was "justified" because "these slow kids lack the basics" and "need easy work to feel successful." In a similar vein, the students in the basic tracks were assigned the most novice teachers and the most watered-down texts. To defend this system, it was argued that the top-track students required a challenge only the most skilled teachers and the toughest textbooks could provide. Any student who wished, we heard each year, had the chance to work hard and "move up."

Ironically, the students arrived at this lighthouse school already trapped in a level. Because the feeder schools practiced ability grouping, the students were predestined for a specific track. One feeder school initiated its grouping as early as the third grade. Using state test scores and teacher recommendations, the students were divided into three math groups at the end of their third year of formal schooling. Group one was slated to continue basic computation through the eighth grade; group two would be introduced to problem solving by grade six; and group three would move on a fast pace through problem solving into pre-algebra and geometry. By the seventh grade, the last group was starting the high school algebra program while the first group was redoing the basic computation it had not yet mastered. To cap the eight years, all of the students took the same entrance test for placement in the high school math ability groups. Given these differences in pace, content, and quality of instruction, is it any wonder that so few students ever even requested a change of ability groups after the first placement in the high school's levels? Theoretically, there was the opportunity for students to change levels. In practice, however, the system strangled any possibility of change. Why then was the distinction so forcefully argued year after year?

> Implicit in the college requirement defense is the notion that students who are slower learners or not perceived as "college material."

2. **The College Requirement.** This argument comes mostly from parents who have high aspirations for their offspring. They recognize that many college admissions officers require solid high school grades and test scores earned in a challenging curriculum. However, implicit in the college requirement defense is the notion that students who are slower learners or not perceived as "college material" are less motivated and will slow down the learning pace or cause teachers to water down the curriculum. If that occurs, the argument continues, the motivated

and bright students will suffer in the eyes of the college admissions officer. Either action might leave the "better" students unready to compete for college placement.

The college requirement argument is essentially political. It is also, as discussed above, systemic. Those who use this college defense ignore the low-expectation practices brought about through the early grade tracking that condemns low-track students to inferior instruction in a slow-paced and unchallenging curriculum. As long as the college-bound student gets the best the school has to offer, even if Peter is robbed to pay Paul, the tracking system is defensible.

> **The battles between elitism and equity are most glaring in metropolitan areas.**

The battles between elitism and equity are most glaring in metropolitan areas. In these large cities, tracking begins with set housing patterns that lock minority and low-income students out of suburbia's more resource-rich schools. Within these urban schools, the poorest students have the highest chance to be placed in the lowest remedial classes from the earliest years of school. In the suburban schools with the greater resources, the poor and the minority students have the greatest chance of being tracked at the bottom. As the primary grade tracking practices described above show, the low-tracked students have the least chance from the earliest school years of sharing the rich resources that will enable them to prepare for the college entrance tests or quality apprenticeship programs.

When we understand that the most powerful ally a young student has in surviving school "competition" is the wealth and education of the mother, it is even more disturbing to accept any argument that suggests all children get to compete on the same, level playing field. When a child is born to wealthy educated parents, the child has a good chance to go into the education game well coached. Once in the game, that child has the best chance for quality education. When born to poor and uneducated parents, the child will most likely lack the early childhood coaching that makes for high success in the game of school. The "ready for school" are tracked for success. The "not ready" are tracked for failure. This is competition?

The voices of the research in this collection tell us that tracking and ability grouping are practices of the past. Systemic change in school structures will require more than an abandonment of these outdated practices. The change will require a shift to new assumptions about learning without the factory assembly line and a committed desire to provide equity in every school for every child. Such changes will require understanding of which barriers are preventing the breakdown of the doors to the factory and a deep commitment to replacing those barriers with an open door to learning for each child.

In the four sections that follow, each article provides a different key. In Section 1, the authors identify the problems associated with tracking and ability grouping. Section 2 paints a more detailed portrait of the effects of tracking on students disadvantaged by poverty and racism. Section 3 invites you to understand that tracking not only harms the low-tracked student, but gives little substantive help to those it is most supposed to help, the gifted and talented child. Lastly, Section 4 suggests some new directions for organizing schools without tracks and ability groups.

In this collection of articles you will find effective tools for helping yourself, parents, and other educators see more clearly the need for a systemic overhaul of school organization that challenges every student equitably.

Tracking: A Systemic Barrier to Success for All Children

The controversial topic of tracking raises many questions. Tracking as an instructional practice began when schools were trying to provide the industrial society with a trained work force sorted by ability levels. In today's society, the sorting prevents many workers from developing minimal skills needed to survive in an increasingly complex system. In effect, the tracking system contributes to the growing numbers of citizens without the knowledge and skills to work.

If the goal of schools is to ensure that all children learn, why do schools retain a system that blocks segments of their student populations from success? Why do so many schools refuse to change the system if evidence shows practices such as cooperative learning, project-based learning, and integrated instruction enable all students from low-functioning to high-functioning to succeed?

The authors of this section pose critical questions about tracking, ability grouping, and the social beliefs that hold these practices in place. They set out to prove that tracking is not beneficial for all students, but rather it is a barrier to their educational success. Jeannie Oakes and Martin Lipton provide a brief background of tracking and explain how it is harmful for many students. They propose ways to "overcome the tracking barrier."

A further explanation of tracking is provided by Adria Steinberg who describes how this practice affects both low- and high-ability achievers. She uses research findings to suggest steps in the right direction, away from tracking. While it won't be a simple process, Steinberg is hopeful when she says, "perhaps it will be possible for students, parents, and teachers to unite behind the goal of making schools more engaging and intellectually stimulating—for all students."

Jeannie Oakes' two-part series completes this section and attempts to solve some essential dilemmas such as what is tracking, why are the effects of tracking so distressing, and why is tracking entrenched in school practice. Oakes offers "directions for change" such as promoting heterogeneity, restructuring the curriculum, altering classroom instruction, and changing commonly held beliefs and assumptions.

Tracking and Ability Grouping: A Structural Barrier to Access and Achievement

by Jeannie Oakes and Martin Lipton

Why, in the light of all the research evidence that tracking is harmful to students in the lower tracks and that high achievers can function well in heterogeneous groups, is the practice so widespread and entrenched in our schools?

Since the 1920s American schools have organized curriculum and instruction by dividing students into ability-grouped classes and curriculum tracks. Since then educators have debated, off and on, whether these practices are necessary and effective, or harmful and discriminatory.

By now, empirical evidence, court decisions, and reform proposals suggest that tracking and rigid ability grouping are generally ineffective, and for many children, harmful. (Reviews by Good and Marshall 1984; Esposito 1973; Findlay and Bryan 1970; Noland 1985; Oakes 1987; Persell 1977; Rosenbaum 1980; Slavin 1986. For court decisions, see, for example *Hobson* v. *Hanson* 1967; *Pennsylvania Association of Retarded Children* v. *Commonwealth of Pennsylvania* 1971; *Mills* v. *Board of Education* 1972; *Dillon* v. *South Carolina Dept. of Education* 1986. For examples of reform proposals, see, for example, Adler 1981; Berman

> Empirical evidence, court decisions, and reform proposals suggest that tracking and rigid ability grouping are generally ineffective, and for many children, harmful.

From *Access to Knowledge*, p. 187–204. Copyright © 1990 by College Entrance Examination Board, New York. Reprinted with permission.

1985; National Commission on Excellence in Education 1983; Achievement Council 1985; Powell, Farrar, and Cohen 1985; Goodlad 1984.) For younger children identified as "low" or "average" ability, and older ones who are not seen as college material, tracked curricula and ability-grouped classes often work against their high achievement. Moreover, though students of all races, classes and genders are publicly identified as low- or average-ability, it is poor, black, and Hispanic children who are disproportionately assigned to these categories.

It is increasingly clear that children are consistently and systematically disadvantaged by a practice that is widely and firmly embedded in school traditions and culture. Consequently, the search for appropriate alternatives to tracking—just beginning to take place in many school districts—is, and will continue to be, fraught with difficulties. Altering tracking practices will not come quickly or easily.

In this paper we explore grouping and tracking from a contextual perspective, arguing that tracking is embedded in a schooling context and a societal context that together help us understand why tracking works to the disadvantage of most students, and why it persists in schools anyway. This contextual view holds that tracking is not as much a response to significant differences among children when they are very young as it is an ongoing contribution to differences as children grow older. (For a fuller explication of the contextual perspective, see Oakes 1987.) At the core of these two cultural contexts we find a fuller appreciation of what school reformers may be up against if they try, as more and more are doing, to change tracking practices without attending to the strongly held assumptions and firm traditions that underlie tracking.

The schooling context includes the day-to-day policies and practices within schools themselves that interact with tracking. The societal context includes the larger society surrounding American schools, that is, the beliefs, values, and circumstances that promoted tracking in the first place and that may continue to shape current practice. This societal context suggests why tracking, and not some other approach, was adopted and persists as the way we organize schools. Despite the intransigence of tracking that these contexts imply, we believe that schools can change, and we offer some suggestions about how constructive change can occur.

PRACTICES, ARGUMENTS, EVIDENCE: A BRIEF REVIEW OF TRACKING

What Is Tracking?

Typically, when schools group students by their "ability," they divide them into separate classes for high, average, and low achievers, and, in high school, into classes for those who are headed for college or for jobs directly after high school. Elementary, middle, and senior high schools divide academic subjects (usually English, mathematics, science, and social studies) into classes at different ability "levels." Most often senior high students in the vocational or general (noncollege) tracks will be in one of the lower levels. Similar overlaps exist for college-bound students and high-ability tracks. But grouping also varies from school to school—in the number of subjects that are tracked, in the number of levels provided, and in the ways placement decisions about students are made.

> Elective subjects, such as art and home economics, often become low-track classes because college preparatory students rarely have time to take them.

Grouping practices also become confounded by "master schedules," which sometimes generate even more tracking than schools intend. Elective subjects, such as art and home economics, often become low-track classes because college preparatory students rarely have time to take them; non-tracked, required classes—health and drivers' education—sometimes become so when students' other classes keep them together for most or all of the day. For example, if students in the remedial reading class move en mass to the next (supposedly) untracked social studies class, social studies becomes a low-track class whether intended to be or not. For similar reasons, one drivers' education class we know of was filled largely with "gifted" students.

Four Conventional Arguments

Those who put forth the usual arguments about tracking admit to some inequity and some unintended administrative glitches associated with its practice. Typically, they are concerned educators, and they work hard to make tracking fairer. But they still contend that *most* children are served best by tracking. They frequently cite extreme cases—and fears—at the prospect of alternatives to tracking. Here, as an important backdrop to what follows, we would like to allay some of those fears. Nowhere will we suggest that calculus be taught to children regardless of their prior math experiences, or that *some* children shouldn't study calculus until all children are ready. Nor would we argue that all children who feel like it should be granted a place in the school's performance jazz band. And we would never suggest that children who need extra or special help should not receive it.

> Tracking often appears to retard the academic progress of children identified as average or slow.

ARGUMENT 1   *Children learn best when they are with others who have similar abilities.*

Response: Tracking does not promote achievement for average- and low-ability children. Students *not* in top tracks (a group that in the early 1980s included about 62 percent of senior high school students) and children in low-ability classes suffer clear and consistent disadvantages from tracking. Tracking often appears to retard the academic progress of children identified as average or slow (see reviews mentioned above). Moreover, high school students in vocational tracks often do not get better jobs as a result of their school placements. Some studies have found that graduates of vocational programs may do about as well in the job market as high school dropouts

(Rubens 1975; Grasso and Shea 1979; Berg 1970; Berryman 1980; Stern et al. 1985).

Neither is tracking required to promote achievement for high-ability students. That tracking can and often does work well for the top students should be obvious. Certainly it is possible to create excellent classes in the midst of mediocre ones: Start by providing the best teachers, the most successful students, and, often, the smallest class size. Add special resources, a sense of superior academic "mission," perhaps a parent support group, and these top students will get the best education in town.

Might tracking yet be worthwhile even if advantages for the top 10 to 30 percent did result in a poorer education for all the rest? Some claim that top students need to be specially "groomed" to be our future scientists, business and government leaders. But what if we could have our cake and eat it too? What if, in addition to the considerable support found for the positive effects on the least-able students of membership in heterogeneous classrooms (Esposito 1973; Noland 1985; Persell 1977; Rosenbaum 1980; Slavin 1983; Slavin and Madden 1983), there was evidence to show that the top students do not necessarily need to learn less even when they are in mixed classes?

Such evidence exists. Many students suggest that high-ability students progress just as well in mixed-ability classes (see reviews by Esposito 1973; Noland 1985; see also Dar and Resh 1986). Further, when advantages to students in the high-ability tracks do accrue, they do not seem to be primarily related to the fact that the students are similar, but to the special curricular and instructional advantages high-ability groups are given. For example, controlled studies of students taking similar subjects in heterogeneous and homogeneous groups show that high-ability students (like other students) rarely benefit from these tracked settings (Esposito 1973; Kulik and Kulik 1983; Noland 1985). Moreover, studies of students learning in small, heterogeneous, cooperative classroom groups provide additional evidence that the achievement of high-ability students actually can be enhanced in heterogeneous settings (Slavin 1983; Webb 1982).

ARGUMENT 2   *Slow or less capable children suffer emotional and educational damage when taught with brighter peers.*

Response: Tracking does not enhance the feelings of slower children. Many times the opposite is true. Rather than helping children feel more comfortable about themselves, being in the low track can foster poor self-esteem, lowered aspirations, and negative attitudes toward school. Some studies conclude that tracking leads low-track children to school misbehavior and eventually to dropping out altogether (Rosenbaum 1980).

ARGUMENT 3   *Tracking greatly eases the teaching task and is the best way to manage student differences.*

Response: This assumption pales in importance when we look at tracking's general ineffectiveness and disproportionate harm to poorer and racial minority students. Even if we could set aside these ethical concerns, and even if we could determine which of the subtle differences among children were truly important for assigning students to tracks, tracking would make sense only if it resulted in truly homogeneous groups. In fact, it doesn't (Oakes 1985).

Within tracks children's differences in learning speed, learning style, interest, effort, and aptitude for various tasks is always great. Often tracking simply makes the fact that instruction for any group of 20 to 35 people requires considerable variety in instructional strategies, tasks, materials, feedback and guidance, and multiple criteria for success and rewards. Unfortunately, tracking deflects attention from these instructional realities. When instruction fails, the problem is too often attributed to the child or perhaps to a "wrong placement." The fact that tracking may make teaching easier for some teachers who prefer to teach as *if* their students were very similar does not mean that any group of children—high, average, or low—will benefit most from that type instruction.

ARGUMENT 4   *Tracking is fair and accurate.*

Response: Tracking *prejudges* how much children will benefit and results in some children being denied the opportunity for academically and socially valued subjects. For example, nearly all children can learn from quality literature; nearly all can learn a second language; and nearly all can benefit from studying the important concepts of algebra. Some will learn more, some less. But tracking serves to exclude many children from ever being in classes where these "high-status" subjects are taught. Furthermore, when errors in judgment are made, they are more likely to underestimate what children can in fact do.

> Younger children who are initially similar in background and achievement become increasingly different in achievement and hopes for the future when they are placed in different tracks.

Fairness is also an issue when we consider well-established links between track placements and student-background characteristics. Poor and racial minority youngsters (principally black and Hispanic) are disproportionately placed in tracks for low-ability or noncollege-bound students; further, minority students are consistently left out of programs for the gifted and talented. Blacks and Hispanics are more frequently enrolled in vocational programs that train for the lowest-level occupations (e.g., building maintenance, commercial sewing, and institutional care). On the other hand, vocational opportunities for white children from wealthier families are more highly valued by society (e.g., accounting, computers, business, law).[1]

Track placements are often based on published, standardized tests. Fundamental concerns with measures of ability are discussed in detail in the chapters in this volume by Asa Hilliard and Kenneth Sirotnik. Here we simply point out the great potential for unfairness with these measures. Those differences that are easily tested and documented may not be the most important.

All the following and more may influence judgments about early track placements and even some in senior high school: social indicators of "maturity"; momentary concerns of "good and bad days"; month of birth that may determine if a child is the youngest or oldest in the group being tested; physical development influencing personal appearance, height, and handwriting; parental interest or influence; specific testing irrelevancies such as when a child's poor reading ability influences his or her math placement; changing schools and being "out of sync" with the new school's curriculum; and so on. However, differences among classes in the different racks are far from subtle. Slight and irrelevant differences at the time of placement can have large consequences in the quality of education children receive.

Over the years of schooling, tracking can exaggerate earlier differences among students (Gamoran 1986). For example, younger children who are initially similar in background and achievement become *increasingly* different in achievement and hopes for the future when they are placed in different tracks. This effect seems to accumulate until, in high school, the differences between students are quite pronounced. One reason for this is that track placements tend to be fixed. Most students placed in low-ability groups in elementary school will continue in these tracks in middle schools and junior highs; in senior high these students are placed in noncollege-preparatory tracks. What is astonishing is how this near-guarantee that children will fall farther behind is so consistently thought of as an opportunity to "catch up."

Certainly, there are notable exceptions. Many teachers know of children who catch on, get inspired, or, by sheer grit, pull themselves out of low-ability classes and succeed in higher classes. But, sadly, these exceptions may occur in spite of track placement, not because of it. For the most part, the evidence suggests that tracking's effects run counter to what school practitioners intend—helping all children learn. To better understand why this situation prevails and why it is so hard to change, we must examine both the school context in which tracking operates and the societal context that places powerful expectations on schools.

THE SCHOOLING CONTEXT OF TRACKING: DAY-TO-DAY PRACTICES

The schooling context of tracking includes conditions and events in schools and classrooms that interact with tracking, suggesting, first, how the tracking system influences the organization of curriculum and instruction generally, and, second, how membership in a particular track influences the experiences and accomplishments of students.

The schooling context of tracking is very complex,[2] including relationships among students' background characteristics, the particular tracking system the school employs, students' track placements, their school and classroom experiences, their responses to those experiences, their cognitive and affective outcomes, and their subsequent track placements. Essentially, tracking involves cycles of interacting policies, practices, and student responses.

The Structure of Opportunity and Accomplishments

School policies determine three structural qualities of the tracking system: *extensiveness* (the number of subjects tracked and the type of distinct curricula offered); *specificity* (the number of track levels offered); and *flexibility* (whether students move from one track to another). Policies also govern how students are classified and placed. Placement criteria (e.g., cut-off scores on standardized tests, prerequisite course requirements, and considerations of students' aspirations) may differ from place to place. Other placement policies determine whether students stay together at a particular level for classes in several subjects ("block scheduling") or are placed separately for each class.

All these policies work together to influence students' access to knowledge at both the school and classroom level. For example, at the school level, we need to look at what classes are available and what, generally, children are expected to learn. Schools that emphasize their vocational or general track are less likely to offer as many advanced courses in science, mathematics, and foreign language as schools with extensive college-preparatory programs. Teacher-assignment policies may influence the quality of instruction. Curriculum guidelines, textbook adoptions, formal decisions (subject departments) and informal decisions (expectations, socializing of new teachers), for example, help establish what knowledge and learning experiences are deemed suitable for particular children.

> Students placed in low-ability classes are usually denied the knowledge that would allow them to move into higher classes.

Depending on the class "level," students will have access to considerably different types of knowledge and have opportunities to develop quite different intellectual skills. Children in high-ability classes, for example, are more likely to be exposed to the topics and skills that will assist them in preparing for college. Critical thinking and problem-solving skills emerge from the high quality of their course content.,

Low-ability classes are taught different knowledge and rarely expected to learn the same skills. Prominent in "low" English classes, for example, are basic reading skills, taught mostly by workbooks, kits, and easy-to-read stories. Learning tasks often require memorizing and repeating answers to the teacher. Critical thinking and problem solving, if they are considerations at all, are more likely taught from a "program" of problem sequences that are unconnected to high-interest, engaging, real-world problems. Since so much of importance is omitted from their curriculum, students placed in low-ability classes are usually denied the knowledge that would allow them to move into higher classes or be successful if they got there.

After considering what courses and knowledge are available, and to whom, we must continue with an equally critical examination of the quality of the teaching and class time different children receive. Teachers in high-ability classes more often encourage independent, questioning, and critical thinking. Children there tend to spend more time on learning activities, and less time on discipline, socializing, and class routines. Children are expected to spend more time doing homework. Their teachers tend to be more enthusiastic, and they make lessons clearer. Teachers in higher classes use strong criticism or ridicule less frequently than teachers of low-ability classes where teachers are often seen as less concerned and more punitive. In high-ability classrooms tasks are often better organized and the children are given a greater variety of things to do, whereas teachers in low-ability classes are more concerned about getting children to follow directions, be on time, and sit quietly.

> **In high-ability classrooms tasks are often better organized and the children are given a greater variety of things to do.**

These differences in learning opportunities portray significant schooling inequities, not to mention schooling's greatest irony: those children who need more time to learn appear to get less; those who have the most difficulty succeeding have fewer of the best teachers; those who could benefit from classrooms with the richest intellectual resources (successful classmates, enriched curricula, etc.) get the poorest.

Although directly influenced by policy, students' responses to schooling are important to the schooling context. These relationships are dynamic and interactive; that is, they are produced as teachers and students respond to one another and to other circumstances in their schools. Understanding tracking simply as a series of inputs, mediating variables, and outcomes is insufficient, and disentangling causes and effects over the long-term may prove impossible. Tracking as a contextual process is likely to spiral. At any point in time, a particular element (placement, student characteristics, classroom experiences, effort, achievement) may be an input, mediator, or outcome; a cause or an effect.

Because track placements begin early (some suggest with assignments to first-grade reading groups), it is likely that these interactive processes cycle repeatedly during a student's schooling experience, not identically, but with successive cycles building on the effects of the previous interactions and effects. Small differences at any one point add up over time. The impact is likely to be cumulative, in a particular direction, and metaphorically, to gather momentum. When the evidence about tracking effects is placed in this cumulative contextual perspective, it becomes apparent how the schooling context structures tracking's long-term effects on student outcomes.

Initial (perhaps relatively small) aptitude differences among students are exacerbated by elementary tracking policies, resulting student placements and experiences, attendant attitudes, interests, and expectations, in elementary school. By middle school or junior high, track placement is more or less crystallized. The process cycles throughout secondary school, with the differences between students growing dramatically wider.

THE SOCIETAL CONTEXT: GOALS, HISTORY AND VALUES

So far we have considered schools and their tracking systems in relative isolation, as if they are untouched by a larger societal context. Tracking also exists within a set of historical circumstances and values that provided the basis for its institution in American secondary schools, and within a current social milieu of norms and expectations about what schools ought to accomplish. If we are to understand why schools track, this context also requires scrutiny. Here we offer additional background to the question of why, in the face of negative effects, tracking continues to make sense to academics, practitioners, parents, and even children themselves.

Tracking as a Means to Achieve Schooling Goals

Both in the past and today tracking policies have been inextricably linked with the most fundamental goals of schooling. For example, the common school probably best represented nineteenth-century curriculum policy. It directed schools to provide universal, publicly supported, common primary school education. This, of course, was intended to form the basis for a literate citizenry—one that shared a set of values and was well-enough informed to participate in democratic decision making.

With the complexity and expansion of universal education came two fundamental interests of school policymakers: first, a child-centered concern required schools to organize curricula to "educate" large, diverse groups of students; and second, a society-centered concern required that schools provide society with politically socialized citizens and human capital. While emphasis on these two goals has ebbed and flowed, policymakers have increasingly attempted to meet both by providing "appropriate" differentiated curricula and separate classes within a *comprehensive* (as distinct from *common*) school: curriculum tracks; ability-grouped classes within subject areas; special programs for the learning-disabled, educational disadvantaged, language minorities, gifted and talented; and the development of courses directed toward having students pass standardized exams for special diplomas or college credit (e.g., New York's Regent's level classes, Advanced Placement, and, perhaps most recently, International Baccalaureate).

Tracking as a Solution to Turn-of-the-Century Problems
Turn-of-the-century problems were responded to with prevailing beliefs, fears, and prejudices, as well as a faith that technological answers could be found to most problems. Schools were no exception. The technology of testing, the factory model of efficiency, the reliance on grades for evaluation, the specialization of "subjects," and the nagging fear that there just weren't enough resources (really good education) to go around characterized the tenor of educational policy. This history helps clarify many of the schooling practices we see today and at least one very central belief that has guided schooling throughout this century: the belief that we best serve children and society when we identify *differences* between children and act on our theories of why the differences exist.

After a long debate about how to educate an increasingly diverse student population for diverse purposes, educators settled on a newly coined view of democracy that defined "opportunity" as the chance to prepare for largely predetermined and certainly different life outcomes. Facing problems they were ill-prepared to solve, schools settled on educational solutions that accommodated prevailing beliefs about racial and ethnic group differences, adopted emerging notions about intelligence, and embraced new theories about managing organizations efficiently. Concurrently, two phenomena supported different schooling for different children: standardized tests and scientific management.

The Influence of Testing. Standardized tests provided a seemingly scientific and meritocratic basis for supporting process in schools. Standardized, psychological testing, founded on principles of individual differences, helped institutionalize beliefs about race and class differences in intellectual abilities. Early testing was designed to support the view that some children's intellectual, moral, and even biological differences were vast and immutable.

Scientific Management. The other development that made sense out of treating children differently was the philosophy of scientific management. Following the principles of scientific management, separating and exaggerating differences made more sense than valuing diversity for the contributions it could make. Time-and-motion studies, organizational centralization with authority concentrated at the top, prescriptions for preferred methods, and so on were touted as the only ways to bring order and efficiency to the apparent disarray of schools. Since the model for efficiency was the well-run factory, children were increasingly seen as "raw materials" out of which would be fashioned the "product"—productive adults. The apex of scientific management was manifest in the assembly line. One line might turn out Fords—to be sure, all running well and doing what Fords should do—and another line would turn out Lincolns—clearly a superior product.[3]

Today's Legacy

Many educators and parents still tend to think that differences in intellectual aptitude and prospects for school performance are profound and, for all practical purposes, unchangeable. Many, too, still link performance differences with biological or cultural influences, with race, or with social class. Most believe that children are so different in ability they cannot be educated within a common schooling experience. Also firmly entrenched is the view that separate school experiences are needed to prepare and certify students for their appropriate roles as adults in the workplace.

The process depicted here suggests that a school's student-body characteristics, assumptions about the educational implications of race and class differences, and prevailing beliefs about secondary schooling's purpose to prepare and certify students for their adult roles in the workplace interact to shape tracking at different types of schools. Schools thus seem to design tracking structures that make sense given the characteristics of student populations and prevailing beliefs about what programs are appropriate for those students.

This process is consistent with some recent evidence documenting systematic differences between schools serving different groups. For example, the greater the percentage of racial minority students, the larger the low-track program; the poorer the students, the less rigorous the college-preparatory program. (See, for example, California State Department of Education 1986). Further, High School and Beyond data show that schools serving predominantly poor and minority populations offer fewer advanced and more remedial courses in academic subjects, and that they have smaller academic tracks and larger vocational programs (National Center for Educational Statistics 1985; Rock et al. 1985).

Of course, minority students and those of low socioeconomic status are, on the average, lower in achievement by the time they reach secondary school, and schools respond to those differences with programs they see as educationally appropriate. But "appropriate schooling" in this case—lower-track and vocational programs—is most often detrimental to these students. Placement in these programs continues a cycle of restricted opportunities, diminished outcomes, and exacerbated differences between low-track students and their counterparts in higher tracks. These placements do not appear either to overcome students' academic deficiencies or to provide them access to high-quality learning opportunities.

Despite this evidence, tracking persists. Furthermore, the tradition of responding to student differences by separation rather than inclusion is so strong that it has followed schools out to the suburbs. There, largely homogeneous populations of white, middle-class children are also subjected to quite needless differences in the quality of their education.

> When a group of the lowest-achieving and most poorly behaved students are together in classrooms, their performance is far below what it might be under other circumstances.

IMPLICATIONS OF A CONTEXTUAL PERSPECTIVE

We have noted so far that the schooling context of tracking consists of a complex set of relationships between structures and events within schools, and these relationships have long-term cognitive and affective consequences for students. We have also asserted that the societal context of tracking—the historically grounded assumptions and shared norms for responding to student diversity—shapes the content and processes of tracking.

The schooling and societal contexts also help explain why practitioners have an ambivalent response to empirical findings on tracking. First, practitioners almost universally recognize and lament the negative consequences of tracking for students in low-track classes; most teachers and administrators have had discouragingly unsuccessful experiences trying to make these programs work. Many suspect that when a group of the lowest-achieving and most poorly behaved students are together in classrooms, their performance is far below what it might be under other circumstances. But practitioners' concerns about protecting the educational opportunities of the top-track students are even more salient. Research conclusions that able students are likely to continue to do well even if they are placed in heterogeneous groups are dissonant with practitioners' experiences. The schooling context of tracking offers clear school advantages to students in the top tracks, and findings that high-achieving students can learn equally well in mixed classes simply don't account for the noticeable, concrete advantages that practitioners, students, and parents can see in high-track classes.

That the effects of tracking occur over many years may contribute to practitioners' and other school observers' "blindness" to those effects. Decisions at any one moment—especially in the early grades—may seem slight and even offer some short-range benefits or relief. The well-intended motives and some actual successes of remediation, for example, often obscure missed elements of mainstream course work. Not until the next school year will child, parent, and teacher have to come to grips with the even wider gulf between what the child and his or her classmates know. The answer is usually more remediation or, eventually, easier or different courses.

> Perhaps the most striking difference between students lies in the speed with which they master skills taught sequentially.

Moreover, the societal context also affects the degree to which practitioners can contemplate change. Definitions of "individual differences" and of what different students "need" are social as well as educational. Students who are identified as less able are more often those who are less advantaged socially and economically. What they need is not seen to be the same abstract knowledge and skills that are suited to their "more able" peers. What they need is more often thought to be functional literacy skills and good deportment that will provide them entry into the lower levels of the work force. Given these *socially influenced* definitions, practitioners are not easily persuaded that a largely common curriculum taught mostly in heterogeneous groups is a promising approach to educating diverse groups of students. Further, alterations in school practice must pass social as well as educational tests. Certifying some for entrance into colleges and universities and preparing others with functional skills and acceptable workplace behaviors are what society expects from its schools. Even if practitioners were convinced of the educational value of "detracking" schools, the tracked curriculum is well suited to certifying students for different futures.

OVERCOMING THE TRACKING BARRIER

Disappointing findings about tracking (and even promising evidence about heterogeneous grouping) should not lead anyone to believe that simply mixing students together will solve the problems of tracking. Tracking is a response to school and social contexts, and because of its central position in the schooling structure, it helps perpetuate those contexts. Exploration of the contexts *and* the alternatives to tracking cannot be separated—so large must be the changes and so sustained the efforts. Schools without tracking will require curriculum and teaching strategies quite different from those now in many schools. In many cases the needed changes are revolutionary.

Mixed-Ability Schooling: A Promising Direction

Creating mixed-ability schools that work for all students is a radical proposition. To be effective these schools will demand fundamental changes in nearly every aspect of teaching and learning. It simply is not possible, for example, to teach diverse groups of students effectively when the curriculum is largely skill-based and rigidly sequential. Perhaps the most striking difference between students lies in the speed with which they master skills taught sequentially. Some students will race ahead; others will lag behind. Quicker students often must be kept busy with make-work; reteaching others becomes a chore; being retaught (and often retaught again) becomes a humiliation, particularly when others are waiting.

The curriculum well suited to mixed-ability schools is of a very different nature. It is organized around central concepts and themes—the "big idea" of a subject area. Mastering these ideas is important, challenging, complex, related to real life, and, most of all, rich with meaning. Indeed it stretches the sense-making of *all* children. Students acquire skills as they become ready within a common conceptual framework. If, on the other hand, conceptual learning is crowded out by rote memorization of facts, trivial assignments, or concerns such as deportment or neatness, then those students who can do more challenging work won't, and those who can't, won't learn how.

In addition to a reconstructed curriculum, mixed-ability schooling requires dramatically altered instructional practice. In tracked schools, classroom teaching typically consists of children of the same age engaged in competitive, whole-group instruction: lecturing, common assignments, uniform due dates and tests, and a single set of standards of competence and criteria for grades. Students in mixed-ability schools, however, benefit by being clustered in small groups exchanging ideas, sometimes working on separate but interrelated tasks, and generally helping each other learn. Teacher talk cannot dominate here; neither can large sessions of question and answer. Teachers function more like orchestra conductors than lecturers; getting things started and keeping them moving along; providing information and pointing to resources; coordinating the diverse but harmonious buzz of activity taking place.[4]

> Successful mixed-ability schools require the belief that all students can and will learn nearly all of what society truly values in an education.

These descriptions are not an attempt to outline a preconceived curriculum suitable for a nontracked, mixed-ability school. Rather, they represent a glimpse of what might be imagined and what occurs in rare and special school moments even today. But a reconstruction of school organization, curriculum, and classroom instruction that can nurture successful mixed-ability classes is a mind-boggling proposition.

More Gradual Approaches

Gradually altering tracking policies is no trivial matter either, regardless of how slowly change might take place. Gradual change may be directed at altering current practices, even while maintaining some tracking: for example, by using low-track classes (e.g., general mathematics) as "prep" courses for successful participation in high-track classes (e.g., algebra); by increasing the mainstreaming of both slow and gifted students; by reducing the number of track levels in academic subjects; by eliminating tracking in some subjects or grades; by team teaching; by ensuring racial and ethnic balances in classes at all track levels; or by blurring the distinction between vocational and academic programs of study. Even these changes require far more than simply tinkering or fine-tuning current practice; these changes require fundamental structural and behavioral changes.

Changing Assumptions: The Bottom Line

These suggested changes largely involve alterations in technological pedagogy. None is easy. Yet it is even more difficult to alter the assumptions about children, learning, and the purposes of schooling on which pedagogy is based. Successful mixed-ability schools require the belief that all students can and will learn nearly all of what society truly values in an education. There are no easy answers or packaged staff-development programs ready to cure tracking problems, or, more accurately, the school and societal problems reflected in tracking. Changing tracking will require more than the commonly accepted strategies for improving schools, that is, conducting needs assessments, developing a one- or two-year plan, or buying the services of a respected staff-development consultant. Instead, these efforts must include extensive school- and district-based data collection about tracking practices, critical reflection on and extended dialogue about the values and assumptions that underlie tracking and teaching, and generous experimentation with organization and teaching.

Practitioners and their communities, informed by research knowledge, must themselves investigate how long-standing traditions, school and district guidelines, standards of common practice, and beliefs about students' abilities and limitations are reflected in their school's tracking system. They must take on the challenge of understanding the nature and power of their school and social contexts. Such democratic, educational endeavors surely will be worth the extraordinary effort they require.

NOTES

1. The evidence of the variation between students within tracked classes has been well documented for decades. See, for example, Goodlad, 1960.

2. The reader should note that this discussion does not represent a model in a strict predictive or causal sense. Rather, it suggests frameworks for better understanding logical and empirically supported interrelationships. Many of these links, moreover, are supported by correlational research and qualitative studies of schools and classrooms. For a review of this research, see Oakes 1987.

3. Fortunately this history has been richly detailed in many fine studies. See, for example, Callahan 1962; Cohen and Lazerson 1972; Gould 1981; Kliebard 1979; Lazerson 1971.

4. See, for example, the vast literature on the effectiveness of cooperative small-group learning strategies, e. g., Slavin 1983. Also note theoretical perspectives on the importance of classroom organization for ability suggested by Cohen 1986; and Rosenholtz and Simpson 1984.

SELECTED REFERENCES

Achievement Council. (1985). *Excellence for whom?* San Francisco: Achievement Council.

Adler, M. (1981). *The paiedia proposal: An educational manifesto.* New York: Macmillan.

Alexander, K., A., Cook, M., and McDill, E. L. (1978). Curriculum tracking and educational stratification: Some further evidence. *American Sociological Review* 43, 47–66.

Berg, I. 1970. *Education and jobs: The great training robbery.* Boston: Beacon Press.

Berman, P. (1985). The next step: The Minnesota plan. *Phi Delta Kappan* 67, 188–193.

Berryman, S. E. (1980). *Vocational education and the work establishment of youth: Equity and effectiveness.* Santa Monica, CA: The Rand Corporation.

California State Department of Education. (1986). *California high school curriculum study: Paths through high school.* Sacramento: California State Department of Education.

Callahan, R. E. (1962). *Education and the cult of efficiency.* Chicago: University of Chicago Press.

Cohen, D. A., & Lazerson, M. K. (1972). Education and the corporate order. *Socialist Revolution* 2, 53.

Cohen, E. G. (1986). On the sociology of the classroom. In J. Hannaway and M. E. Lockeed, eds., *The contributions of the social sciences to educational policy and practice: 1965–1985,* 127–152. Berkeley, CA: McCutchan.

Dar, Y., & Resh, N. (1986). Classroom intellectual composition and academic achievement. *American Educational Research Journal* 23, 357–374.

Dillon v. *South Carolina Department of Education*, (1986).

Esposito, D. (1973). Homogeneous and heterogeneous ability grouping: Principal findings and implications for evaluating and designing more effective educational environments. *Review of Educational Research* 43, 163–179.

Findlay, W. G., & Bryan, M. M. (1970). *Ability grouping: 1970 status, impact, and alternatives.* Athens, GA: University of Georgia, Center for Educational Improvement.

Gamoran, A. (1986). The stratification of high school learning opportunities. Paper presented at the annual meeting of the American Education Research Association, San Francisco.

Goldman, E. (1952). *Rendezvous with destiny.* New York: Random House.

Good, T. L., & Marshall, S. (1984). Do students learn more in heterogeneous or homogeneous groups? In *The Social Context of Instruction*, edited by P. P. Peterson, L. C. Wilkinson, and M. T. Hallinan, 15–28. New York: Academic Press.

Goodlad, J. I. (1960). Classroom organization. In *Encyclopedia of Educational Research*, edited by C. Harris, 221–226. Third edition. New York: Macmillan.

Goodlad, J. I. (1984). *A place called school: Prospect for the future.* New York: McGraw-Hill.

Gould. S. J. (1981). *The mismeasure of man.* New York: Norton.

Grasso, J., & Shea, J. (1979). *Vocational education and training: Impact on youth.* Berkeley, CA: Carnegie Council on Policy Studies in Higher Education.

Hobson v. *Hanson*, 269 F. Supp. 401, (1967).

Kliebard, H. M. (1979). The drive for curriculum change in the United States, 1890–1958. *Curriculum Studies* 11, 191–202.

Kulik, C. C., & Kulik, J. A. (1982). Effects of ability grouping on secondary school students: A meta-analysis of evaluation findings. *American Educational Research Journal* 19, 415–428.

Lazerson, M. (1971). *The origins of the urban school.* Cambridge, MA: Harvard University Press.

Mills v. *Board of Education*, 348 F. Supp. 866, (1972).

National Center for Educational Statistics. (1985). *Analysis of course offerings and enrollments as related to school characteristics.* Washington, D.C.: U. S. Government Printing Office.

National Commission on Excellence in Education. (1983). *A nation at risk.* Washington, D.C.: U. S. Government Printing Office.

Noland, T. K. (1985). The effects of ability grouping: A meta-analysis of research findings. Ph.D. dissertation, University of Colorado, Boulder.

Oakes, J. (1985). *Keeping track: How schools structure inequality*. New Haven: Yale University Press.

Oakes, J. (1987). Tracking in secondary schools: A contextual perspective. *Educational Psychologist* 22, 129–153.

Pennsylvania Association of Retarded Children (PARC) v. *Commonwealth of Pennsylvania*, 334 F. Supp. 1257 (1971) and 343 F. Supp. 279, (1972).

Persell, C. J. (1977). *Education and inequality: The roots and results of stratification in America's schools*. New York: Free Press.

Pillsbury, W. B. (1921). Selection—an unnoticed function of education. *Scientific Monthly* 12, 71.

Powell, A. G., Farrar, E. & Cohen, D. I. (1985). *The shopping mall high school: Winners and losers in the educational marketplace*. Boston: Houghton Mifflin.

Rock, D. A., et al. (1985). *Study of excellence in high school education: Longitudinal study, 1980–82. Final report*. Princeton, NJ: Educational Testing Service.

Rosenbaum, J. E. (1980). Social implications of educational grouping. In *Review of Research in Education*, edited by D. C. Berliner, 8, 361–401. Washington, D. C.: American Educational Research Association.

Rosenholtz, S. J., & Simpson, C. (1984). The formation of ability conceptions: Developmental trend or social construction. *Review of Educational Research* 54, 31–63.

Rubens, B. (1975). Vocational education for all in high school? In *Work and the quality of life*, edited by J. O'Toole, 299–337. Cambridge, MA: MIT Press.

Slavin, R. E. (1983). *Cooperative learning*. New York: Longman.

Slavin, R. E. (1986). *Ability grouping and student achievement in elementary schools: A best evidence synthesis*. Report of the National Center for Effective Elementary Schools. Baltimore: Johns Hopkins University.

Slavin, R. E., and Madden, N. (1983). Mainstreaming students with mild handicaps: Academic and social outcomes. *Review of educational research* 53, 519–569.

Stern, D., et al. (1985). *One million hours a day: Vocational education in California public secondary schools*. Report to the California Policy Seminar. Berkeley: University of California School of Education.

Vanfossen, B. E., Jones, J. D., & Spade, J. Z. (1987). Curriculum tracking and status maintenance. *Sociology of education* 60, 104–122.

Webb, N. M. (1982). Group composition and group interaction and achievement in small groups. *Journal of Educational Psychology* 74, 475–484.

The Tracking Wars: Is Anyone Winning?

by Adria Steinberg

No issue in education touches off more intense feelings than whether, and to what extent, students should be grouped into different classes according to their abilities and probably futures. Although arguments about tracking go back at least 75 years, today the debate is more intense, and potentially more divisive, than at any time in our recent history.

One of the most disturbing aspects of the tracking issue is its potential to divide communities along racial and social class lines. In 1986, when Noward Roussell became the first African-American superintendent of the Selma, Alabama, schools, 90 percent of the white students and only 3 percent of the African-American students were in the top track. After he mandated that placement be based on stated criteria (grade point average and test scores), 10 percent of the black students became eligible for the highest track. The school board then decided not to renew Roussell's contract, a move that sparked protests from Selma's black community reminiscent of the civil rights struggles of the 1960s.

> One of the most disturbing aspects of the tracking issue is its potential to divide communities along racial and social class lines.

Similar—if less dramatic—scenarios are unfolding elsewhere. The curtain opens on a spokesperson citing accumulating evidence that racking harms those on the

From *The Harvard Education Letter*, May/June 1992 (Vol. VIII, No. 3, 1–4). Copyright President and Fellows of Harvard College. Reprinted with permission.

bottom. This is followed by cries of alarm from parents of high achievers, who want to protect their children from becoming the "sacrificial lambs" of what they see as a misdirected effort to place equity over excellence.

Teachers enter the act, concerned that they will once again be pawns in a political game—asked to teach ever more diverse groups of students without additional support. Researchers come on next, waving pages of evidence to show that tracking cannot be justified on educational grounds. Finally, a chorus of school officials offers the show-stopping line: "We don't have tracking in our school. All our classes are heterogeneous—except for the advanced placement and remedial ones."

DEFINITION SOUP

This vehement denial by school officials that their schools are tracked may seem like deliberate obfuscation, but in most cases the confusion probably arises from differences in the way the term is defined. Historically, "tracking" described the practice of offering different secondary school programs—with different requirements and courses—to students looking to different futures. When officials say the schools are not tracked, they usually mean that students are not placed—on the basis of test scores or grade point average—into all college preparatory or all vocational classes.

But most high schools do offer courses at a number of levels, from honors to remedial. And even when students are given a choice as to which level to take, recommendations from counselors and teachers have a major influence on where kids end up, as do the prerequisites for getting into particular courses. Furthermore, the schedule often creates de facto tracking—a student who takes practical math may end up in remedial English simply because it's all that is available at the time he has open.

Tracking is "any effort to organize a system that results in students who seem to be alike in ability being taught together, separated from others," suggests Jeannie Oakes, whose extensive research reveals both the prevalence and the harmful effects of such practices. By this definition it would be difficult indeed to find a high school in America that is not tracked.

TRACKED VS. UNTRACKED

Rather than dispelling myths and laying the foundation for a new policy consensus, the infusion of research evidence into the tracking debate often seems to exacerbate the tensions. An increasing number of policymakers appear to be persuaded that tracking, at least in its most rigid forms, should be eliminated. But this view is not shared by many of those most affected—students, parents, and teachers.

> The central argument in favor of tracking is that it allows teachers to give top groups the challenge and low groups the support they need to learn.

The central argument in favor of tracking is that it allows teachers to differentiate instruction appropriately and give top groups the challenge and low groups the support they need to learn. If this argument is valid, then a school that is tracked should evidence better overall achievement than one that is not.

The available evidence, according to Robert Slavin of Johns Hopkins University, fails to support this position. Searching for the "best evidence" about tracking in secondary schools, Slavin found 29 studies comparing tracked to untracked classes or schools. Because of today's paucity of untracked situations in secondary education, almost all of the studies were of grades 7-9 and dated from before 1970.

Overall, students in tracked and untracked situations showed comparable average achievement on standardized tests. Slavin found the effect of tracking to be essentially zero. Only five of the studies used random assignment of students to tracked or untracked classes. In all five the results favored heterogeneity, but the effects were very small.

HIGH VS. LOW GROUPS

Both those who favor and those who oppose tracking tend to cite more recent evidence that focuses on its *relative* impact on high-achieving and low-achieving groups of students. Unlike the earlier studies that compared tracked and untracked students, most studies since the early 1970s simply correlate students' track placements with their gains in achievement.

Drawing from large representative data sets like the High School and Beyond (HSB) longitudinal study, researchers rely on students' self-reports to divide them into tracks—usually delineated as "academic," "general," and "vocational." Attempting to control for IQ, scores on pretests, and socioeconomic status, researchers analyze the gains in achievement test scores of students in each of these tracks.

> **Being in the top track appears to accelerate achievement and being in the low track to reduce it.**

Although such surveys offer interesting data, a basic problem limits how much can be learned from them: students may not know their own track placement because their schools may offer each major subject at several levels, avoiding overall labels like "academic track" or "general track."

Despite the possibility that students' responses do not accurately reflect course-by-course sources of stratification, the survey data show a clear pattern of a widening gap between high and low achievers in secondary schools. According to this research, being in the top track appears to accelerate achievement and being in the low track to reduce it.

It is this finding, perhaps more than any other, that leads people to adopt particular postures in the debate. Many parents (usually middle class) see it as confirmation of the need for tracking. They want to protect the advantages their children have, or at least protect their children from suffering the disadvantages of being in a low group. Parents or advocates who speak for lower-track (and usually lower-income or minority) students reach the opposite conclusion—that tracking is harmful to children and should be eliminated.

The survey research says nothing about how high- or low-group students would fare in an untracked situation. It is possible, however, to draw some general guidance from the findings. As Adam Gamoran of the University of Wisconsin puts it: "Average achievement would be higher if all kids belonged to a program like the college track but lower if everyone's program were like those currently offered to the noncollege bound."

EXPLAINING THE GAP

The challenge is to figure out just what it is about the academic or college track that accelerates learning. Here, there are several strands of research that offer insight.

An obvious way in which academic and nonacademic tracks differ is in the kinds and number of courses that students take. In an analysis of the HSB data, Gamoran and Mark Berends concluded that the effects of track on achievement in math and science can be explained, at least in part, by the fact that kids in academic tracks take more courses in math and science, including more advanced courses.

In explaining why the average scores on some standardized achievement tests favor Catholic schools over public schools, James Coleman and others have confirmed the importance of course-taking patterns. It appears that a broader range of students in Catholic schools than in public schools take the more rigorous academic courses (See "Catholic Schools" in this issue.)

Another difference that bears investigation is the distribution of teachers among the tracks. Joan Talbert and Michele Ennis recently used HSB data to assess the prevalence of what they call "teacher tracking." They discovered that low-track students are taught largely by teachers assigned only to low-level classes. Talbert and Ennis concluded that students in low-track classes are likely to have teachers with a lower opinion of their own efficacy, lower status in the school, and fewer resources for professional growth.

Like many aspects of tracking, this one poses a chicken-egg problem. It is not clear whether inexperienced, ineffective teachers are assigned to teach low-track classes or whether the teachers assigned to these classes come to feel ineffective. Either way, there is a good chance that students who have the most difficulty in school are

being taught by teachers with the fewest resources—
personal or institutional—on which to draw.

This research raises an interesting question: If teachers were reassigned, could a school eliminate some of the
ills that have been attributed to tracking? Unfortunately,
this hypothesis would be very difficult to test. Tracking
almost always results in stratification of staff as well as
students. As critics of tracking are quick to point out, the
conditions of teaching and learning in low-track classes are
so bad that teachers with any clout try to avoid such
assignments. Furthermore, high-track students and their
parents are a very vocal group; they demand, and are likely
to get, the best.

HOW CLASSES DIFFER

Potentially, the most powerful explanation for the growing
achievement gap between high and low classes lies in what
actually goes on in the classroom. It is thus necessary to
look beyond the survey data—which provide virtually no
information on the quality of instruction—and review a
third strand of research: observations and case studies of
classrooms.

Such portraits offer a consistent view of how upper-
and lower-track classes differ. Jeannie Oakes and a number
of other researchers have documented that high-level
classes cover more complex material, at a faster pace, with
more on-task engagement than do low-level ones. This
difference in what Oakes calls "access to valued knowledge" explains why early judgments of low ability become
permanent assignments to lower tracks and limited
futures. Once a student is denied access, it is very difficult
ever to catch up.

Studies also reveal crucial differences in the kinds of
instruction offered in different tracks. Instruction in the
low tracks tends to be fragmented, often requiring students to memorize small bits of information and fill out
worksheets. Although many upper-track classes share
some of these traits, they are more likely to offer opportunities for discussion, writing, and other meaning-making
activities.

In a recent study, Gamoran, Berends, and Martin Nystrand attempted to quantify such differences. They found that students in low-achieving eighth-grade English classes were assigned fill-in-the-blank exercises five times as often and true-false or multiple choice questions four times as often as peers in high-track classes. On writing assignments, low groups were twice as likely as high groups to receive teacher comments about spelling and grammar and half as likely to get comments about content.

> **The high groups consistently engaged in more writing and discussion than the low groups.**

The researchers also identified dimensions for rating the quality of instructional discourse in high, low, and untracked eighth-grade English classes. Observers looked for evidence of (1) coherence (do teachers frame lessons in terms of previous ones? does today's classroom talk refer to yesterday's? do students discuss what they have read, write about it, discuss the essays, etc.?); (2) uptake (do teachers pick up on student responses, incorporating answers into subsequent questions?); and (3) authenticity (do teachers ask questions that build on student interests?).

They found that the high groups consistently engaged in more writing and discussion than the low groups, and experienced more uptake and more authentic questions from teachers. Among the heterogeneous classes, some more closely resembled the high groups, some the low.

In a follow-up study of 54 classes of ninth graders, Gamoran and Nystrand found a slightly different pattern. Although high-achieving classes devoted less time to seatwork and more time to question-and-answer, the large majority of questions in both types of classes called for conventional recitation; few were open-ended, or what the researchers termed authentic.

But analysis of these authentic questions revealed a difference between high- and low-track classes. In high-level classes, the focus was usually on ideas and issues embedded in literary texts the class had read. In contrast, questions in remedial classes tended to be about topics unrelated to literature. For example, one teacher asked a string of questions about how students felt about tests and grades. While such questions may interest students, they fail to draw their attention to the subject matter.

The burden of proof should be on those who want to preserve it.

Current theory suggests the value of active and authentic learning, in which students understand why they are studying a problem or text and how it relates to their prior and future knowledge and experiences. The research suggests that it may be possible to find evidence linking such instructional differences to the growing achievement gap between high and low tracks.

TOWARD DETRACKING

Although tracking is the established practice, the burden of proof should be on those who want to preserve it. Because tracking is most detrimental to children who come to school with the fewest advantages, it undermines the promise of equal opportunity. If this type of sorting is to continue, an overriding case must be made for its educational advantages. And this case certainly cannot be made from current research.

But the research also does not make the opposite case—that simply abolishing tracking would improve educational opportunities or outcomes. A current trend in urban districts is to eliminate the lowest track. This seems to be a step in the right direction—*if* such top-down detracking is accompanied by resources and support for the teachers who will implement it.

The research contains an implicit warning that schools would do well to heed. If untracked classes re-semble low-track ones—in reduced content, slower pace, and drill-oriented instruction—the results will probably be an overall reduction in achievement. When schools move to reduce tracking, they must also accept responsibility for changing classroom practices in ways that accommodate and challenge diverse learners.

As Oakes and Martin Lipton point out, detracking is not simply a technical matter of learning new strategies or techniques. Teachers need time to reexamine the beliefs and norms that underlie current practice. This process will allow them to view the changes not as a political imposition but as an opportunity to act on new, vital knowledge about intelligence and learning.

Clearly, detracking is not an end in itself but part of a larger vision for the school—a vision of the learning experiences, relationships, and outcomes the school seeks to achieve. Viewed in this light, the tracking debate may not have to result in a splintering of the school community. Perhaps it will be possible for students, parents, and teachers to unite behind the goal of making schools more engaging and intellectually stimulating—for all students.

FOR FURTHER INFORMATION

Gamoran, A., & Berends, M. (Winter 1987). The effects of stratification in secondary schools: Synthesis of survey and ethnographic research. *Review of Educational Research.*

_____. (Forthcoming). Taking students seriously. In F. Newmann, ed., *Student Engagement and achievement in American secondary schools.* New York: Teachers College Press.

Gamoran, A., Berends, M., & Nystrand, M. (1990). Classroom instruction and the effects of ability grouping: A structural model. Paper presented at the annual meeting of the American Educational Research Association, Boston.

Oakes J., & Lipton, M. (February 1992). Detracking schools: Early lessons from the field. *Phi Delta Kappan,* 73(6).

Slavin, R. (1990). Achievement effects of ability grouping in secondary schools: A best-evidence synthesis. Madison: National Center on Effective Secondary Schools, University of Wisconsin.

Talbert, J., with Ennis, M. (1990). Teacher tracking: Exacerbating inequalities in the high school. Paper presented at the annual meeting of the American Educational Research Association, Boston.

"Tracking and ability grouping." Newsletter of the National Center on Effective Secondary Schools 5, no. 1 (Spring 1990).

Keeping Track, Part 1
The Policy and Practice of Curriculum Inequality
by Jeannie Oakes

The basic features of schools may lock them into patterns that make it difficult to achieve either excellence or equality, says Ms. Oakes. The practice of tracking, for example, contributes to mediocre schooling for most secondary students.

The idea of educational equality has fallen from favor. In the 1980s policy makers, school practitioners, and the public have turned their attention instead to what many consider a competing goal: excellence. Attempts to "equalize" schooling in the sixties and seventies have been judged extravagant and naive. Worse, critics imply that those well-meant efforts to correct inequality may have compromised the central mission of the schools: teaching academics well. And current critics warn that, given the precarious position of the United States in the global competition for economic, technological, and military superiority, we can no longer sacrifice the quality of our schools to social goals. This view promotes the judicious spending of limited educational resources in ways that will produce the greatest return on "human capital." Phrased in these economic terms, special provisions for underachieving poor and minority students become a bad investment. In short, equality is out; academic excellence is in.

On the other hand, many people still argue vociferously that the distinction between promoting excellence

From *Phi Delta Kappan*, vol. 68, no. 1, p. 12–17, September 1986. Reprinted with permission.

and providing equality is false, that one cannot be achieved without the other. Unfortunately, whether "tight-fisted" conservatives or "fuzzy-headed" liberals are in the ascendancy, the heat of the rhetoric surrounding the argument largely obscures a more serious problem: the possibility that the unquestioned *assumptions* that drive school practice and the *basic features of schools* may themselves lock schools into patterns that make it difficult to achieve *either* excellence *or* equality.

> Even as they voice commitment to equality and excellence, schools organize and deliver curriculum in ways that advance neither.

The practice of tracking in secondary schools illustrates this possibility and provides evidence of how schools, even as they voice commitment to equality and excellence, organize and deliver curriculum in ways that advance neither. Nearly all schools track students. Because tracking enables schools to provide educational treatments matched to particular groups of students, it is believed to promote higher achievement for all students under conditions of equal educational opportunity. However, rather than promoting higher achievement, tracking contributes to mediocre schooling for *most* secondary students. And because it places the greatest obstacles to achievement in the path of those children least advantaged in American society—poor and minority children—tracking forces schools to play an active role in perpetuating social and economic inequalities as well. Evidence about the influence of tracking on student outcomes and analyses of how tracking affects the day-to-day school experiences of young people support the argument that such basic elements of schooling can *prevent* rather than *promote* educational goals.

WHAT IS TRACKING?

Tracking is the practice of dividing students into separate classes for high-, average-, and low-achievers; it lays out different curriculum paths for students headed for college and for those who are bound directly for the workplace. In most senior high schools, students are assigned to one or another *curriculum track* that lays out sequences of courses for college-preparatory, vocational, or general track students. Junior and senior high schools also make use of *ability grouping*—that is, they divide academic subjects (typically English, mathematics, science, and social studies) into classes geared to different "levels" for students at different abilities. In many high schools these two systems overlap, as schools provide college-preparatory, general, and vocational sequences of courses and also practice ability grouping in academic subjects. More likely than not, the student in the vocational curriculum track will be in one of the lower ability groups. Because similar overlapping exists for college-bound students, the distinction between the two types of tracking is sometimes difficult to assess.

But tracking does not proceed as neatly as the description above implies. Both curriculum tracking and ability grouping vary from school to school in the number of subjects that are tracked, in the number of levels provided, and in the ways in which students are placed. Moreover, tracking is confounded by the inflexibilities and idiosyncrasies of "master schedules," which can create unplanned tracking, generate further variations among tracking systems, and affect the courses taken by individual students as well. Elective subjects, such as art and home economics, sometimes become low-track classes because college-preparatory students rarely have time in their schedules to take them; required classes, such as drivers' training, health, or physical education, though they are intended to be heterogeneous, become tracked when the requirements of other courses that *are* tracked keep students together for large portions of the day.

Despite these variations, tracking has common and predictable characteristics:

- The intellectual performance of students is judged, and these judgments determine placement with particular groups.

• Classes and tracks are labeled according to the performance levels of the students in them (e.g., advanced, average, remedial) or according to students' postsecondary destinations (e.g., college-preparatory, vocational).

• The curriculum and instruction in various tracks are tailored to the perceived needs and abilities of the students assigned to them.

• The groups that are formed are not merely a collection of different but equally-valued instructional groups. They form a hierarchy, with the most advanced tracks (and the students in them) seen as being on top.

• Students in various tracks and ability levels experience school in very different ways.

UNDERLYING ASSUMPTIONS

First, and clearly most important, teachers and administrators generally assume that tracking promotes overall student achievement—that is, that the academic needs of all students will be better met when they learn in groups with similar capabilities or prior levels of achievement. Given the inevitable diversity of student populations, tracking is seen as the best way to address individual needs and to cope with individual differences. This assumption stems from a view of human capabilities that includes the belief that students' capacities to master schoolwork are so disparate that they require different and separate schooling experiences. The extreme position contends that some students cannot learn at all.

A second assumption that underlies tracking is that less-capable students will suffer emotional as well as educational damage from daily classroom contact and competition with their brighter peers. Lowered self-concepts and negative attitudes toward learning are widely considered to be consequences of mixed-ability grouping for slower learners. It is also widely assumed that students can be placed in tracks and groups both accurately and fairly. And finally, most teachers and administrators contend that tracking greatly eases the teaching task and is, perhaps, the *only* way to manage student differences.

THE RECORD OF TRACKING

Students clearly differ when they enter secondary schools, and these differences just as clearly influence learning. But separating students to better accommodate these differences appears to be neither necessary, effective, nor appropriate.

Does tracking work? At the risk of oversimplifying a complex body of research literature, it is safe to conclude that *there is little evidence to support any of the assumptions about tracking.* The effects of tracking on student outcomes have been widely investigated, and the bulk of this work *does not* support commonly-held beliefs that tracking increases student learning. Nor does the evidence support tracking as a way to improve students' attitudes about themselves or about schooling.[1] Although existing tracking systems *appear* to provide advantages for students who are placed in the top tracks, the literature suggests that students at all ability levels can achieve at least as well in heterogeneous classrooms.

> The net effect of tracking is to exaggerate the initial differences among students rather than to provide the means to better accommodate them.

Students who are *not* in top tracks—a group that includes about 60% of senior high school students—suffer clear and consistent disadvantages from tracking. Among students identified as average or slow, tracking often appears to retard academic progress. Indeed, one study documented the fact that the lowered IQ scores of senior high school students followed their placement in low tracks.[2] Students who are placed in vocational tracks do not even seem to reap any benefits in the job market. Indeed, graduates of vocational programs may be less employable and, when they do find jobs, may earn lower wages than other high school graduates.[3]

Most tracking research does not support the assumption that slow students suffer emotional strains when enrolled in mixed-ability classes. Often the opposite result has been found. Rather than helping students feel more comfortable about themselves, tracking can reduce self-esteem, lower aspirations, and foster negative attitudes toward school. Some studies have also concluded that tracking leads low-track students to misbehave and eventually to drop out altogether.[4]

The net effect of tracking is to exaggerate the initial differences among students rather than to provide the means to better accommodate them. For example, studies show that senior high school students who are initially similar in background and prior achievement become *increasingly* different in achievement and future aspirations when they are placed in different tracks.[5] Moreover, this effect is likely to be cumulative over most of the students' school careers, since track placements tend to remain fixed. Students placed in low-ability groups in elementary school are likely to continue in these groups in middle school or junior high school; in senior high school these students are typically placed in non-college-preparatory tracks. Studies that have documented increased gaps between initially comparable high school students placed in different tracks probably capture only a fraction of this effect.

> **Minority students are consistently underrepresented in programs for the gifted and talented.**

Is tracking fair? Compounding the lack of empirical evidence to support tracking as a way to enhance student outcomes are compelling arguments that favor exposing all students to a common curriculum, *even if differences among them prevent all students from benefiting equally.* These arguments counter both the assumption that tracking can be carried out "fairly" and the view that tracking is a legitimate means to ease the task of teaching.

Central to the issue of fairness is the well-established link between track placements and student background characteristics. Poor and minority youngsters (principally black and Hispanic) are disproportionately placed in tracks for low-ability or non-college-bound students. By the same token, minority students are consistently underrepresented in programs for the gifted and talented.

In addition, differentiation by race and class occurs within vocational tracks, with blacks and Hispanics more frequently enrolled in programs that train students for the lowest-level occupations (e.g., building maintenance, commercial sewing, and institutional care). These differences in placement by race and social class appear regardless of whether test scores, counselor and teacher recommendations, or student and parent choices are used as the basis for placement.[6]

Even if these track placements are ostensibly based on merit—that is, determined by prior school achievement rather than by race, class, or student choice—they usually come to signify judgments about supposedly fixed abilities. We might find appropriate the disproportionate placements of poor and minority students in low-track classes if these youngsters were, in fact, known to be innately less capable of learning than middle- and upper-middle-class whites. But that is not the case. Or we might think of these track placements as appropriate *if* they served to remediate the obvious educational deficiencies that many poor and minority students exhibit. If being in a low track prepared disadvantaged students for success in higher tracks and opened future educational opportunities to them, we would not question the need for tracking. However, this rarely happens.

The assumption that tracking makes teaching easier pales in importance when held up against the abundant evidence of the general ineffectiveness of tracking and the disproportionate harm it works on poor and minority students. But even if this were not the case, the assumption that tracking makes teaching easier would stand up *only if* the tracks were made up of truly homogeneous groups. In fact, they are not. Even within tracks, the variability of students' learning speed, cognitive style, interest, effort, and aptitude for various tasks is often considerable. Tracking simply masks the fact that instruction for any group of 20 to 35 people requires considerable variety in instructional strategies, tasks, materials, feedback, and guidance. It also requires multiple criteria for success and a variety of rewards. Unfortunately, for many schools and teachers, tracking deflects attention from these instructional realities. When instruction fails, the problem is too often attributed to the child or perhaps to a "wrong placement." The fact that tracking *may* make teaching easier for some teachers should not cloud our judgment about whether that teaching is best for any group of students—whatever their abilities.

> In the three areas we studied—curriculum content, instructional quality, and classroom climate—we found remarkable and disturbing differences between classes in different tracks.

Finally, a profound ethical concern emerges from all the above. In the words of educational philosopher Gary Fenstermacher, "[U]sing individual differences in aptitude, ability, or interest as a basis for curricular variation denies students equal access to the knowledge and understanding available to humankind." He continues, "[I]t is possible that some students may not benefit equally from unrestricted access to knowledge, but this fact does not entitle us to control access in ways that effectively prohibit all students from encountering what Dewey called 'the funded capital of civilization.' "[7] Surely educators do not intend any such unfairness when by tracking they seek to accommodate differences among students.

WHY SUCH DISAPPOINTING EFFECTS?

As those of us who were working with John Goodlad on A Study of Schooling begun to analyze the extensive set of data we had gathered about 38 schools across the U.S., we wanted to find out more about tracking.[8] We wanted to gather specific information about the knowledge and skills that students were taught in tracked classes, about the learning activities they experienced, about the ways in which teachers managed instruction, about the classroom relationships, and about how involved students were in their learning. By studying tracked classes directly and asking over and over whether such classes differed, we hoped to begin to understand why the effects of tracking have been so disappointing for so many students. We wanted to be able to raise some reasonable hypotheses about the ways in which the good intentions of practitioners seem to go wrong.

We selected a representative group of 300 English and mathematics classes. We chose these subjects because they are most often tracked and because nearly all secondary students take them. Our sample included relatively equal numbers of high-, average-, low-, and mixed-ability groups. We had a great deal of information about these classes because teachers and students had completed extensive questionnaires, teachers had been interviewed, and teachers had put together packages of materials about their classes, including lists of the topics and skills they taught, the textbooks they used, and the ways in which they evaluated student learning. Many teachers also gave us sample lesson plans, worksheets, and tests. Trained observers recorded what students and teachers were doing and documented their interactions.

The data gathered on these classes provided some clear and consistent insights. In the three areas we studied—curriculum content, instructional quality, and classroom climate—we found remarkable and disturbing differences between classes in different tracks. These included important discrepancies in student access to knowledge, in their classroom instructional opportunities, and in their classroom learning environments.

Access to knowledge. In both English and math classes, we found that students had access to considerably different types of knowledge and had opportunities to develop quite different intellectual skills. For example, students in high-track English classes were exposed to content that can be called "high-status knowledge." This included topics and skills that are required for college. High-track students studied both classic and modern fiction. They learned the characteristics of literary genres and analyzed the elements of good narrative writing. These students were expected to write thematic essays and reports of library research, and they learned vocabulary that would boost their scores on college entrance exams. It was the high-track students in our sample who had the most opportunities to think critically or to solve interesting problems.

Low-track English classes, on the other hand, rarely, if ever, encountered similar types of knowledge. Nor were they expected to learn the same skills. Instruction in basic reading skills held a prominent place in low-track classes, and these skills were taught mostly through workbooks, kits, and "young adult" fiction. Students wrote simple paragraphs, completed worksheets on English usage, and practiced filling out applications for jobs and other kinds of forms. Their learning tasks were largely restricted to memorization or low-level comprehension.

The differences in mathematics content followed much the same pattern. High-track classes focused primarily on mathematical concepts; low-track classes stressed basic computational skills and math facts.

These differences are not merely curricular adaptations to individual needs, though they are certainly thought of as such. Differences in access to knowledge have important long-term social and educational consequences as well. For example, low-track students are probably prevented from *ever* encountering at school the knowledge our society values most. Much of the curriculum of low-track classes was likely to lock students into a continuing series of such bottom-level placements because important concepts and skills were neglected. Thus these students were denied the knowledge that would enable them to move successfully into higher-track classes.

Opportunities to learn. We also looked at two classroom conditions known to influence how much students will learn: instructional time and teaching quality. The marked differences we found in our data consistently showed that students in higher tracks had better classroom opportunities. For example, all our data on classroom time pointed to the same conclusion: students in high tracks get more; students in low tracks get less. Teachers of high-track classes set aside more class time for learning, and our observers found that more actual class time was spent on learning activities. High-track students were also expected to spend more time doing homework, fewer high-track students were observed to be off-task during class activities, and more of them told us that learning took up most of their class time, rather than discipline problems, socializing, or class routines.

Instruction in high-track classes more often included a whole range of teacher behaviors likely to enhance learning. High-track teachers were more enthusiastic, and their instruction was clearer. They used strong criticism or ridicule less frequently than did teachers of low-track classes. Classroom tasks were more various and more highly organized in high-track classes, and grades were more relevant to student learning.

> We discovered a distressing pattern of advantages for high-track classes and disadvantages for low-track classes.

These differences in learning opportunities portray a fundamental irony of schooling: those students who need more time to learn appear to be getting less; those students who have the most difficulty learning are being exposed least to the sort of teaching that best facilitates learning.

Classroom climate. We were interested in studying classroom climates in various tracks because we were convinced that supportive relationships and positive feelings in class are more than just nice accompaniments to learning. When teachers and students trust one another, classroom time and energy are freed for teaching and learning. Without this trust, students spend a great deal of time and energy establishing less productive relationships with others and interfering with the teacher's instructional agenda; teachers spend their time and energy trying to maintain control. In such classes, less learning is likely to occur.

The data from A Study of Schooling permitted us to investigate three important aspects of classroom environments: relationships between teachers and students, relationships among the students themselves, and the intensity of student involvement in learning. Once again, we discovered a distressing pattern of advantages for high-track classes and disadvantages for low-track classes. In high-track classes students thought that their teachers were more concerned about them and less punitive.

Teachers in high-track classes spent less time on student behavior, and they more often encouraged their students to become independent, questioning, critical thinkers. In low-track classes teachers were seen as less concerned and more punitive. Teachers in low-track classes emphasized matters of discipline and behavior, and they often listed such things as "following directions," "respecting my position," "punctuality," and "learning to take a direct order" as among the five most important things they wanted their class to learn during the year.

We found similar differences in the relationships that students established with one another in class. Students in low-track classes agreed far more often that "students in this class are unfriendly to me" or that "I often feel left out of class activities." They said that their classes were interrupted by problems and by arguing in class. Generally, they seemed to like each other less. Not surprisingly, given these differences in relationships, students in high-track classes appeared to be much more involved in their classwork. Students in low-track classes were more apathetic and indicated more often that they didn't care about what went on or that failing didn't bother most of their classmates.

In these data, we found once again a pattern of classroom experience that seems to enhance the possibilities of learning for those students already disposed to do well—that is, those in high-track classes. We saw even more clearly a pattern of classroom experience likely to inhibit the learning of those in the bottom tracks. As with access to knowledge and opportunities to learn, we found that those who most needed support from a positive, nurturing environment got the least.

Although these data do show clear instructional advantages for high-achieving students and clear disadvantages for their low-achieving peers, other data from our work suggest that the quality of the experience of *average* students falls somewhere between these two extremes. Average students, too, were deprived of the best circumstances schools have to offer, though their classes were typically more like those of high-track students. Taken together, these findings begin to suggest *why* students who are not in the top tracks are likely to suffer because of their placements: their education is of considerably lower quality.

It would be a serious mistake to interpret these data as the "inevitable" outcome of the differences in the students who populate the various tracks. Many of the mixed-ability classes in our study showed that high-quality experiences are very possible in classes that include all types of students. But neither should we attribute these differences to consciously mean-spirited or blatantly discriminatory actions by schoolpeople.

Obviously, the content teachers decide to teach and the ways in which they teach it are greatly influenced by the students with whom they interact. And it is unlikely that students are passive participants in tracking processes. It seems more likely that students' achievements, attitudes, interests, perceptions of themselves, and behaviors (growing increasingly disparate over time) help produce some of the effects of tracking. Thus groups of students who, by conventional wisdom, seem less able and less eager to learn are very likely to affect a teacher's ability or even willingness to provide the best possible learning opportunities. The obvious conclusion about the effects of these track-specific differences on the ability of the schools to achieve academic excellence is that students who are exposed to less content and lower-quality teaching are unlikely to get the full benefit out of their schooling. Yet this less-fruitful experience seems to be the norm when average- and low-achieving students are grouped together for instruction.

> **Schools seem to have locked themselves into a structure that may unnecessarily buy the achievement of a few at the expense of the many.**

I believe that these data reveal frightening patterns of curricular inequality. Although these patterns would be disturbing under any circumstances (and though many white, suburban schools consign a good number of their students to mediocre experiences in low-ability and general-track classes), they become particularly distressing in light of the prevailing pattern of placing disproportionate numbers of poor and minority students in the lowest-track classes. A self-fulfilling prophecy can be seen to work at the institutional level to prevent schools from providing equal educational opportunity. Tracking appears to teach and reinforce the notion that those not defined as the best are *expected* to do less well. Few students and teachers can defy those expectations.

TRACKING, EQUALITY, AND EXCELLENCE

Tracking is assumed to promote educational excellence because it enables schools to provide students with the curriculum and instruction they need to maximize their potential and achieve excellence on their own terms. But the evidence about tracking suggests the contrary. Certainly students bring differences with them to school, but, by tracking, schools help to widen rather than narrow these differences. Students who are judged to be different from one another are separated into different classes and then provided knowledge, opportunities to learn, and classroom environments that are vastly different. Many of the students in top tracks (only about 40% of high-schoolers) do benefit from the advantages they receive in their classes. But, in their quest for higher standards and superior academic performance, schools seem to have locked themselves into a structure that may *unnecessarily* buy the achievement of a few at the expense of many. Such a structure provides but a shaky foundation for excellence.

At the same time, the evidence about tracking calls into question the widely held view that schools provide students who have the "right stuff" with a neutral environment in which they can rise to the top (with "special" classes providing an extra boost to those who might need it). Everywhere we turn we find that the differentiated structure of schools throws up barriers to achievement for poor and minority students. Measures of talent clearly seem to work against them, which leads to their disproportionate placement in groups identified as slow. Once there, their achievement seems to be further inhibited by the type of knowledge they are taught and by the quality of the learning opportunities they are afforded. Moreover, the social and psychological dimensions of classes at the bottom of the hierarchy of schooling seem to restrict their chances for school success even further.

Good intentions, including those of advocates of "excellence" and of "equity," characterize the rhetoric of schooling. Tracking, because it is usually taken to be a neutral practice and a part of the mechanics of schooling, has escaped the attention of those who mean well. But by failing to scrutinize the effects of tracking, schools unwittingly subvert their well-meant efforts to promote academic excellence and to provide conditions that will enable all students to achieve it.

NOTES

1. Some recent reviews of studies on the effects of tracking include: Robert C. Calfee and Roger Brown, "Grouping Students for Instruction," in *Classroom Management* (Chicago: 78th Yearbook of the National Society for the Study of Education, University of Chicago Press, 1979); Dominick Esposito, "Homogeneous and Heterogeneous Ability Grouping: Principal Findings and Implications for Evaluating and Designing More Effective Educational Environments," *Review of Educational Research*, vol. 43, 1973, pp. 163–79; Jeannie Oakes, "Tracking A Contextual Perspective on How Schools Structure Differences," *Educational Psychologist*, in press; Caroline J. Persell, *Education and Inequality: The Roots and Results of Stratification in America's Schools* (New York: Free Press, 1977); and James E. Rosenbaum, "The Social Implications of Educational Grouping," in David C. Berliner, ed., *Review of Research in Education, Vol. 8* (Washington, D.C.: American Educational Research Association, 1980), pp. 361–401.

2. James E. Rosenbaum, *Making Inequality: The Hidden Curriculum of High School Tracking* (New York: Wiley, 1976).

3. See, for example, David Stern et al., *One Million Hours a Day: Vocational Education in California Public Secondary Schools* (Berkeley: Report to the California Policy Seminar, University of California School of Education, 1985).

4. Rosenbaum, "The Social Implications…"; and William E. Shafer and Carol Olexa, *Tracking and Opportunity* (Scranton, Pa.: Chandler, 1971).

5. Karl A. Alexander and Edward L. McDill, "Selection and Allocation Within Schools: Some Causes and Consequences of Curriculum Placement," *American Sociological Review*, vol. 41, 1976, pp. 969–80; Karl A. Alexander, Martha Cook, and Edward L. McDill, "Curriculum Tracking and Educational Stratification: Some Further Evidence," *American Sociological Review*, vol. 43, 1978, pp. 47–66; and Donald A. Rock et al., *Study of Excellence in High School Education: Longitudinal Study, 1980–82* (Princeton, N.J.: Educational Testing Service, Final Report, 1985).

6. Persell, *Education and Inequality…*; and Jeannie Oakes, *Keeping Track: How Schools Structure Inequality* (New Haven, Conn.: Yale University Press, 1985).

7.   Gary D. Fenstermacher, "Introduction," in Gary D. Fenstermacher and John I. Goodlad, eds., *Individual Differences and the Common Curriculum* (Chicago: 82nd Yearbook of the National Society for the Study of Education, University of Chicago Press, 1983), p. 3.

8.   John I. Goodlad, *A Place Called School* (New York: McGraw-Hill, 1984).

Keeping Track, Part 2
Curriculum Inequality and School Reform
by Jeannie Oakes

Why does tracking persist? Why is the empirical evidence about its negative effects largely ignored? "De-tracking" schools will require difficult adjustments, explains Ms. Oakes, in this sequel to her September article.

In last month's *Kappan*, I offered a hypothesis that challenges conventional school practice. Tracking and ability grouping, both widely accepted as means of adapting curriculum and instruction to individual differences among students, may *obstruct* efforts to achieve two highly valued goals of schooling: helping students reach high levels of academic excellence and providing equal opportunities for all students to reach those levels.

I argued that compelling evidence indicates that the curricular and instructional *inequalities* that accompany tracking may actually foster mediocre classroom experiences for *most* students and erect special barriers to the educational success of poor, black, and Hispanic students. I also suggested that, despite this evidence, a largely unquestioned acceptance of the educational "soundness" of tracking has kept it firmly entrenched in school practice.

> A largely unquestioned acceptance of tracking has kept it firmly entrenched in school practice.

Here I will attempt to shed some light on this dilemma. First, I will sketch briefly some of the circumstances and beliefs that led to the institution of tracking

From *Phi Delta Kappan*, vol. 68, no. 2, p. 148–154, October 1986. Reprinted with permission.

(rather than to some *other* practice) for managing student diversity, and I will suggest how these social, political, and historical factors can continue to sustain deleterious tracking practices.

Second, I will offer some promising directions for altering ability grouping and tracking. However, if educators and policy makers choose to undertake such changes, they must reconsider much of what now takes place in their schools. Because of the profundity of the social and educational forces that support tracking, any change in this area will require an intensity not commonly seen in school reform.

UNLOCKING THE TRADITION

Schools and tracking systems do not exist in isolation, untouched by the larger societal context. The beliefs, values, and circumstances that originally influenced the institution of tracking in comprehensive secondary schools may continue to shape current practice. A careful look at earlier conditions can help us discover why tracking (and not some other approach) developed in response to student diversity and why tracking is so resistant to change. Since today's educational problems, social context, and students do resemble those of 90 years ago in some ways, we must ask whether we are satisfied with the outcomes of this school practice and whether we should make the same choices today as were made then.

In the late 19th and early 20th centuries, the widespread practice of tracking and ability grouping developed as a response to a complex series of events: dramatically increased immigration from southern and eastern Europe, rapidly expanding and shockingly deteriorating cities, burgeoning factory-based industry and the decline of home-based manufacturing. These events combined to trigger a social crisis of major proportions.

Then as now, society looked to the schools for salvation. The expansion of a then quite rare institution—the free public high school—was seen as a solution to a whole array of problems: socializing new immigrants, providing an avenue for upward mobility, training workers for the factories, and providing proper supervision for footloose urban youth. But how could these new schools possibly accommodate either this new array of expectations or this diverse new school population?

The solution for schools was tracking and ability grouping—providing a differentiated curriculum to accommodate the needs of these "new" students, as well as fulfilling the more traditional function of providing "high-status" preparation for upper-class students. This solution emerged from a long and vigorous debate that engaged, in addition to educators, university presidents, social reformers, industrialists, and leaders of labor unions. Within this debate, such prevailing social ideas as social Darwinism, Americanization of immigrants, and scientific management contributed to a major shift in the commitment of American education to the idea of the common school as a central force in building a democratic society.

Although no simple conspiracy was at work to consign poor and ethnic minority students to inferior and unequal schooling, high schools that were tracked along the lines of race and class provided an acceptable solution to the considerable social disequilibrium. Among the vast array of social forces, three sets of beliefs stand out as the rationale that reconciled differentiation with democracy: the belief in the immutability of vast differences between population groups, the belief that secondary schooling should serve as a preparation for work, and the belief that democratic principles required the extension of secondary schooling to all.

Group differences. Among the educational and political leaders who shaped the new public secondary school at the turn of the century, there were those who believed that the intellectual, moral, and even biological differences among various groups of adolescents were vast and immutable. For example, a misguided social Darwinism posited that darker-skinned, recently arrived immigrants were on a fundamentally lower rung of the evolutionary ladder than were the children of the "native" stock—that is, northern Europeans.

These supposedly inherent group differences were seen to include enormous differences in students' potential for school learning. Moreover, the curriculum that was thought to be suitable for a more advanced group (white Protestants, for the most part) was viewed as entirely inappropriate for those of lesser capabilities (predominantly Catholic and Jewish immigrants from southern and eastern Europe). For example, intelligence test pioneer Lewis Terman wrote of the latter group, "Their dullness seems to be racial.... Children of this group should be segregated in special classes.... They cannot master abstractions, but they can often be made efficient workers."[1] Although Terman's views did not go uncontested, school tracking practices eventually corresponded to these assumptions.

> Industrial employers wanted to hire immigrants who were trained in certain technical skills and who had acquired the work habits and attitudes required to fit in as factory workers.

Purposes of schooling. Terman's statement also responded to an emerging belief that a critical role of public secondary schooling was the preparation and certification of students for work. For the first time, students who would not become scholars, professionals, or members of the elite were attending secondary schools. The traditional academic curriculum seemed a mismatch for such students, particularly for immigrant youth. Industrial employers wanted to hire immigrants who were trained in certain technical skills and who had acquired the work habits and attitudes required to fit in as factory workers. That is, employers needed students who possessed proper deportment, punctuality, and willingness to be supervised and managed.

These requirements of industry coincided with the absence of a curriculum that seemed appropriate for lower-class and immigrant youth. The link between schooling and work provided the substance of a differentiated curriculum: college-preparatory tracks prepared and certified some students for further education, while vocational programs readied others for work. Commenting on these new curriculum tracks, one school administrator wrote, "We can picture the educational system as having a very important function as a selecting agency, a means of selecting the men of best intelligence from the deficient and mediocre."[2]

Democratic education. Ellwood Cubberly, one of the most prominent educational scholars of the time, wrote in 1909, "Our city schools will soon be forced to give up the exceedingly democratic idea that all are equal, and our society devoid of classes... and to begin a specialization of educational effort along many lines in an attempt to adapt the school to the needs of these many classes."[3]

Though consistent with Cubberly's prescription, the prevailing response of the schools was more in keeping with American values of fairness and opportunity. Tracking was seen as a way to incorporate student differences and the sorting function of schools into a new form of democratic schooling. In 1908 the superintendent of schools in Boston articulated this shift: "Until very recently [the schools] have offered equal opportunity for all to receive *one kind* of education, but what will make them democratic is to provide opportunity for all to receive education as will fit them *equally well* for their particular life work."[4]

The rich and intriguing history that I have barely touched on here provides the context for understanding why tracked schools made sense to turn-of-the-century policy makers and practitioners charged with providing educational opportunities for a new population of students.[5]

The problem of educating diverse groups of students, compounded by entrenched beliefs about racial and ethnic differences, was met with a solution that relied on a newly coined view of democracy and the emerging function of school as the accepted preparation for varying adult opportunities. This solution defined student differences and appropriate educational treatments in *social* as well as *educational* terms. At the same time, the use of standardized tests provided a seemingly scientific and meritocratic basis for the sorting process in schools. But surely tracking was more than a technical solution to an instructional problem. Tracking helped to institutionalize beliefs about race and class differences in intellectual abilities and to erect structural obstacles to the future social, political, and economic opportunities of those who were not white and native-born.

THE LEGACY IN TODAY'S SCHOOLS

Today, too, many people, both in and out of school, hold that intellectual aptitude and prospects for school performance are not only linked to race and class, but also are profound and, for all practical purposes, unchangeable. Although biology is less often blamed for these differences today than environmental factors, the commonly held judgment that poor blacks and Hispanics will *characteristically* face insurmountable learning difficulties and that Asians are *by nature* prone to achieve well in school provide two contemporary examples.

Furthermore, it is widely believed that the differences among students cannot be accommodated within a common schooling experience. Witness the proliferation of "pull-out" compensatory programs for the poor and of separate programs for limited-English speakers, as well as the all-too-frequent placement of black students with severe learning problems in programs for the "educationally retarded," while whites with similar difficulties are placed in classes for the "learning disabled." All these practices, moreover, are carried out under the banner of providing "special help" to the students. The view is also firmly entrenched that separate and differentiated curricula are needed to prepare and certify students for their appropriate roles as adults in the workplace.

So powerful is the tradition of tracking and so unquestioned is its general efficacy that even schools with largely homogeneous populations often track their students as rigidly as schools with diverse populations. This is not to say, however, that all schools track in the same way.

For example, tracking tends to vary among schools serving students of different backgrounds in ways that recall turn-of-the-century views of group differences. Schools serving predominantly poor and minority populations typically offer fewer advanced courses and a greater number of remedial courses in academic subjects; they have smaller academic tracks and larger vocational programs; in some cases their college-preparatory classes are less rigorous.[6] Vocational programs often reveal characteristic differences as well, with schools serving middle-class whites offering more classes in business and in science-related fields and schools serving poor minority students offering more classes in low-level preparation for trades and such essentially unskilled work as agricultural crop-picking and building maintenance.[7] In these ways schools use tracking to design programs that "make sense," that are in keeping with their views of their student populations and of the kind of education deemed appropriate for them.

> **Lower-track and vocational programs are often detrimental to the students in them. Ample evidence suggests that placement in these programs begins a cycle of restricted opportunities, diminished outcomes, and growing achievement differences.**

This phenomenon should not be viewed as a simple case of discrimination by race or class. Minority students and poor students *are* typically lower in achievement by the time they reach secondary school, and the secondary schools respond to these differences with largely well-meant programs that they judge to be educationally appropriate for these students.

What is critically important, however, is that lower-track and vocational programs are often detrimental to the students in them. Ample evidence suggests that placement in these programs begins a cycle of restricted opportunities, diminished outcomes, and growing achievement differences between low-track students and their counterparts in higher tracks. These placements do not appear either to overcome students' academic deficiencies or to provide them with future access to high-quality learning opportunities.

Why, then, despite these disappointing outcomes, does tracking persist? And why is the empirical evidence about its negative effects largely ignored? One possible answer is embedded in the historical use of tracking for social as well as educational purposes.

Although tracking, ability grouping, and differentiated curricula are generally regarded as *educational* decisions, these conventional and little-questioned responses to student differences stem from a tradition that has far less to do with education that it does with providing what society-at-large believes to be "appropriate" for different types of students. Tracking may stem more from what society perceives as *its* needs than from what would most benefit students. Because of these important social meanings, evidence about the educational effects of tracking is only partly relevant to the ongoing operation of schools. Consequently, schoolpeople are frustrated in their attempts to achieve *educational* ends (academic excellence) by means of *socially influenced* definitions of appropriate school practice.

> **Well-intentioned, hard-working people appear locked into a school structure that contradicts the expressed goals of schooling.**

DIRECTIONS FOR CHANGE

School practitioners support tracking largely because they are convinced that, considering the tradeoffs, it is best for students. Because tracking enables schools to provide differentiated curricula and instruction, practitioners believe that students placed in the "right track" will have the best opportunity for success in school.

Empirical evidence suggests that a substantial gap exists between these intentions and the effects of tracking. Well-intentioned, hard-working people appear locked into a school structure that contradicts the expressed goals of schooling. This is surely testimony to the power and complexity of tracking and should foreshadow the difficulties of reform.

As long as race and class inequities exist in the larger society, it is unlikely that schooling opportunities and benefits for the disadvantaged will ever equal those of more privileged whites. Nevertheless, schools are not condemned to exacerbate these differences by funneling students into tracks, and some promising directions for altering the practice of tracking do exist.

Promoting heterogeneity. The first and most obvious way to undo the negative effects of tracking is to reorganize schools so that "similar" students are not grouped for instruction. This is obvious enough, and it follows not only from the detrimental effects of tracking, but from the considerable educational promise of heterogeneous classrooms, as well.

The bulk of the research literature on tracking (discussed in Part 1 of this article, which appeared in the September *Kappan*) indicates that *even under usual circumstances* nearly all students can learn as well in heterogeneous groups as in tracked classrooms and that students identified as average or below average often do better in heterogeneous settings. In addition, we found in A Study of Schooling that heterogeneous classes can provide a positive alternative in many ways.[8] In important areas of curriculum and classroom instruction, heterogeneous classes were considerably better off than low tracks. More than half of these mixed-ability classes were among those with the friendliest relationships among peers.

This is good news for teachers and administrators. Practitioners almost universally recognize and lament the negative consequences of tracking on students in low-track classes; most have had discouragingly unsuccessful experiences trying to make these programs work. Many suspect that, when the lowest-achieving and worst-behaved students are grouped together for instruction, everyone in that class performs far below potential.

But the concerns of educators about protecting the educational opportunities of the top-track students are even more salient in the school culture. Research findings that show that able students are likely to continue to do well even when placed in heterogeneous groups do not seem to make sense to practitioners.

As we saw in the classrooms we observed for A Study of Schooling, tracking offers clear educational and social advantages to students in the top tracks. The contrary finding that top students can learn equally well in mixed-ability classes doesn't seem to account for the noticeable and concrete advantages offered by high tracks that practitioners, students, and parents can see in their own schools. Where tracking exists, the top tracks offer more opportunities to the students in them; it is difficult to give up that particular "bird in the hand" for promises that top students would do "no worse" if tracking were stopped. In addition, since parents and teachers of high-track students are often the most visible, vocal, and respected school constituencies, the concerns for "all the others" who might benefit tend not to be as fully represented.

> Much of the practical concern about tracking reform centers on the extreme difficulty of teaching classes with a wide range of student ability.

Promising findings about heterogeneous classrooms should not lead us to believe that all the problems of schooling would be solved simply by mixing students up and leaving everything else in schools untouched. Tracking reform must go beyond simply exchanging heterogeneous for homogeneous classes. Even if such a simple scenario were possible, it would be unlikely to be effective. What these findings do provide, however, is evidence that curricular inequality is *not* inevitable.

Reconstructing the curriculum. Much of the practical concern about tracking reform centers on the extreme difficulty of teaching classes with a wide range of student ability. As long as curriculum is presented as a sequence of topics and skills that require prerequisite knowledge and prior mastery of certain skills, teaching heterogeneous groups of students will remain problematic.

Students do differ, and the most striking differences among them seem to be in the speed with which they master sequentially presented skills. Sequentially arranged material is better suited for students who are grouped according to ability. For, unless students are similar in learning "speed," such a curriculum raises horrendous problems of pacing. Some students are ready to race ahead; others lag behind. Enrichment for the quicker students often involves extra work; reteaching the slower students becomes a chore; being retaught (and often retaught again) becomes a humiliation for the slower students, particularly if others are simply waiting for them to catch up.

Many curriculum experts argue that this "scope and sequence" approach does a disservice to students, regardless of whether they are slow or quick and regardless of whether they are in heterogeneous or tracked classes. They suggest that the curriculum that is well-suited to diverse groups of students is the curriculum to be preferred in all settings.

> Instruction in secondary schools (regardless of track) is grounded in the assumption that the students are grouped homogeneously.

For example, John Goodlad suggests that curriculum might better be organized around central ideas and themes and that these be the focus of what students learn throughout their schooling. Students can then acquire specific knowledge and skills as they are ready *within a common conceptual framework*. In mathematics, Thomas Romberg suggests a common curriculum organized around the major mathematical processes of abstracting, inventing, proving, and applying.[9] With such a concept-based approach to curriculum, the range of skill differences becomes a far less formidable obstacle to teaching and learning. It is also important to remember that these are sound curricular approaches for *all* students—not compromises in order to "do good" for the disadvantaged.

Restructuring classroom instruction. Maintaining current instructional practices in heterogeneous classrooms is a mind-boggling proposition to practitioners already struggling with too many students and ever-increasing expectations for improved achievement. Instruction in secondary schools (regardless of track) is grounded in the assumption that the students are grouped homogeneously. It is characterized by competitive whole-group instruction, lecturing as the prevailing teaching strategy, common assignments, uniform due dates and tests for all students, and a single set of standards of competence and criteria for grades. Diversity among students *within* tracks is evident, but it is not thought to be great enough to require different learning experiences.

Practitioners do not resist an end to tracking because they have had extensive experiences *trying* to teach heterogeneous groups at the secondary level; indeed, few have had such experiences at all. Rather, they resist because they cannot imagine mixing what they believe to be two or three distinctly different groups of students and maintaining the high quality of instruction that they now see *high-ability* groups receiving. However, there *are* approaches to working productively with heterogeneous classroom groups. But these approaches require a reconsideration of the ways in which classrooms are currently organized.

> **Genuine tracking reform will demand dramatically altered assumptions about students, about learning, and about the purpose of schooling.**

Although this sounds overwhelming, recent research on the sociology of the classroom has identified specific kinds of changes in the task and reward structures of classrooms, in student interaction, and in evaluation processes that can greatly facilitate learning in heterogeneous classrooms. These classroom changes are particularly promising because they not only enable students to learn the task at hand, but they can also alter teachers' and students' conceptions of the intellectual ability of low-achieving students.[10] Furthermore, many of these concepts are currently being developed into specific and transportable strategies for teaching and learning. Cooperative learning is one such strategy that is embraced enthusiastically by many practitioners.[11]

Going beyond technology. Alterations in school organization, curriculum, and classroom instruction, as described above, are promising. But they touch only the *technological* side of tracking, and these technological changes, though major, are likely to be the easiest aspect of tracking reform.

Seriously considering "de-tracking" schools will require changes far more difficult than applying altered technologies. Genuine tracking reform will demand dramatically altered assumptions about students, about learning, and about the purpose of schooling.

Just as the implicit assumption that some students can't or won't learn underlies the practice of tracking, so the belief that all students can and will learn underlies the successful implementation of heterogeneous grouping. With such a shift in thinking, the commonly accepted view of intelligence as a "standardized" dimension on which students can be compared and ranked according to their performance on particular tasks may prove to be dysfunctional. It may be more useful to view intelligence as a standard that all students are capable of attaining. For example, intelligence might be more appropriately defined as "competence"—the ability to use learning environments to develop cognitive processes, to acquire knowledge, and to refine skills at problem solving.[12] With such a definition, all students could be considered intelligent and, perhaps even more important, educable.

Moreover, to "de-track" schools effectively, we must reconsider our views of the purpose of schools. For just as tracking is central and essential to a system that separates winners from losers and certifies students for adult work roles, so schools without tracking will be able to focus on educational goals to be achieved by all children. To reform tracking practices, schools will need to place less emphasis on identifying, labeling, sorting, and certifying for roles in larger social and political settings and more emphasis on providing opportunities for individual development.

But, as our brief foray into history illustrated, schools and school reform operate within a social context. Definitions of "individual differences," prescriptions of what students "need," and determinations of the purpose of schooling are as much *social* as they are *educational* choices. Students who are identified as *less able* are often those who have less, both socially and economically. These children are often seen as more disposed to working with their hands rather than their heads. What they "need" is not seen to be the same abstract knowledge and skills that are needed by their abler (and often more affluent) peers.

What they need is often thought to be the rudimentary skills of functional literacy and good deportment that will provide them entry into the lower levels of the workforce.

Given these socially influenced definitions, the public and practitioners alike will not be easily persuaded that a largely common curriculum taught mostly in heterogeneous groups is a promising approach to educating diverse groups of students. Changes in school practice must pass "social" as well as "educational" tests. Certifying some for entrance into colleges and universities and preparing others with basic functional skills and acceptable workplace behaviors are the job that society *expects* its schools to perform. Even if all practitioners were convinced of the educational value of de-tracking schools, the tracked curriculum might continue to be well-suited for fulfilling the social purposes of schooling. Indeed, some radical critics of the schools suggest that attempts to change tracking are futile without concomitant efforts to alter the social structures and ideologies that sustain it.

HOW DO WE GET THERE?

Schools are not "stuck" with tracking simply because it's a complex and difficult problem to solve. Nor are they compelled to continue a practice that reinforces educational inequalities simply because it matches the inequalities in the larger society. Because of these complexities, however, the type of change required to do away with tracking is not commonly attempted in schools.

The directions for reform suggested above should, if nothing else, make clear the enormity of the challenge that tracking and ability grouping present. My recommendations here will not satisfy many. They are likely to frustrate those well-intentioned educators and policy makers who would like to undo the "bad effects" of tracking without disrupting everything else. These are the people who ask such "practical" questions as, "How can we de-track schools and still maintain our Advanced Placement program?" or "Should all ninth-graders take algebra regardless of their mastery of the prerequisite skills?" or "How can we use heterogeneous groups when our basal

reading series is organized by reading levels?" or
"Wouldn't tracking work just fine if we could persuade
teachers (especially those who teach in low tracks) to raise
their expectations and to improve their classroom management skills?"

Instead of providing "realistic" or "practical" solutions, the recommendations I have offered challenge the
conventional wisdom of practitioners,
the accepted modus operandi of school
policy makers, and the vested interests
of many parents. They suggest that
reform will require the rethinking and
restructuring of much of what is now
taken for granted about schooling. They
also suggest that changing tracking will
require more than the use of such
commonly accepted strategies for
improving schools as conducting needs
assessments, developing a one- or two-
year plan, and buying the services of a consultant for staff
development.

> Unless research knowl-
> edge is supported by
> inquiry within schools,
> local school districts,
> and state education
> agencies themselves,
> little change is likely
> to occur.

There is still much to be learned about how tracking
works and why it persists in schools. For change to occur,
these questions must become the objects of intense
inquiry. We must discover how long-standing traditions,
school and district guidelines, standards of common
practice, and beliefs about students' abilities and limitations translate into day-to-day decisions about which
tracks schools should offer, which tracks students should
be assigned to, and what students should learn in different
tracks. We must discover how students' family backgrounds, motivations, peer-group influences, and self-
concepts interact with their track placements to produce
differences in achievement and attitudes. We must
discover the extent to which turn-of-the-century beliefs
about race and class differences continue to affect teachers' and administrators' responses to poor and minority
children. These are appropriate questions for research,
and researchers can (and increasingly will) shed useful
light on these tracking processes and effects.

But essential and useful as answers to such questions may be, it is unlikely that, given the history of tracking, information alone will spur significant reform. Unless research knowledge is supported by *inquiry within schools, local school districts, and state education agencies themselves,* little change is likely to occur. Those in and around schools must make efforts to understand how tracking works and what values and interests it represents. These efforts will probably need to include extensive school- or district-based data collection about tracking practices, critical reflection and extended dialogue about the values and assumptions that underlie these practices, and liberal experimentation with countervailing organizational and instructional processes.

Such activities go far beyond typical improvement processes that focus largely on the technical and managerial aspects of school problems. But they are likely to provide a rich store of knowledge, values, and experiences that will enable practitioners to tackle the problem of tracking.[13] While this may sound like an unrealistic and impractical approach to school change, schools and districts that have attempted tracking reforms (although their number is small) often report that this kind of inquiry process ultimately proves to be more "realistic" and "practical" than conventional approaches because it makes it easier for practitioners and their communities to recognize and alter previously unquestioned practices that conflict with their commitment to educate all students well.[14]

Values, history, and politics that include, but go far beyond, matters of pedagogy and human learning underlie school tracking practices. Changing such practices will require the careful, open, tolerant, and generous probing of the experiences, assumptions, values, and knowledge of those whose lives are most affected by it: students, teachers, administrators, and communities. Inquiry, reflection, and thoughtful dialogue among policy makers, practitioners, and their constituents is an arduous and rarely attempted undertaking in education. But we should expect to do no less if we intend to make schools humane, equitable, and truly educational places.

NOTES

1. Lewis Terman, *Intelligence Tests and School Reorganization* (New York: World Book Co., 1923), p. 28.

2. William B. Pillsbury, "Selection: An Unnoticed Function of Education," *Scientific Monthly*, vol. 12, 1921, p. 71.

3. Ellwood P. Cubberly, *Changing Conceptualizations of Education* (Boston: Houghton Mifflin, 1909), pp. 15–16.

4. Boston Schools, *School Documents*, No. 7, 1908.

5. Fortunately, this history has been richly detailed in many fine studies. See, for example, Raymond E. Callahan, *Education and the Cult of Efficiency* (Chicago: University of Chicago Press, 1962); David A. Cohen and Marvin K. Lazerson, "Education and the Corporate Order," *Socialist Revolution*, vol. 2, 1972, p. 53; Stephen Jay Gould, *The Mismeasure of Man* (New York: Norton, 1982); Herbert M. Kliebard, "The Drive for Curriculum Change in the United States, 1890–1958," *Curriculum Studies*, vol. 11, 1979, pp. 191–202; and Marvin K. Lazerson, *The Origins of the Urban School* (Cambridge, Mass.: Harvard University Press, 1971).

6. Susan Hanson, "The College Preparatory Curriculum Across Schools: Access to Similar Types of Knowledge?," paper presented at the annual meeting of the American Educational Research Association, San Francisco, 1986; Jeannie Oakes, *Keeping Track: How Schools Structure Inequality* (New Haven, Conn.: Yale University Press, 1985); and Donald A. Rock et al., *Study of Excellence in High School Education: Longitudinal Study, 1980–82* (Princeton, N.J.: Final Report, Educational Testing Service, 1985).

7. Oakes, *Keeping Track...*

8. John I. Goodlad, *A Place Called School: Prospects for the Future* (New York: McGraw-Hill, 1984).

9. Thomas A. Romberg, "A Common Curriculum for Mathematics," in Gary D. Fenstermacher and John I. Goodlad, eds., *Individual Differences and the Common Curriculum* (Chicago: 82nd Yearbook of the National Society for the Study of Education, University of Chicago Press, 1983).

10. Elizabeth G. Cohen, "On the Sociology of the Classroom," in Jane Hannaway and Marlaine E. Lockheed, *The Contributions of the Social Sciences to Educational Policy and Practice: 1965–1985* (Berkeley, Calif.: McCutchan, 1986; and Susan Rosenholtz and Carl Simpson, "The Formation of Ability Conceptions: Developmental Trend or Social Construction," *Review of Educational Research*, vol. 54, 1984, pp. 31–63.

11. Robert E. Slavin, *Cooperative Learning* (New York: Longman, 1983).

12. See, for example, the alternatives posed in Richard K. Wagner and Robert J. Sternberg, "Alternative Conceptions of Intelligence and Their Implications for Education," in Tommy M. Tomlinson and Herbert J. Walberg, eds., *Academic Work and Educational Excellence: Raising Student Productivity* (Berkeley, Calif.: McCutchan, 1986).

13. The justification for this argument and discussion of processes of school change can be found in a number of sources, including Seymour Sarason, *The Culture of the School and the Problem of Change* (Boston: Allyn & Bacon, 1971); John I. Goodlad, *The Dynamics of Educational Change* (New York: McGraw-Hill, 1979); Kenneth A. Sirotnik and Jeannie Oakes, "Critical Inquiry for

School Renewal: Liberating Theory and Practice," in Kenneth A. Sirotnik and Jeannie Oakes, eds., *Critical Perspectives on the Organization and Improvement of Schooling* (Hingham, Mass.: Kluwer-Nijhoff, 1986).

14. See, for example, an account of data collection in the San Diego City Schools in Donna G. Davis, "A Pilot Study to Assess Equity in Selected Curricular Offerings Across Three Diverse Schools in a Large Urban School District: A Search for Methodology," paper presented at the annual meeting of the American Educational Research Association, San Francisco, 1986. Some recently developed university/school collaborations are also exemplary, including a critical inquiry into educational equity between the Puget Sound Consortium and the University of Washington, reported in Kenneth A. Sirotnik and Richard W. Clark, "Operationalizing Equity and Excellence in Concept and Practice," unpublished manuscript, University of Washington, 1986.

The Research Speaks About the Effects of Tracking

Although the importance of using research to identify methods that help children is widely agreed upon, it is amazing how selective the application of this research can be—especially when the research challenges the very heart of the system. This is true for the practice of tracking. Even though research indicates a change is greatly needed, the practice still persists.

In this section, leading researchers explore the negative and systemic nature of tracking and ability grouping. The authors all challenge the arguments used to defend the tracking system and examine why tracking persists in spite of their research findings. Their research and analyses speak of change, reorganization, and alternatives. Robert Slavin's overview details the detrimental effects of ability grouping and tracking on student achievement. Concentrating on secondary schools, Slavin condenses the research to draw helpful conclusions for school reorganization.

Jomills Braddock focuses on the disastrous results of ability grouping on minority students. He points out the dangers of this practice: inappropriate placement, unequal resource allocation, differential teacher behavior, and restricted learning opportunities. The author also outlines the trends, implications, and alternatives to tracking.

Along the same lines, Jeannie Oakes and her co-authors attempt to discover how the achievement of disadvantaged and minority students is affected by teachers' curriculum goals and instructional strategies. The authors document one of the most damaging and critical aspects of tracking: its effects on the equal opportunity for all students to learn math and science. Their studies span elementary and secondary schools.

Concluding this section is Daniel Gursky's study of tracking as a heated, civil rights issue of the '90s. Opponents of tracking contend that an over-representation of minority students in low-level classes exists, and that this inequality produces "a form of resegregation, even in schools with seemingly mixed student populations." Gursky cites many researchers who attest to the harmful effects of tracking on minority students and offers insight as to how some schools are beginning to combat the problem.

Achievement Effects of Ability Grouping in Secondary Schools
A Best-Evidence Synthesis

by Robert E. Slavin

For more than seventy years, ability grouping has been one of the most controversial issues in education. Its effects, particularly on student achievement, have been extensively studied over the time period, and many reviews of the literature have been written. In recent years, a comprehensive review of the achievement effects of ability grouping in elementary schools was published by Slavin (1987), but only brief meta-analyses by Kulik and Kulik (1982, 1987) have reviewed the evidence on ability grouping and heterogeneous placement in secondary schools.

The purpose of this paper is to present a comprehensive review of all research published in English which evaluated the effects of ability grouping on student achievement in secondary schools. "Secondary schools" are defined here as middle, junior, or senior high schools in the U.S., or similarly configured secondary schools in other countries. Secondary schools can include grades as low as five, but they usually begin with sixth or seventh grades. Ability grouping is defined as any school or classroom organization plan which is intended to reduce the heterogeneity of instructional groups; between-class ability grouping reduces the hetero-

> **Ability grouping is defined as any school or classroom organization plan which is intended to reduce the heterogeneity of instructional groups.**

This study was supported and first published in 1990 by the National Center on Effective Secondary Schools, University of Wisconsin, Madison, WI, 53706. Reprinted with permission.

geneity of each class for a given subject and within-class ability grouping reduces the heterogeneity of groups within the class (e.g., reading groups).

Unlike the situation in elementary schools, ability grouping in secondary schools is overwhelmingly between-class grouping (McPartland, Coldiron, & Braddock, 1987). Several closely related forms of ability grouping are used. Sometimes students are assigned to a track within which all courses are taken, based on some combination of composite achievement, IQ, and teacher judgments. For example, senior high school students are often assigned to academic, general, and vocational tracks; middle/junior high school students are often assigned to advanced, basic, and remedial tracks (in either case, the number of tracks and the names used to describe them vary widely). This type of grouping plan is generally called tracking in the U.S. or streaming in Europe. It is an example of what Slavin (1987) called "ability-grouped class assignment." In additional to assignment to higher and lower sections of the same courses, tracking in senior high schools usually also involves different courses or course requirements. For example, a student in the academic track may have to take more years of mathematics than a student in the general track, or may take French III rather than metal shop.

A particular form of tracking often seen in middle/junior high schools is block scheduling, where students spend all or most of the day with one homogeneous group of students. Some schools rank-order students from top to bottom and assign them to, say, 7-1, 7-2, 7-3, and so on. Many senior high schools allow students to choose their track or to choose the level they wish to take in each subject, but in plans of this kind counselors tend to steer students into the level of classes to which they would have been assigned if the school were not allowing students a choice (Rosenbaum, 1978).

Another form of ability grouping common in secondary schools involves assigning students to ability-grouped classes for all academic subjects, but allows for the possibility that students will be placed in a high-ranking group for one subject and a low-ranking group for another. In practice, scheduling constraints often make this type of grouping similar to plans in which all courses are taken within the same track. In some cases schools group by ability for some subjects and not for others; for example, students may be in ability-grouped math and English classes but in heterogeneous social studies and science classes. Ability grouping usually involves higher and lower sections of the same course, but sometimes consists of assignment to completely different courses, as when ninth graders are assigned either to Algebra I or to general math. When high achievers are assigned to markedly different courses usually offered to older students (as when seventh graders take algebra), this is called acceleration. More commonly, high achievers may be assigned to "honors" or "advanced placement" sections of a given course, while low achievers may be assigned to special "remedial" sections.

While between-class ability grouping is by far the most common type of ability grouping in secondary schools, forms of within-class grouping are also occasionally seen. These are plans in which students are assigned to homogeneous instructional groups within their classes. Within-class ability grouping, such as use of reading or math groups, is the most common form of grouping at the elementary level (McPartland et al., 1987). Complex plans, such as plans that involve grouping across grade lines, flexible grouping for particular topics, and part-time grouping, are also occasionally seen in secondary schools. In general, a wider range of grouping plans are used in middle/junior high schools than in senior high schools.

Arguments for and against ability grouping have been essentially similar for seventy years. For example, Turney (1931), summarizing writings of the 1920s, listed the following advantages and disadvantages:

ADVANTAGES (ACCORDING TO TURNEY, 1931)
1. It permits pupils to make progress commensurate with their abilities.
2. It makes possible an adaptation of the technique of instruction to the needs of the group.

3. It reduces failures.
4. It helps to maintain interest and incentive, because bright students are not bored by the participation of the dull.
5. Slower pupils participate more when not eclipsed by those much brighter.
6. It makes teaching easier.
7. It makes possible individual instruction to small slow groups.

DISADVANTAGES (ACCORDING TO TURNEY, 1931)
1. Slow pupils need the presence of the able students to stimulate them and encourage them.
2. A stigma is attached to low sections, operating to discourage the pupils in these sections.
3. Teachers are unable, or do not have time, to differentiate the work for different levels of ability.
4. Teachers object to the slower groups.

A research symposium, school board meeting, or PTA meeting on the topic of ability grouping in 1990 is likely to bring up much the same arguments on both sides, with two important additions: the argument that ability grouping discriminates against minority and lower-class students (e.g., Braddock, 1989; Rosenbaum, 1976), and the argument that the low tracks receive a lower pace and lower quality of instruction than do students in the higher tracks (e.g., Gamoran, 1989; Oakes, 1985).

In essence, the argument in favor of ability grouping is that grouping will allow teachers to adapt instruction to the needs of a diverse student body, with an opportunity to provide more difficult material to high achievers and more support to low achievers. For high achievers, the challenge and stimulation of other high achievers is felt to be beneficial (see Feldhusen, 1989). Arguments opposed to ability grouping focus primarily on the perceived damage to low achievers, who experience a slower pace and lower quality of instruction; teachers who are less experienced or able and who do not want to teach low-track classes; low expectations for performance; and few positive behavioral models (e.g., Gamoran, 1989; Oakes, 1985; Persell, 1977; Rosenbaum, 1980). Because of the demoralization, low expectations, and poor behavioral models, students in the low tracks are felt to be more prone to delinquency, absenteeism, dropping out, and other social problems (Crespo & Michelna, 1981; Wiatrowski, Hansell, Massey, & Wilson, 1982). With few college-bound peers, students in the low tracks are found to be less likely to attend college than other students (Gamoran, 1987). Ability grouping is perceived to perpetuate social class and racial inequities because lower-class and minority students are disproportionally represented in the lower tracks. Ability grouping is often considered to be a major factor in the development of elite and underclass groups in society (Persell, 1977; Rosenbaum, 1980). Perhaps most importantly, tracking is felt to work against egalitarian, democratic ideals by sorting students into categories from which escape is difficult or impossible.

> Tracking is felt to work against egalitarian, democratic ideals by sorting students into categories from which escape is difficult or impossible.

There are important differences between the pro-grouping and anti-grouping positions that go beyond the arguments themselves. Arguments in favor of ability grouping focus on *effectiveness*, saying in effect that as distasteful as grouping may be, it so enhances the learning of students (particularly but not only high achievers) that its use is necessary. In contrast, arguments opposed to grouping focus at least as much on *equity* as on effectiveness, on democratic values as much as on outcomes. In one sense, then, the burden of proof is on those who favor grouping, for if grouping is not found to be clearly more effective than heterogeneous placement, none of the pro-grouping arguments apply. The same is not true of anti-grouping arguments, which provide a rationale for abolishing grouping that would be plausible even if grouping were found to have no adverse effect on achievement.

Research on the achievement effects of ability grouping has taken two broad forms. One type of research compares the achievement gains of students who were in one or another form of grouping to those of students in ungrouped, heterogeneous placements. Another type of research compares the achievement gains made by students in high-ability groups to those made by students in the low groups.

Reviews of the grouping vs. non-grouping literature have consistently found ability grouping to have little or no impact on student achievement overall in elementary and secondary schools (e.g., Borg, 1965; Esposito, 1973; Findley & Bryan, 1971; Good & Marshall, 1984; Heathers, 1969; Kulik & Kulik, 1982). Based primarily on his own empirical research, Borg (1965) claimed that ability grouping had a slight positive effect on the achievement of high achievers and a slight negative effect on low achievers, but Kulik and Kulik (1987) found no such trend.

> It is difficult to compare "quality of instruction" in high- and low-track classes.

In contrast, researchers who have compared gains made by students in different tracks have generally concluded that when ability level, socioeconomic status, and other factors are controlled, high-track assignment accelerates achievement while low-track assignment significantly reduces achievement (Alexander, Cook, & McDill, 1978; Dar & Resh, 1986; Gamoran & Berends, 1987; Gamoran & Mare, 1989; Oakes, 1982; Persell, 1977; Sorensen & Hallinan, 1986). In fact, many researchers and theorists in the sociological tradition maintain that tracking is a principal engine of social inequality in society and that it causes or greatly magnifies differences along lines of class and ethnicity (e.g., Braddock, 1990; Jones, Erickson, & Crowell, 1972; Schafer & Olexa, 1971; Vanfossen, Jones, & Spade, 1987).

One area of research has investigated the quality of instruction offered to students in high- and low-ability groups, usually concluding that low-ability group classes receive a quality of instruction that is significantly lower than that received by students in high-track classes (e.g., Evertson, 1982; Gamoran, 1989; Oakes, 1985; Trimble & Sinclair, 1987). However, it is difficult to compare "quality

of instruction" in high- and low-track classes. For example, teachers typically cover less material in a low-track
class (e.g., Oakes, 1985). Is this an indication of poor
quality of instruction or an appropriate pace of instruction? Students in low-track classes are more off-task than
those in high-track classes (e.g., Evertson, 1982). Is this
due to the poor behavioral models and low expectations in
the low-track classes, or would low achievers be more off-
task than high achievers in any grouping arrangement?
However, evidence that low-track classes are often taught
by less experienced or less qualified teachers or that they
manifest other indicators of lower-quality instruction
could justify the conclusion that regardless of measurable
effects on learning, students in the lower tracks do not
receive equal treatment.

In addition to synthesizing research on overall effects
of ability grouping on the achievement of high- average-
and low-achieving secondary students, this review will
attempt to reconcile research comparing achievement
gains in different tracks with research comparing grouped
and ungrouped settings.

REVIEW METHODS

This article uses a review procedure called "best-evidence
synthesis" (Slavin, 1986), which incorporates the best
features of meta-analytic and traditional reviews. Best-
evidence syntheses specify clear, well-justified methodological and substantive criteria for inclusion of studies in
the main review and describe individual studies and
critical research issues in the depth typical of good-quality
narrative reviews. However, whenever possible, effect sizes
are used to characterize study outcomes, as in meta-
analyses (Glass, McGaw, & Smith, 1981). Systematic
literature search procedures, also characteristic of meta-
analysis, are similarly applied in best-evidence syntheses.

CRITERIA FOR STUDY INCLUSION

The studies on which this review is based had to meet a set
of a priori criteria with respect to relevance to the topic
and methodological adequacy. First, all students had to
involve comprehensive ability grouping plans, which

incorporated most or all students in the school. This excludes studies of special programs for the gifted or other high achievers as well as studies of special education, remedial programs, or other special programs for low achievers. Studies of within-class ability grouping are included, but studies of such grouping-related programs as individualized instruction, mastery learning, cooperative learning, and continuous-progress groupings are excluded.

Studies had to be available in English, but otherwise no restrictions were placed on study location or year of publication. Every attempt was made to locate dissertations and other unpublished documents in addition to the published literature.

METHODOLOGICAL REQUIREMENTS FOR INCLUSION

Criteria for inclusion of studies in the main review were essentially identical to those used in an earlier review of elementary ability grouping (Slavin, 1987). These were as follows:

1. Ability-grouped classes were compared to heterogeneously grouped classes. This requirement excluded a few studies that correlated "degree of heterogeneity" with achievement gain (e.g., Millman & Johnson, 1964; Wilcox, 1963). Studies that compared achievement gains for students in different tracks (e.g., Alexander, Cook, & McDill, 1978) were excluded from the main review but are discussed in a separate section.

2. Achievement data from standardized or teacher-made tests were presented. This excluded many anecdotal reports and studies which used grades as the dependent measure. Teacher-made tests, used in a very small number of studies, were accepted only if there was evidence that they were designed to assess objectives taught in all classes.

3. Initial comparability of samples was established by use of random assignment or matching of students or classes. When individual students in intact schools

or classes were matched, evidence had to be presented that the intact groups were comparable.

4. Ability grouping had to be in place for at least a semester.

5. At least three ability-grouped and three control classes were involved.

The criteria outlined above excluded very few studies comparing comprehensive ability grouping plans to heterogeneous placements. Every study located which satisfied criteria 1, 2, and 3 also satisfied criteria 4 and 5. Excluding studies of special programs for high achievers (e.g., Atkinson & O'Connor, 1963), all but two of the studies included in meta-analyses by Kulik and Kulik (1982, 1987) were also included in the present review. The exception was a study by Adamson (1971) which had substantial IQ differences favoring the ability-grouped school, and one by Wilcox (1963) which compared more and less heterogeneously tracked classes.

One major category of studies included in the present review but excluded by the Kuliks are those which did not present data from which effect scores could be computed (e.g., Borg, 1965; Ferri, 1971; Lovell, 1960; Postlethwaite & Denton, 1978). These studies are discussed in terms of the direction and statistical significance of their findings.

LITERATURE SEARCH PROCEDURES
The studies included in this review were located in an extensive search. Principal sources included the Educational Resources Information Center (ERIC), Dissertation Abstracts, and citations made in other reviews, meta-analyses, and primary sources. Every attempt was made to obtain a complete set of published and unpublished studies that met the criteria outline above.

COMPUTATION OF EFFECT SIZES
Effect sizes were generally computed as the difference between the experimental and control means divided by the control group's standard deviation (Glass et al., 1981).

In the ability grouping literature, the heterogeneous group is almost always considered the control group, and this convention is followed in the present article; positive effective sizes are ones that favored ability grouping, while negative effect sizes indicated higher means in the heterogeneous groups. The standard deviation of the heterogeneous group is also preferred as the denominator because of the possibility that ability grouping may alter the distribution of scores. However, when means or standard deviations were omitted in studies that otherwise met the inclusion criteria, effect sizes were estimated when possible from t's, F's, exact p values, sums of squares in factorial designs, or other information, following procedures described by Glass et al. (1981).

Several of the studies included in this review presented data comparing gain scores without reporting actual pre- or post-test means. Standard deviations of gain scores are typically lower than those of raw scores (to the degree that pre-post correlations exceed + 0.5), so effect sizes computed on gain scores are often inflated. If pre-post correlations are known, effect sizes from all scores can be transformed to the scale of posttest values. However, because none of the studies using gain scores also provided pre-post correlations, a pre-post correlation of +0.8 was assumed (following Slavin, 1987). Using a formula from Glass et al. (1981), this correlation produces a multiplier of 0.632, which was used to deflate effect size estimates from gain score data. The purpose of this and other procedures was to attempt to put all effect size estimates in the same metric, the unadjusted standard deviation of the heterogeneous classes. However, because this multiplier is only a rough approximation, effect sizes from studies using gain scores should be interpreted with even more caution than that which is warranted for effect sizes in general.

Another deviation from the usual meta-analytic procedure used in the present review involved adjustments of posttest scores for any pretest differences. This was done either by subtracting pretest means from posttests (if the same tests were used), by converting pre- and post-test means to z-scores and then subtracting (if different tests were used), or by using covariance-adjusted scores. However, even when such adjustments were made affecting the numerator of the effect size formula, the denominator remained the unadjusted posttest standard deviation.

One effect size is reported for each study (see Bangert-Drowns, 1986). When multiple subsamples, subjects, or tests were used, medians were computed across the data points. For example, if four measures were used with three subgroups (e.g., high, middle, and low achievers), the effect size for the study as a whole would be the median of the twelve (4 x 3) resulting effect sizes. Whenever possible, findings were also broken down by achievement level (high, average, low), and separate effect sizes were also computed for each major subject.

In pooling findings across studies, medians rather than means were used, principally to avoid giving too much weight to outliers. However, any measure of central tendency in a meta-analysis or best-evidence synthesis should be interpreted in light of the quality and consistency of the studies from which it was derived, not as a finding in its own right.

RESEARCH ON ABILITY GROUPING IN SECONDARY SCHOOLS

A total of 29 studies of tracking or streaming in secondary schools met the inclusion criteria listed earlier. The studies, their major characteristics, and their findings are listed in Table 1.

The studies listed in Table 1 are organized in three categories according to their research designs. Six studies used random assignment of students to ability-grouped or heterogeneous classes. Nine studies took groups of students, matched them individually on IQ, composite achievement, and other measures, and then assigned one of each matched pair of students to an ability-grouped class, one to a heterogeneous class. The quality of these randomized or matched experimental designs is very high, and the findings of the 15 studies using such designs must be given special weight. The remaining 14 studies investi-

Table 1
Studies of Secondary Tracking

Article	Grades	Location	Sample Size	Duration	Design	Effect Sizes By Achievement			Effect Sizes By Subject		Total

Randomized Experimental Studies

| Marascuilo & McSweeney, 1972 | 8-9 | Berkeley, CA | 603 Students | 2 yrs | Students randomly assigned to 3-group AG or hetero social studies classes. Compared students on teacher-made and standardized tests. | HI +0.14 AV -0.37 LO -0.43 | Social Studies -0.22 | -0.22 |
| Drews, 1963 | 9 | Lansing, MI | 4 Schools 432 Students | 1 yr. | Students randomly assigned to 3-group AG or hetero English classes compared on standardized tests. | HI -0.16 AV +0.01 LO -0.01 | Reading -0.11 Language 0.00 | -0.05 |

Key: AG = Ability Grouping
Hetero = Heterogeneous Assignment
HI = High Achieving Students
AV = Average Achieving Students
LO = Low Achieving Students

			Sample			Effect Sizes		
Article	Grades	Location	Size	Duration	Design	By Achievement	By Subject	Total
Fick, 1963	7	Olathe, KS	1 School 168 Students	1 yr.	Students randomly assigned to 3-group AG or hetero "core" classes. Both classes taught by same teacher. Iowa Tests of Basic Skills used as posttests.	HI +0.01 AV 0.00 LO -0.04	Reading -0.01 Language 0.00	-0.01
Peterson, 1966	7-8	Chisholm, MN	1 School 152 Students	1 yr.	Students randomly assigned to AG or hetero classes. AG based on composite achievement and grades. Compared on standardized tests.	HI +0.05 AV -0.44 LO -0.06	Reading +0.02 Language -0.01 Math -0.25 Social Studies -0.07	-0.04
Ford, 1974	9	New York, NY (Low SES minority)	80 Students	1 sem.	Students randomly assigned to 2-group AG or hetero math classes. Same teachers taught both types of classes. Students compared on Metropolitan Achievement Test.		Math (0)	(0)
Bicak, 1962	8	Minneapolis, MN (lab school)	1 School 75 Students	1 sem.	Students randomly assigned to 2-group AG or hetero science classes at university lab school.	HI -0.39 LO -0.10	Science -0.25	-0.25

Matched Experimental Studies

Article	Grades	Location	Sample Size	Duration	Design	By Achievement	Effect Sizes By Subject	Total
Lovell, 1960	10	Panama City, FL	500 Students	1 yr.	Matched students assigned to 5-group AG or hetero English, biology, and algebra classes.	HI (+) AV (0) LO (0)	Language (+) Math (0) Biology (0)	(0)
Billett, 1928	9	Painesville, OH	408 Students	1 yr.	In three successive years, matched students assigned to 3-group AG or hetero English classes. Compared gains on standardized tests.	HI -0.11 AV +0.03 LO +0.18	English +0.04	+0.04
Platz, 1965	9	?	298 Students	1 sem.	Matched students assigned to 3-group AG or hetero science classes. Students compared on standardized science test.	HI +0.24 AV -0.10 LO +0.22	Science +0.22	+0.22
Bailey, 1968	9	St. Louis, MO	255 Students	1 yr.	Matched students assigned to 2-group AG or hetero algebra classes. Same teachers taught both types of classes. Students compared on gains on standardized algebra measure.	HI +0.18 LO -0.24	Math -0.03	-0.03

Article	Grades	Location	Sample Size	Duration	Design	Effect Sizes By Achievement		Effect Sizes By Subject		Total
Thompson, 1974	11	Suburban VA	240 Students	1 yr.	Compared students in 2 schools, one AG in social studies, one hetero. Students matched. Compared gain scores on teacher-made tests.	HI HI AV LO AV LO	-0.50 -0.47 -0.43 -0.54	Social Studies	-0.48	-0.48
Barton, 1964	9	Rural UT	204 Students	1 yr.	Matched students assigned to 4-group AG or hetero English classes, compared on California Achievement Test gains.	HI HI AV LO AV LO	+0.22 -0.03 -0.13 -0.20	Reading Language	+0.06 -0.13	-0.04
Wilcutt, 1969	7	Bloomington, IN (lab school)	156 Students	1 yr.	Matched students assigned to 4-group flexible AG in math or to hetero. Grouping changed 8 times in the year.			Math	-0.15	-0.15
Holy & Sutton, 1930	9	Marion, OH	148 Students	1 sem.	Matched students assigned to AG, hetero algebra classes. Same teacher taught all classes.			Math	+0.28	+0.28

Article	Grades	Location	Sample Size	Duration	Design	Effect Sizes By Achievement	By Subject	Total
Martin, 1927	7	New Haven, CT	83 Students	1 yr.	Matched students assigned to 3-group AG or hetero.	HI +0.12 AV -0.06 LO +0.23	Reading +0.17 Math +0.13 Language +0.03 Social Studies 0.00 Science -0.04	+0.10
Correlational Studies								
Kerckhoff, 1986	5-10	Britain	8,500 Students	5 yrs.	Longitudinal study of students throughout Britain who attended streamed or unstreamed secondary schools.		Reading +0.02 Math +0.03	+0.03
Fogelman, Essen & Tibbenham 1978	6-10	Britain	5,923 Students	4 yrs.	Retrospective study compared students who had been in streamed, partially streamed, or heterogeneous schools through-out secondary school, controlling for grade 5 general ability.		Reading +0.02 Math +0.03	+0.03

Article	Grades	Location	Sample Size	Duration	Design	Effect Sizes By Achievement		By Subject		Total
Borg, 1965	6-9 7-10 8-11 9-12	Utah	2,934 Students	4 yrs.	Longitudinal study of students in districts using AG compared to students in neighboring district using heterogeneous grouping, controlling for pretests.	HI AV LO	(0) (0) (0)	Math Science	(0) (0)	(0)
Ferri, 1971	5-6	Britain	28 Schools 1,716 Students	2 yrs.	Streamed and non-streamed schools matched on 7+ (grade 2) reading, followed 4 years in junior school, 2 years in secondary.	HI AV LO	(0) (0) (0)	Math Science	(0) (0)	(0)
Breidenstine, 1936	7-9	Soudersburg, PA	11 Schools 860 Students	1 yr.	Compared students in 4 AG, 7 hetero schools matched on IQ.			Composite Achievement		-0.19
Purdom, 1929	9	?	700 Students	1 sem.	Matched students in AG, hetero English and algebra classes compared in achievement.	HI AV LO	-0.02 -0.08 +0.07	English Algebra	-0.02 0.00	+0.01

Article	Grades	Location	Sample Size	Duration	Design	Effect Sizes By Achievement	Effect Sizes By Subject	Total
Postlethwaite & Denton, 1978; Newbold, 1977	5-7	Britain	1 School 450 Students	2 yrs.	Students within one secondary school assigned to streamed or unstreamed halls. Achievement assessed on national examinations.	HI (0) AV (0) LO (0)	Math (0) English (0) Social Studies (0) French (0)	(0)
Bachman, 1968	7	Portland, OR	15 Schools 23 Teachers 404 students	1 yr.	Math classes in schools using AG compared to hetero classes, controlling for IQ.		Math (0)	(0)
Kline, 1964	9-12	St. Louis, MO	4 Schools	4 yrs.	Retrospective study of successive cohorts of students, one in 3- or 4-group AG, one in hetero, in 4 schools. Compared on standardized tests after 4 years of AG or hetero placement.	V.HI -0.02 HI +0.08 AV 0.00 LO -0.02	Reading -0.05 Language +0.07 Math +0.01	+0.01
Stoakes, 1964	7	Cedar Rapids, IA	3 Schools	1 yr.	Matched mentally advanced and slow-learning students compared in schools using AG or hetero assignment. Compared on standardized tests.	HI (0) LO (0)	Reading (0) English (0) Math (0)	(0)

Article	Grades	Location	Sample Size	Duration	Design	By Achievement		Effect Sizes By Subject		Total
Martin, 1959	6-8	Nashville, TN	3 Schools	2 yrs.	Retrospective study compared gains on Stanford Achievement Tests for 2 AG and 1 hetero school from grades 6-8.	HI AV LO	(0) (0) (0)	Reading Language Math	(0) (0) (0)	(0)
Chiotti, 1961	9	Issaquah, WA	3 Schools	1 yr.	Matched students in 3-group AG and hetero schools compared in math achievement.	HI AV LO	+0.14 +0.06 +0.35	Math	+0.18	+0.18
Fowlkes 1931	7	Glendale, CA	2 Schools	1 sem.	Students in schools using 3-group AG based on IQ matched with students in hetero school. Compared gains on Stanford Achievement Tests.	HI AV LO	-0.45 -0.18 -0.05	Reading Language Math Social Studies	-0.04 -0.17 -0.17 -0.21	-0.20
Cochrane, 1961	8	Kalamazoo, MI	1 School	1 yr.	Compared students grouped separately for English, math, to previous year (hetero) students matched in IQ, age, sex, achievement.	HI AV LO	(0) (0) (0)	Math English	(0) (0)	(0)

gated existing schools or classrooms which used or did not use ability grouping, and then either selected matched groups of students from within each type of school or used analyses of covariance or other statistical procedures to equate the groups. The difficulty inherent in such designs is that any differences between schools that are systematically related to ability grouping would be confounded with the practice of ability grouping per se. For example, a secondary school that used heterogeneous grouping might have a staff, principal, or community more concerned about equity, affective development, or other goals than would a "matched" school that used ability grouping. However, several of the correlational studies used very large samples and longitudinal designs, and these provide important additional information not obtainable from the typically smaller and shorter experimental studies.

There are few consistent patterns in the study findings.

Within each category students are listed in descending order of sample size. All other things being equal, therefore, studies near the top of Table 1 should be considered as better evidence of the effects of ability-grouping than studies near the end of the Table. However, the nature and quality of the studies are discussed in more detail in the following sections.

OVERALL FINDINGS

Across the 29 studies listed in Table 1, the effects of ability grouping on student achievement are essentially zero. The median effect size for the 20 studies from which effect sizes could be estimated was -.02, and none of the nine additional studies found statistically significant effects. Counting the studies with nonsignificant differences as though they had effect sizes of .00, the median effect size for all 29 studies would be .00. Results from the 15 randomized and matched experimental studies were not much different; the median effect size was -.06 for the 13 studies from which effect sizes could be estimated. In nine of these thirteen studies (including all five of the randomized studies) results favored the heterogeneous groups, but these effects are mostly very small.

There are few consistent patterns in the study findings. Most of the studies involved grades 7-9, with ninth graders sometimes in junior high schools and sometimes in senior high schools. No apparent trend is discernable within this range. Above the ninth grade the evidence is too sparse for firm conclusions. Lovell (1960) found that high achievers performed significantly better in ability-grouped English classes, but there were no effects in biology or algebra and no effects for average or low achievers. In a four-year study of students in grades 9-12, Borg (1965) found significant positive effects of ability grouping for average and low achievers in math, but found no differences in science or for high achievers. Cohorts followed from grades 7-10 and 8-11 showed no significant differences on any measure for any ability level. On the other hand, Thompson (1974), in a study of eleventh-grade social studies, found the largest effects favoring heterogeneous grouping of all studies located (ES = -.48), while Kline (1964), in another four-year study of students in grades 9-12, found no differences.

Twelve of the 29 studies tracked students for all subjects according to one composite ability or achievement measure. The remaining seventeen studies grouped on the basis of performance in one or more specific subjects. However, there were no differences in the outcomes of these different forms of ability grouping. In addition, there were no consistent patterns in terms of the number of ability groups to which students were assigned (the great majority of studies used three). Study duration had no apparent impact on outcome. Studies which used adjusted gain scores produced the same effects as other studies, and the use of the adjustment of gain scores described above made no difference in outcomes.

There was no discernible pattern of findings with respect to different subjects, with one possible exception. Studies by Marascuilo and McSweeney (1972), Thompson (1974), and Fowlkes (1931) found relatively strong effects favoring heterogeneous grouping in social studies, and three additional studies by Peterson (1966), Martin (1927), and Postlethwaite and Denton (1978) found no differences or slight effects in the same direction. This is not enough evidence to conclusively point to a positive effect of heterogeneous grouping in social studies, but it is important to note that all three of the randomized or matched experimental studies found differences in this direction.

There were no consistent effects according to study location. All four of the British studies found no differences between streamed and unstreamed classes. A large, longitudinal Swedish study by Svensson (1962), not shown in Table 1 because it lacked adequate evidence of initial equality, also found no differences between streamed and unstreamed classes. Urban, suburban, and rural schools had similar outcomes. The one study which involved large numbers of minority students, a randomized experiment in a New York City high school by Ford (1974), found no differences between ability-grouped and heterogeneous math classes.

Studies conducted before 1950 were no more likely than more recent studies to find achievement differences. On this topic, it is interesting to note that experimental-control studies of ability grouping have not been done in recent years. The only study of the 1980s, by Kerckhoff (1986), was done by a sociologist who focused his attention on differences between students in different streams. This study is described in more detail later on. Otherwise, the most recent experimental-control comparisons were done in the early 1970s.

DIFFERENTIAL EFFECTS ACCORDING TO ACHIEVEMENT LEVELS

One of the most important questions about ability grouping in secondary schools concerns the degree to which it affects students at different achievement levels differently. As noted earlier, many researchers and reviewers, particularly those working in the sociological tradition, have emphasized the *relative* impact of grouping for different groups of students far more than the average effect for all students.

Twenty-one of the 29 studies presented in Table 1 presented data on the effects of ability grouping on students of different ability levels. Most studies broke their samples into three categories (high, average, and low achievers), but some used two or four categories.

Across the 15 studies from which effect sizes could be computed, the median effect size was +.01 for high achievers, -.08 for average achievers, and -.02 for low achievers. Effects of this size are indistinguishable from zero, and if all the nonsignificant differences found in studies from which effect sizes could not be computed are counted as effect sizes of .00, the median effect size for each level of student becomes .00. In addition, only one of seven studies from which effect sizes could not be computed (Lovell, 1960) found significantly positive effects of ability grouping for high achievers, and none of these studies found significant effects in either direction for average and low achievers. The randomized and matched experimental studies provided slightly more support for the idea that ability grouping has a differential effect; the median effects sizes for high, average, and low achievers were +.05, -.10, and -.06, respectively. It is interesting to note that the study by Borg (1965), which is often cited to support the differential effect of ability grouping on students of different ability levels, in fact provides very weak support for this phenomenon. Across two measures given to members of four-year cohorts which principally included secondary years, significant effects favoring ability grouping were found for high achievers in one out of eight comparisons, for average achievers in three out of eight, and for low achievers in one out of eight. Only in a cohort that went from grades 4 to 7 were there significant effects favoring heterogeneous grouping for low achievers.

It might be expected that differential effects of track placement would build over time, and that longitudinal studies would show more of a differential impact than one-year studies. The one multi-year randomized study, by Marascuilo and McSweeney (1972), did find that over a two-year period, students in the top social studies classes

> One of the most important questions about ability grouping in secondary schools concerns the degree to which it affects students at different achievement levels differently.

gained slightly more than similar students in heterogeneous classes (ES=+.14), while middle (ES=-.37), and low
(ES=-.43) groups gained significantly less than their
ungrouped counterparts. However, across seven multi-
year correlational studies of up to five years' duration, not
one found a clear pattern of differential effects.

A few studies provided additional information on
differential impacts of ability grouping by investigating
effects of grouping on high or low achievers only. For
example, Torgelson (1963) randomly assigned low-
achieving students in grades 7-9 to homogeneous or
heterogeneous classes. Across several performance measures, the median effect size was +.13 (non-significantly
favoring ability grouping). Similarly, Borg and Prpich
(1966) randomly assigned low-achieving tenth graders to
ability-grouped or heterogeneous English classes, and
found that there were no differences in one cohort. In a
second cohort, differences favoring ability grouping on a
writing measure were found, but there were no differences
on eight other measures.

Studies of ability grouping of high achievers are
difficult to distinguish from studies of special programs for
the gifted. Well-designed studies of programs for the gifted
generally find few effects of separate programs for high
achievers unless the programs include acceleration (exposure to material usually taught at a higher grade level)
(Fox, 1979; Kulik & Kulik, 1984). That is, grouping per se
has little effect on the achievement of high achievers. An
outstanding study that illustrates this is a dissertation by
Mikkelson (1962), who randomly assigned high-achieving
seventh and eighth graders to ability-grouped or heterogeneous math classes. The seventh-grade homogeneous
classes were given enrichment, but the eighth graders were
accelerated, skipping to ninth-grade algebra. No effects
were found for the seventh graders. The accelerated eighth
graders of course did substantially better than similar
students who were not accelerated on an algebra test, and
they did no worse on a test of eighth grade math.

Taken together, research comparing ability-grouped
to heterogeneous placements provides little support for

the proposition that high achievers gain from grouping while low-achievers lose. However, there is an important limitation to this conclusion. In most of the studies which compared tracked to untracked grouping plans (including all of the randomized and matched experimental studies), tracked students took different levels of the same courses (e.g., high, average, or low sections of Algebra 1.) Yet much of the practical impact of tracking, particularly at the senior high school level, is on determining the nature and number of courses taken in a given area. The experimental studies do not compare students in Algebra 1 to those in Math 9, or students who take four years of math to those who take two. The conclusions drawn in this section are limited therefore, to the effects of between-class grouping *within the same courses*, and should not be read as indicating a lack of differential effects of tracking as it affects course selection and course requirements.

OTHER FORMS OF ABILITY GROUPING

The studies discussed above and summarized in Table 1 evaluated the most common forms of ability grouping in secondary schools; full-time, between-class ability grouping for one or more subjects. However, a few studies have evaluated other grouping plans.

The most widely used form of grouping in elementary schools, within-class ability grouping, has also been evaluated in a few studies involving middle and junior high schools. Campbell (1965) compared the use of three math groups within the class to heterogeneous assignment in two Kansas City junior high schools. There were no differences between the two programs in achievement. Harrah (1956) compared five types of within-class grouping in grades 7-9 in West Virginia, and found ability grouping to be no more successful than other grouping methods. Note that these findings conflict with those of studies of within-class ability grouping in mathematics in the upper elementary grades, which tended to support the use of math groups (Slavin, 1987).

Vakos (1969) evaluated the use of a combination of heterogeneous and homogeneous instruction in eleventh-grade social studies classes in Minneapolis. Students were grouped by ability two days each week, but heterogeneously grouped the other three days. No achievement differences were found. Zweibelson, Bahnmuller, & Lyman (1965) evaluated a similar mixed approach to teaching ninth-grade social studies in New Rochelle, New York, and also found no achievement differences. Chiotti (1961) compared a flexible plan for grouping junior high school students across grade lines for mathematics to both ability-grouped and heterogeneous grouping plans, and again found no differences in achievement. A cross-grade grouping arrangement similar to the Joplin Plan (Slavin, 1987) was compared to within-class grouping in reading by Chismar (1971) in grades 4-8. Significantly positive effects of this program were found in grades 4 and 7 but not 5, 6, and 8.

RECONCILING TRACK/NO TRACK AND HIGH TRACK/LOW TRACK STUDIES

As noted earlier in this review, two very different traditions of research have dominated research on ability grouping. One involves comparisons of ability-grouped to heterogeneous placements. The other involves comparisons of the progress made by students in different ability groups or tracks. While there has been little experimental research comparing ability-grouped to heterogeneous placements since the early 1970s, research comparing the achievement of students in different tracks largely began in the 1970s and continues to the present.

The findings of high track/low track studies of ability grouping conflict with those emphasized in this review, in that they generally find that even after controlling for IQ, socioeconomic status, pretests, and other measures, students in high tracks gain significantly more in achievement than do students in low tracks, especially in mathematics (see Gamoran & Berends, 1987, for a review). How can these findings be reconciled with those of the experimental studies?

One important difference between experimental and correlational studies of ability grouping is that, as mentioned earlier, correlational studies (especially at the senior high school level) often include not only the effects of being in a high, average, or low class, but also the effects of differential course-taking. Students in academic tracks may score better than those in general or vocational classes because they take more courses or more advanced courses. The experimental studies comparing grouped and ungrouped classes are all studies of grouping per se, holding course-taking and other factors constant, while the correlational studies examine tracking as it is in practice, where track placement implies differences in course requirements, course-taking patterns, and so on. Also, experimental track vs. no track studies are rare beyond the ninth grade, while most correlational studies comparing students in high vs. low tracks involve senior high schools. The lack of track vs. no track studies at the senior high school level is hardly surprising given the nearly universal use of some form of tracking at that level. However, tracking usually has a different meaning in senior than in junior high school. While junior high school tracking mostly involves different levels of courses (e.g., high English vs. low English), senior high tracking is more likely to involve completely different patterns of coursework (e.g., metal shop vs. French III). Also, the problem of dropouts becomes serious in senior high school; a study of twelfth graders unavoidably excludes the students who may have suffered most from being in the low track and left school (see Gamoran, 1987). This could reduce observed differences between high- and low-track students.

> Junior high school tracking mostly involves different levels of courses (e.g., high English vs. low English), senior high tracking is more likely to involve completely different patterns of coursework (e.g., metal shop vs. French III).

There is limited evidence, however, that differences in course-taking or grade level account for the different conclusions of the track/no track and high track/low track studies. Four-year longitudinal studies in U.S. senior high schools by Kline (1964) and Borg (1965) found no differential effects of track placement for high, average, and low achievers (as compared to similar students in untracked placements). Presumably, course-taking patterns in these senior high school studies varied by track. A correlational study by Alexander and Cook (1982) found that while taking more courses in senior high school did increase achievement (net of background factors), different course-taking patterns in different tracks did not account for track differences in achievement. Gamoran (1987) found that track effects on math and science achievement were explained in part by the fact that students in the academic tracks take more math and science courses and, in particular, more *advanced* courses in these areas. However, no such patterns were seen on reading, vocabulary, writing, or civics achievement measures. Gamoran notes the difficulty of disentangling track and course-taking, which are highly correlated in math and science (and of course both track and course-taking are strongly correlated with ability, socioeconomic status, and other factors). It is certainly logical to expect correlational studies of senior high school tracking to find different effects of different track placements because of different course-taking patterns, but because of confounding of tracking, course-taking, and student background factors, this is difficult to determine conclusively.

Students in higher tracks tend to achieve at much higher levels than those in lower tracks.

Another likely explanation for different findings of track/no track and high track/low track studies has to do with the difficulty of statistically controlling for large differences. Students in higher tracks tend to achieve at much higher levels than those in lower tracks (both before and after taking secondary courses), and statistically controlling for these differences is probably not enough to completely remove the influence or ability or prior performance on later achievement. Further, students in higher tracks are also likely to be higher in such attributes as motivation, internal locus of control, academic self-esteem, and effort; factors which are not likely to be controlled in correlational studies, measures of prior ability and achievement.

To understand the difficulty of controlling for large initial differences between students, imagine an experiment in which a new instructional method was to be evaluated. The experimenter selects a group of students who have high test scores and high IQ scores, and are nominated by their teachers as being hard-working, motivated, and college material. This group becomes the experimental group, and the remaining students serve as the control group. To control for the differences between the groups, prior composite achievement and socioeconomic status are used as covariates or control variables.

> Students in higher tracks are also likely to be higher in such attributes as motivation, internal locus of control, academic self-esteem, and effort.

In such an experiment, no one would doubt that regardless of the true effectiveness of the innovative treatment, the experimental group would score far better than the control group, even controlling for prior achievement and socioeconomic status. No journal, or dissertation committee would accept such a study. Yet this "experiment" is essentially what is being done when researchers compare students in different tracks. When there are significant pretest differences, use of statistical controls through analysis of covariance or regression are considered inadequate to equate the groups. Most often, the statistical controls will undercontrol for true differences (Lord, 1960; Reichardt, 1979). Yet high- and low-track students usually differ in pretests or IQ by one to two standard deviations, an enormous systematic difference for which no statistical procedure can adequately control.

The only study which compared both tracked to untracked schools and high-track to low-track students was a five-year longitudinal study of Kerckhoff (1986) in Britain. This study illustrates the problem of controlling for large differences. For example, in mathematics, boys in the high track of 3-group ability-grouping programs gained about 11 z-score points from a test given at age 11 to one given at age 16, while students in a remedial track gained 18 z-score points. Yet the regression coefficient comparing the high track to ungrouped students was +2.34, indicating performance about 42% of a standard deviation above "predicted" performance. In contrast, the remedial-track boys had a regression coefficient (in comparison to ungrouped students) of –.72, indicating performance about 13% of standard deviation below "predicted" performance, despite the fact that the remedial students actually gained more than the top-track students. The reason for this is that the remedial students started out (at age 11) scoring 1.64 standard deviations below the ungrouped students, while top-track students started out 1.02 standard deviations above the ungrouped students, a total difference between top-track and remedial students at 2.66. No regression or analysis of covariance can adequately control for such large pretest differences. Because of unreliability in the measures and less than perfect within-group correlations of pre- and posttests, "predicted" scores based on pretests and other covariates will (other things being equal) be too low for high achievers and too high for low achievers.

Another factor that can contribute to overestimates of the effects of curriculum track on achievement in studies lacking heterogeneous comparison groups is fan spread. Put simply, high achievers usually gain more per year than do low achievers, so over time the gap between high and low achievers grows. This increasing gap cannot be unambiguously ascribed to ability grouping or other school practices, as it occurs under virtually all circumstances. A student who is performing at the 16th percentile in the sixth grade and is still at the 16th percentile in twelfth grade will be further "behind" the twelfth-grade mean in grade equivalents, for example (Coleman & Karweit, 1972).

An additional factor that can contribute to spurious findings indicating a benefit of being in the high track is that factors other than test scores influence placement decisions. For example, a study by Balow (1964) found that on math tests not used for group placement, there was enormous overlap between students in supposedly homogeneous seventh-grade math classes. More than 72% of the students scored between the lowest score in the top group and the highest score in the bottom group. Among these students in the "area of overlap," students who were in the top group gained the most in math achievement over the course of the year, while those in the low group gained the least.

On its surface this study provides support to the "self-fulfilling prophecy" argument. Yet consider what is going on. Imagine two students with identical scores, one assigned to the high group and one to the low group. Why were they so assigned? Random error is a possibility, but all the systematic possibilities weigh in the direction of higher performance for the student assigned to the high group. Since teacher judgment was involved, teachers may have accurate knowledge to enable them to predict who will do well and who will not. The actual assignments were done on different tests than those used in the Balow study; it is likely that students who scored low on Balow's pretests but were put in the high groups scored high on the test used for placement, and then regressed to a higher mean on Balow's posttest.

What this discussion is meant to convey is not that different tracks do or do not have differential impact on student achievement, but that comparisons of students in existing tracks cannot tell us one way or another. To learn about the differential impacts of track placement, there are two types of research that might be done. One would be to randomly assign students at the margin to different tracks, something that has never been done. The other is to compare similar students randomly assigned to ability-grouped or ungrouped systems. This has been done several times, and, as noted earlier in this review, there is no clear trend indicating that students in high-track classes learn any more than high-achieving students in heterogeneous classes, or that students in low-track classes learn any less than low-achieving students in heteroge-neous classes.

WHY IS ABILITY GROUPING INEFFECTIVE?

The evidence summarized in Table 1 and discussed in this review is generally consistent with the conclusions of earlier reviews comparing homogeneous and heterogeneous grouping (e.g., Kulik & Kulik, 1982, 1987; Noland, 1985), but runs counter to two quite different kinds of "common sense." On one hand, it is surprising to find that assignment to the low ability group is not detrimental to student learning. A substantial literature has indicated the low quality of instruction in low groups (e.g., Evertson, 1982; Gamoran, 1989; Oakes, 1985), and a related body of research has documented the negative impact of ability grouping on the motivations and self-esteems of students assigned to low groups (e.g., Cottle, 1974; Schafer & Olexa, 1971; Trimble & Sinclair, 1987). How can the effect of ability grouping on low-achieving students be zero, as this review concludes?

On the other hand, another kind of "common sense" would argue that, at least in certain subjects, ability grouping is imperative in secondary schools. How could an eighth-grade math teacher teach a class composed of students who are fully ready for algebra and students who are still not firm in subtraction and multiplication? How does an English teacher teach literature and writing to a class in which reading levels range from third to twelfth grade? Yet study after study, including randomized experiments of a quality rarely seen in educational research, finds no positive effect of ability grouping in any subject or at any grade level, even for the high achievers most widely assumed to benefit from grouping.

The present review cannot provide definitive answers to these questions. However, it is worthwhile to speculate on them.

One possibility is that the standardized tests used in virtually all the studies discussed in this review are too insensitive to pick up effects of grouping. This seems particularly plausible in looking at tests of reading, because reading has not generally been taught as such in secondary schools. However, standardized tests of mathematics do have a great deal of face validity and curricular relevance, and these show no more consistent a pattern of outcomes. Marasculio & McSweeney (1972) used both teacher-made and standardized measures of social studies achievement and found similar results with each.

Another possibility is that it simply does not matter whom students sit next to in a secondary class. Secondary teachers use a very narrow range of teaching methods, overwhelmingly using some form of lecture/discussion (Goodlad, 1983). In this setting, the direct impact of students on one another may be minimal. If this is so, then any impacts of ability grouping on students would have to be mediated by teacher characteristics or behaviors or by student perceptions and motivations.

Study after study finds no positive effect of ability grouping in any subject or at any grade level, even for the high achievers most widely assumed to benefit from grouping.

Studies contrasting teaching behaviors in high- and low-track classes usually find that the low tracks have a slower pace of instruction and lower time on-task (e.g., Evertson, 1982; Oakes, 1982). Yet, as noted earlier, the meaning and impact of these differences are not self-evident. It may be that a slower pace of instruction is appropriate with lower-achieving students, or that pace is relatively unimportant because a higher pace with lower mastery is essentially equivalent to a lower pace with higher mastery. Higher time on-task should certainly be related to higher achievement (Brophy & Good, 1986), but the comparisons of time on task between high and low tracks are misleading. What would be important to compare is time on task *for low achievers* in homogeneous and heterogeneous classes, because low achievers may simply be off-task more than high achievers regardless of their class placement. In this regard, it is important to note that Evertson, Sanford, & Emmer (1981) found time on-task to be lower in extremely heterogeneous junior high school classes than in less heterogeneous ones because teachers had difficulty managing the more heterogeneous classes.

The lesson to be drawn from research on ability grouping may be that unless teaching methods are systematically changed, school organization has little impact on student achievement. This conclusion would be consistent with the equally puzzling finding that substantial reductions in class size have little impact on achievement (Slavin, 1989); if teachers continue to use some form of lecture/discussion/seatwork/quiz, then it may matter very little in the aggregate which students the teachers are facing or how many of them there are. In contrast, forms of ability grouping which were found to make a difference in the upper elementary grades, the Joplin Plan (cross-grade grouping in reading to allow for whole-class instruction) and within-class grouping in mathematics (Slavin, 1987) both significantly change time allocations and instructional activities within the classroom.

> The lesson to be drawn from research on ability grouping may be that unless teaching methods are systematically changed, school organization has little impact on student achievement.

ALTERNATIVES TO ABILITY GROUPING

If the effects of ability grouping on student achievement are zero, then there is little reason to maintain the practice. As noted earlier in this article, arguments in favor of ability grouping depend on assumptions about the effectiveness of grouping, at least for high achievers. In the absence of any evidence of effectiveness, these arguments cannot be sustained.

Yet there is also no evidence that simply moving away from traditional ability grouping practices will in itself enhance student achievement, and there are legitimate concerns expressed by teachers and others about the practical difficulties of teaching extremely heterogeneous classes at the secondary level. How can schools moving away from traditional ability grouping use this opportunity to contribute to student achievement?

One alternative to ability grouping often proposed (e.g., Oakes, 1985) is use of cooperative learning methods, which involve students working in small, heterogeneous learning groups. Research on cooperative learning consistently finds positive effects of these methods if they incorporate two major elements: group goals and individual accountability (Slavin, 1990). That is, the cooperating groups must be rewarded or recognized based on the sum or average of individual learning performances. Cooperative learning methods of this kind have been successfully used at all grade levels, but there is less research on them in grades 10-12 than in grades 2-9 (see Newmann & Thompson, 1987). Cooperative learning methods have also had consistently positive impacts on such outcomes as self-esteem, race relations, acceptance of mainstreamed academically handicapped students, and ability to work cooperatively (Slavin, 1990).

One category of cooperative learning methods may be particularly useful in middle schools moving toward heterogeneous class assignments. These are Cooperative Integrated Reading and Composition (Stevens, Madden, Slavin, & Farnish, 1987) and Team Assisted Individualization-Mathematics (Slavin, Madden, & Leavey, 1984; Slavin & Karweit, 1985). Both of these methods are designed to accommodate a wide range of student performance levels in one classroom, using both homogeneous and heterogeneous within-class groupings. These programs have been successfully researched in grades 3-6, but are often used up to the eighth grade level.

> Cooperative learning methods have also had consistently positive impacts on such outcomes as self-esteem, race relations, acceptance of mainstreamed academically handicapped students, and ability to work cooperatively.

Other alternatives to between-class ability grouping have also been found to be successful in the upper elementary grades (see Slavin, 1987) and could probably be effective in middle schools as well. These include within-class ability grouping in mathematics (e.g., teaching two or three math groups within a heterogeneous class), and the Joplin Plan in reading. The Joplin Plan involves regrouping students for reading across grade levels but according to reading level, so that no within-class reading groups are necessary. However, while these alternatives to between-class grouping are promising because of their success in the upper elementary grades, the few studies of within-class ability grouping at the junior high school level have not found this practice to be effective

(Campbell, 1965; Harrah, 1956) and the one middle
school study of the Joplin Plan found only inconsistent
positive effects (Chismar, 1971).

For descriptions of secondary schools implementing
alternatives to traditional ability grouping, see Slavin,
Braddock, Hall, & Petza, 1989.

LIMITATIONS OF THIS REVIEW

It is important to note several limitations of the present
review. Perhaps the most important is that in none of the
studies reviewed here were there systematic observations
made of teaching and learning. Observational studies and
outcome studies have proceeded on parallel tracks; it
would be important to be able to relate evidence of
outcomes to changes in teacher behaviors or classroom
characteristics. Another limitation, mentioned earlier, is
that almost all studies reviewed here used standardized
tests of unknown relationship to what was actually taught.
A third limitation is the age of most of the studies reviewed. It is possible that schools, students, or ability
grouping have changed enough since the 1960s or 1970s to
make conclusions from these and older studies tenuous.

As noted earlier, the results reported in this review
mainly concern the effects of grouping per se, with little
regard for the effects of tracking on such factors as course-
taking. Effects of tracking on differential course-taking are
most important in senior high schools. There is a need for
additional research comparing tracked to untracked
situations at the senior high school level, particularly
research designed to disentangle the effects of tracking
from those of differential course-tracking.

In addition, it would add greatly to the understanding of ability grouping in secondary schools to have
evaluations or even descriptions of a wider range of
alternatives to traditional ability grouping. The few studies
of within-class grouping, cross-grade grouping, and
flexible grouping plans are not nearly adequate to explore
alternatives. Cooperative learning, often proposed as an
alternative to ability grouping, has frequently been found
to increase student achievement in ability grouped as well

as ungrouped secondary classes (Slavin, 1990; Newmann & Thompson, 1987), but no study has yet compared cooperative learning in heterogeneous classes to traditional instruction in homogeneous ones. Descriptions of creative alternatives to ability grouping currently exist only at the anecdotal level (Slavin, Braddock, Hall, & Petza, 1989).

CONCLUSIONS

While there are limitations to the scope of this review and to the studies on which it is based, there are several conclusions that can be advanced with some confidence. These are as follows:

1. Comprehensive between-class ability grouping plans have little or no effect on the achievement of secondary students. This conclusion is most strongly supported in grades 7-9, but the more limited evidence that does exist from studies in grades 10-12 also fails to support any effect of ability grouping.
2. Different forms of ability grouping are equally ineffective.
3. Ability grouping is equally ineffective in all subjects, except that there may be a negative effect of ability grouping in social studies.
4. Assigning students to different levels of the same course has no consistent positive or negative effects on students of high, average, or low ability.

For the narrow but extremely important purpose of determining the impact of ability grouping on standardized achievement measures, the studies reviewed here are exemplary. Six of them randomly assigned individual students to ability-grouped or heterogeneous classes, and nine more individually matched students and then assigned them to one or the other grouping plan. Many of the studies followed students for two or more years. If there were any true effect of ability grouping on student achievement, this set of studies would surely have detected it.

For practitioners, the findings summarized above mean that decisions about whether or not to group by ability must be made on bases other than likely impacts on achievement. Given the antidemocratic, antiegalitarian nature of ability grouping, the burden of proof should be on those who would group rather than those who favor heterogeneous grouping, and in the absence of evidence that grouping is beneficial, it is hard to justify continuation of the practice. The possibility that students in the low groups are at risk for delinquency, dropping out, and other social problems (e.g., Rosenbaum, 1980) should also weigh against the use of ability grouping. Yet schools and districts moving toward heterogeneous grouping have little basis for expecting that abolishing ability grouping will in itself significantly accelerate student achievement unless they also undertake changes in curriculum or instruction likely to improve actual teaching.

There is much research still to be done to understand the effects of ability grouping in secondary schools on student achievement. Studies of grouping at grades 10-12, studies of a broader range of alternatives to grouping, and studies relating observations to outcomes of grouping are areas of particular need. Enough research has been done comparing tracked to heterogeneous classes and achievement in high, middle, and low tracks, at least up through the ninth grade. It is time to move beyond these simple comparisons to consider more fully how secondary schools can adapt instruction to the needs of a heterogeneous student body.

REFERENCES

Adamson, D.P. (1971). *Differentiated multi-track grouping vs. uni-track education grouping in mathematics.* Unpublished doctoral dissertation, Brigham Young University, Salt Lake City, UT.

Alexander, K.L., Cook, M.A., & McDill, E.L. (1978). Curriculum tracking and educational stratification. *American Sociological Review, 43,* 47–66.

Alexander, K.L., Cook, M.A. (1982). Curricula and coursework: A surprise ending to a familiar story. *American Sociological Review, 47,* 626–640.

Atkinson, J.W., & O'Conner, P. (1963). Effects of ability grouping in schools related to individual differences in achievement-related motivation. *Final Report*, Cooperative Research Project No. OE-2-10-024, U.S. Dept. of H.E.W.

Bachman, A.M. (1968). *Factors related to the achievement of junior high school students in mathematics*. Unpublished doctoral dissertation, University of Oregon, Eugene, OR.

Bailey, H.P. (1968). A study of the effectiveness of ability grouping on success in first-year algebra. *Dissertation Abstracts, 28*, 3061 A. (University Microfilms No. 68-1249).

Balow, I. (1964). The effects of "homogeneous" grouping in seventh grade arithmetic. *Arithmetic Teacher, 12*, 186–191.

Bangert-Drowns, R.L. (1986). Review of developments in meta-analytic method. *Psychological Bulletin, 99*, 388–399.

Barton, D.P. (1964). A evaluation of ability grouping in ninth grade English. *Dissertation Abstracts, 25*, 1731 (University Microfilms No. 64–9939).

Bicak, L.J. (1962). *Achievement in eighth grade science by heterogeneous and homogeneous classes*. Unpublished doctoral dissertation, University of Minnesota.

Billett, R.O. (1928). A controlled experiment to determine the advantages of homogeneous grouping. *Educational Research Bulletin, 7*, 139.

Borg, W. (1965). Ability grouping in the public schools. *The Journal of Experimental Education, 34*, 1–97.

Borg, W. & Prpich, T. (1966). *Grouping of slow learning high school pupils.*

Braddock, J.H. (1990). *Tracking: Implications for student race-ethnic subgroups* (Tech. Rep. No. 1). Baltimore, MD: Center for Research on Effective Schooling for Disadvantaged Students.

Breidenstine, A.G. (1936). The educational achievement of pupils in differentiated and undifferentiated groups. *Journal of Experimental Education, 5*, 91–135.

Brophy, J.E. & Good, T.C. (1986). Teacher behavior and student achievement. In M.C. Wittrock (ed.), *Handbook for Research on Teaching* (3rd ed.) (pp.328–375). New York: Macmillan.

Campbell, A.L. (1965). A comparison of the effectiveness of two methods of class organization for the teaching of arithmetic in junior high school. *Dissertation Abstracts International, 26*, 813–814. (University Microfilms, No. 65-6726).

Chiotti, J.F. (1961). *A progress comparison of ninth grade students in mathematics from three school districts in the State of Washington with varied methods of grouping*. Unpublished doctoral dissertation, University of Northern Colorado, Greeley, CO.

Chismar, M.H. (1971). *A study of the effectiveness of cross-level grouping of middle school underachievers for reading instruction*. Unpublished doctoral dissertation, Kent State University, Kent, OH.

Cochran, J. (1961). Grouping students in junior high school. *Educational Leadership*, 18, 414–419.

Coleman, J.S., & Karweit, N.L. (1972). *Information systems and performance measures in schools*. Englewood Cliffs, NJ: Educational Technology Publications.

Cottle, T.J. (1974). What tracking did to Ollie Taylor. *Social Policy, 5*, 21–24.

Crespo, M. & Michelna, J. (1981). Streaming, absenteeism, and dropping out. *Canadian Journal of Education, 6*, 40–55.

Dar, Y., & Resh, N. (1986). Classroom intellectual composition and academic achievement. *American Educational Research Journal, 23*, 357–374.

Drews, E.M. (1963). *Student abilities, grouping patterns, and classroom interaction*. Cooperative Research Project No. 608, U.S. Department of Health, Education, and Welfare.

Esposito, D. (1973). Homogeneous and heterogeneous ability grouping: Principal findings and implications for evaluating and designing more effective educational environments. *Review of Educational Research, 43*, 163–179.

Evertson, C.M. (1982). Differences in instructional activities in higher- and lower-achieving junior high English and math classes. *Elementary School Journal, 82*, 329–350.

Evertson, C., Sanford, J., & Emmer, E., (1981). Effects of class heterogeneity in junior high school. *American Educational Research Journal*, 18, 219–232.

Feldhusen, J.F. (1989). Synthesis of research on gifted youth. *Educational Leadership, 46*,(6), 6–11.

Ferri, E. (1971). *Streaming: Two years later*. London: National Foundation for Educational Research in England and Wales.

Fick, W.W. (1963). The effectiveness of ability grouping in seventh grade core classes. *Dissertation Abstracts, 23*, 2753.

Findley, W.G., & Bryan, M. (1971). *Ability grouping: 1970 Status, impact, and alternatives*. Athens, GA: Center for Educational Improvement, University of Georgia. (ERIC Document Reproduction Service No. ED 060 595).

Fogelman, K., Essen, J. & Tibbenham, A. (1978). Ability-grouping in secondary schools and attainment. *Educational Studies, 4*, 201–212.

Ford, S. (1974). *Grouping in mathematics: Effects on achievement and learning environment*. Unpublished doctoral dissertation, Yeshiva University, New York, NY.

Fowlkes, J.G. (1931). Homogeneous or heterogeneous grouping — which? *The Nation's Schools, 8*, 74–78.

Fox, L.H. (1979). Programs for the gifted and talented: An overview. In A.H. Passow (ed.), *The gifted and talented: Their education and development* (pp. 104–126). Chicago: University of Chicago Press.

Gamoran, A. (1987). The stratification of high school learning opportunities. *Sociology of Education, 60,* 135–155.

Gamoran, A. (1989). Measuring curriculum differentiation. *American Journal of Education, 97,* 129–143.

Gamoran, A., & Berends, M. (1987). The effects of stratification in secondary schools: Synthesis of survey and ethnographic research. *Review of Educational Research, 57,* 415–435.

Gamoran, A., & Mare, R.D. (1989). Secondary school tracking and educational inequality: Compensation, reinforcement, or neutrality? *American Journal of Sociology, 94,* 1146–1183.

Glass, G., McGaw, B., & Smith, M.L. (1981). *Meta-analysis in social research.* Beverly Hills, CA: Sage.

Good, T., & Marshall, S. (1984). Do students learn more in heterogeneous or homogeneous groups? in P. Peterson, L.C. Wilkinson, & M. Hallinan (Eds.) *The social context of instruction: Group organization and group processes* (pp. 15–38). New York: Academic Press.

Goodlad, J.I. (1983). *A place called school.* New York: McGraw-Hill.

Harrah, D.D. (1956). A study of the effectiveness of five kinds of grouping in the classroom. *Dissertation Abstracts, 17,* 715. (University Microfilms No. 56–1114).

Heathers, G. (1969). Grouping. In R. Ebel (Ed.). *Encyclopedia of educational research.* (4th ed.). New York: Macmillan.

Holy, T.C., & Sutton, D.H. (1930). Ability grouping in the ninth grade. *Educational Research Bulletin, 9,* 419–422.

Jones, J.D., Erickson, E.L., & Crowell, R. (1972). Increasing the gap between whites and blacks: Tracking as a contribution source. *Education and Urban Society, 4,* 339–349.

Kerckhoff, A.C. (1986). Effects of ability grouping in British secondary schools. *American Sociological Review, 51,* 842–858.

Kline, R.E. (1964). A longitudinal study of the effectiveness of the track plan in the secondary schools of a metropolitan community. *Dissertation Abstracts, 25,* 324. (University Microfilms No. 64-4257).

Kulik, C.L., & Kulik, J. (1982). Effects of ability grouping on secondary school students: A meta-analysis of evaluation findings. *American Educational Research Journal, 19,* 415–428.

Kulik, C., & Kulik, J. (1984). Effects of accelerated instruction on students. *Review of Educational Research, 54,* 409–425.

Kulik, J.A., & Kulik, C.L. (1987). Effects of ability grouping on student achievement. *Equity and Excellence, 23,* 22–30.

Lord, F.M. (1960). Large-sample covariance analysis when the control variable is fallible. *Journal of the American Statistical Association, 55,* 307–321.

Lovell, J.T. (1960). The Bay High School experiment. *Educational Leadership, 17,* 383–387.

Martin, W.H. (1927). *The results of homogeneous grouping in the junior high school.* Unpublished doctoral dissertation, Yale University, New Haven, CT.

Martin, W.B. (1959). Effects of ability grouping on junior high school achievement. *Dissertation Abstracts, 20,* 2810. (University Microfilms No. 59-1108).

Marascuilo, L.A., & McSweeney, M. (1972). Tracking and minority student attitudes and performance. *Urban Education, 6,* 303–319.

McPartland, J.M., Coldiron, J.R., Braddock, J.H. (1987). *School structures and classroom practices in elementary, middle, and secondary schools.* Baltimore, MD: Johns Hopkins University, Center for Research on Elementary and Middle Schools.

Mikkelson, J.E. (1962). *An experimental study of selective grouping and acceleration in junior high school mathematics.* Unpublished doctoral dissertation, University of Minnesota.

Millman, J., & Johnson, M. (1964). Relation of section variance to achievement gains in English and mathematics in grades 7 and 8. *American Educational Research Journal, 1,* 47–51, 54.

Newbold, D. (1977). *Ability-grouping, the Banbury enquiry.* Slough, England: National Foundation for Educational Research in England and Wales.

Newmann, F.M. & Thompson, J. (1987). *Effects of cooperative learning on achievement in secondary schools: A summary of research.* Madison, WI: University of Wisconsin, National Center on Effective Secondary Schools.

Noland, T.K. (1985). *The effects of ability grouping: A meta-analysis of research findings.* Unpublished doctoral dissertation, University of Colorado, Boulder, CO.

Oakes, J. (1982). The reproduction of inequity: The content of secondary school tracking. *Urban Review, 14,* 107–120.

Oakes, J. (1985). *Keeping track: How schools structure inequality.* New Haven, CT: Yale University Press.

Persell, C.H. (1977). *Education and inequality: A theoretical and empirical synthesis.* New York: Free Press.

Peterson, R.L. (1966). *An experimental study of the effects of ability grouping in grades 7 and 8.* Unpublished doctoral dissertation, University of Minnesota, Minneapolis, MN.

Platz, E.F. (1965). The effectiveness of ability grouping in general science classes. *Dissertation Abstracts, 26,* 1459–1460A. (University Microfilms No. 65-6914).

Postlethwaite, K., & Denton, C. (1978). *Streams for the future?* Slough, England: National Foundation for Educational Research.

Purdom, T.L. (1929). *The value of homogeneous grouping.* Baltimore, MD: Warwick & York.

Reichardt, C.S. (1979). The statistical analysis of data from nonequivalent group designs. In T.C. Cook & D.T. Campbell, *Quasi-experimentation: Design and analysis issues for field settings* (pp. 147–205). Chicago: Rand McNally.

Rosenbaum, J.E. (1976). *Making inequality: The hidden curriculum of high school tracking.* New York: Wiley.

Rosenbaum, J.E. (1978). The structure of opportunity in school. *Social Forces, 57,* 236–256.

Rosenblum, J.E. (1980). Social implications of educational grouping. *Review of Research in Education, 8,* 361–401.

Schafer, W. & Olexa, C. (1971). *Tracking and opportunity: The locking-out process and beyond.* Scranton, PA: Chandler.

Slavin, R.E. (1986). Best evidence synthesis: An alternative to meta-analytic and traditional reviews. *Educational Researcher, 15*(9), 5–11.

Slavin, R.E. (1987). Ability grouping and student achievement in elementary schools: A best-evidence synthesis. *Review of Educational Research, 57,* 347–350.

Slavin, R.E. (1989). Achievement effects of substantial reductions in class size. In R.E. Slavin (Ed.), *School and classroom organization* (pp. 247–257). Hillsdale, NJ: Erlbaum.

Slavin, R.E. (1990). *Cooperative learning: Theory, research, and practice.* Englewood Cliffs, NJ: Prentice-Hall.

Slavin, R.E., Braddock, J.H., Hall, C., & Petza, R.J. (1989). *Alternatives to ability grouping.* Baltimore, MD: Johns Hopkins University, Center for Research on Effective Schooling for Disadvantaged Students.

Slavin, R.E., Karweit, N.L. (1985). Effects of whole-class, ability grouped, and individualized instruction on mathematics achievement. *American Educational Research Journal, 22,* 351–367.

Slavin, R.E., Madden, N.A., & Leavey, M.B. (1984). Effects of team assisted individualization on mathematics achievement of academically handicapped and non-handicapped students. *Journal of Educational Psychology, 76,* 813–819.

Sorensen, A.B., & Hallinan, M.T. (1986). Effects of ability grouping on growth in academic achievement. *American Educational Research Journal, 23,* 543–557.

Stevens, R.J., Madden, N.A., Slavin, R.E., & Farnish, A.M. (1987). Cooperative integrated reading and composition: Two field experiments. *Reading Research Quarterly, 22,* 433–454.

Stoakes, D.W. (1964). *An educational experiment with the homogeneous grouping of mentally advanced and slow learning students in the junior high school.* Unpublished doctoral dissertation, University of Colorado, Boulder, CO.

Svensson, N.E. (1962). *Ability grouping and scholastic achievement.* Stockholm: Almqvist & Wirsell.

Thompson, G.W. (1974). The effects of ability grouping upon achieve-
    ment in eleventh grade American history. *Journal of Experimental
    Education, 42,* 76–79.

Torgelson, J.W. (1963). *A comparison of homogeneous and heterogeneous
    grouping for below-average junior high school students.* Unpublished
    doctoral dissertation, University of Minnesota, Minneapolis, MN.

Trimble, K.D., & Sinclair, R.L. (1987), On the wrong track: Ability
    grouping and the threat to equity. *Equity and Excellence, 23,* 15–21.

Turney, A.H. (1931). The status of ability grouping. *Educational
    Administration and Supervision, 17,* 21–42, 110–127.

Vakos, H.N. (1969). The effect of part-time grouping on achievement
    in social studies. *Dissertation Abstracts, 30,* 2271. (University
    Microfilms No. 69-20, 066).

Vanfossen, B.E., Jones, J.D., & Spade, J.Z. (1987). Curriculum tracking
    and status maintenance. *Sociology of Education, 60,* 104–122.

Wiatrowski, M., Hansell, S., Massey, C.R., & Wilson, D.L. (1982).
    Curriculum tracking and delinquency. *American Sociological
    Review, 47,* 151–160.

Wilcox, J. (1963). A search for the multiple effects of grouping upon the
    growth and behavior of junior high school pupils. *Dissertation
    Abstracts, 24,* 205.

Willcutt, R.E. (1969). Ability grouping by content topics in junior high
    school mathematics. *Journal of Educational Research, 63,* 152–156.

Zweibelson, I., Bahnmuller, M., Lyman, L. (1965). Team teaching and
    flexible grouping in the junior high-school social studies. *Journal
    of Experimental Education, 34,* 20–32.

Tracking: Implications for Student Race-Ethnic Subgroups

by Jomills Henry Braddock II

S tudies of tracking and ability grouping have called attention to their potential harmful effects on low income and racial and ethnic student subgroups who are often overrepresented among the low tracks and classes (Oakes, 1983, 1985; Slavin 1989). Yet very little is known about the prevalence of tracking and ability grouping in schools or about the actual dispersion of African American, American Indian, Asian, and Hispanic students across school programs or classes of different ability levels. Thus, a major objective of this paper is to clarify the magnitude of the problem of African American, American Indian, Asian and Hispanic students' maldistributions across tracks and ability groups.

> The term "tracking" is typically used to refer to between-class homogeneous grouping of students.

We address these issues by using several different sources of large national survey data to (1) summarize current national profiles of school's practices of tracking and ability grouping across the grades using recent survey data (2) analyze recent trends in secondary-level tracking of major race-ethnic student subgroups (3) discuss the implications of tracking for race-ethnic student subgroups' educational outcomes, including adult literacy and (4) consider alternative strategies that schools can use to address problems of instruction and student diversity.

From Report No. 1, Center for Research on Effective Schooling for Disadvantaged Students, February 1990, The Johns Hopkins University, Baltimore, MD. Reprinted with permission.

BACKGROUND

The term "tracking" is typically used to refer to between-class homogeneous grouping of students, including the program differentiation in high schools as well as the separate ability-grouped classes based on evaluations of students' current academic preparation found with different frequencies at all levels of schooling. In theory, tracking is used to accommodate instruction to the diversity of student needs, interests, and abilities found in most schools. The theory is that students will learn best when the instructional content is matched well to current individual knowledge and abilities, thus it is necessary to divide students into homogeneous learning groups to have an effective learning program. With homogeneous groups, a teacher can offer a lesson that no student finds too hard or too easy, which in theory should maximize student motivation and learning.

> Tracking continues to be among the most controversial issues in American education.

Tracking continues to be among the most controversial issues in American education. Education researchers and school practitioners probably disagree more about the need for and the effects of tracking than any other single feature of public schools. Many researchers and theorists advocate the elimination of tracking and between-class ability grouping. They note that ability grouping is unfair to low achievers, citing problems of poor peer models, low teacher expectations, concentration of minority students in low tracts, and slow instructional pace. Proponents typically counter that ability grouping lets high achievers move rapidly and gives low achievers attainable goals and extra help.

The effects of various forms of between-class ability grouping (such as course and program tracking) have been extensively studied (e.g., Findley & Bryan, 1971; Good & Marshall, 1984; Slavin, 1987). According to Slavin (1988), the research evidence indicates, almost without exception, that between-class ability grouping or tracking has few if any benefits for student achievement.

Nevertheless, tracking continues to be routinely used at all levels of schooling. Teachers report both using and believing in ability grouping (e.g., NEA, 1968; Wilson & Schmits, 1978). However, recent events indicate that some of the problems of tracking may be finally addressed in practice. As a result of the major efforts for school restructuring recommended by both school practitioners and education policy makers, or often out of a concern for social justice, many districts are reexamining their ability grouping practices. And challenges to ability grouping have often become a major issue in school desegregation cases (e.g., *Hobson* vs. *Hansen, 1967 U.S. Department of Education* v. *Dillon County School District No. 1, 1986*).

Curriculum tracking in American high schools acts as an allocation mechanism that sorts students into vocational, academic, and general education programs. Vocational programs are designed to develop specific occupational skills that lead to direct entry into the labor market; academic programs are designed to develop the more advanced academic skills and knowledge which are prerequisites for postsecondary schooling prior to labor force entry; general education programs lack the specialized focus of either the vocational or college prep curriculum—serving mainly as a holding pen prior to graduation or dropping out. Thus, tracking may operate as a key mediating mechanism in the link between education and adult career success. Recently, corporate leaders and educators have focused increased attention on the relationship between the type and level of skill brought by American high school graduates to the U.S. workforce and the content and quality of their courses and programs of study. Or as Gamoran (1987) notes, students' "opportunities to learn" are directly related to their course and track placements. Thus there is a growing concern about the impact of tracking and educational stratification generally on the well being of our national economy.

PATTERNS, TRENDS, AND INEQUITIES IN TRACKING AND ABILITY GROUPING

How pervasive are tracking and between-class ability

grouping? And to what extent are African American, Hispanic, American Indian and Asian students maldistributed across curriculum tracks and ability-grouped classes? We will shed some light on these questions by first, presenting descriptive profiles that show the status of high school curriculum tracking of race-ethnic subgroup students in 1982 compared to 1972, based on High School and Beyond (HSB) data and National Longitudinal Study of the High School Class of 1972 (NLS) data. Second, we will present national distributions that show the overall prevalence of between-class grouping and curriculum tracking in American schools, based on data from the NLS, the HSB, and the Johns Hopkins University 1988 National Survey of Middle Grades Principals. Third, we will use data from the 1986 National Assessment of Educational Progress (NAEP) Young Adult Literacy Survey to examine the effects of track placement on young adult literacy.

HIGH SCHOOL PROGRAM PLACEMENT

Table 1 presents nationally representative data that show the status of curriculum track placement for Hispanic, American Indian, Asian, African American and White high school students in 1982 (HSB data, top panel) and 1972 (NLS data, bottom panel). These data allow us to examine two aspects of tracking—first, the recent status of tracking (1982) and the dissimilar distributions among the various populations; second, trends in curriculum program tracking among these populations during the ten-year period from 1972 to 1982.

We will examine these data to compare the curriculum track status of African American and Hispanic high school seniors with the curriculum track status of White high school seniors in 1982 and in 1972, and we will identify trends over the ten-year period for these populations. We will then report the status of American Indian and Asian subgroups compared to Whites in 1982; no comparable 1972 data are available for these populations.

Table 1

Curricular Program Enrollments of 1982 and 1972
High School Seniors by Race-Ethnic Group

Race-Ethnic Category

Cohort and Curriculum Track	Hispanic	American Indian	Asian	African American	White	Total
1982 Seniors	(N=1759)	(N=198)	N=178)	(N=1743)	(N=9503)	(N=13382)
ACADEMIC						
Percent	26.5*	18.8*	58.0*	35.9*	40.9	38.3
Parity Index	0.65	0.46	1.42	0.88	1.00	
GENERAL						
Percent	29.6	48.8*	22.4*	25.5*	30.2	29.7
Parity Index	0.98	1.62(a)	0.74	0.84	1.00	
VOCATIONAL						
Percent	43.9*	32.4	19.6*	38.7*	28.9	32.1
Parity Index	1.52	1.12	0.68	1.34	1.00	
1972 Seniors	(N=631)	(b)	---	(N=1594)	(N=3491)	(N=5715)
ACADEMIC						
Percent	28.1*	---	---	33.0*	52.5	44.3
Parity Index	0.54	---	---	0.63	1.00	
GENERAL						
Percent	42.4*	---	---	33.9*	28.2	31.3
Parity Index	1.50	---	---	1.20	1.00	
VOCATIONAL						
Percent	29.5*	---	---	33.1*	19.4	24.3
Parity Index	1.52	---	---	1.71	1.00	

Sources : Data for 1982 seniors based on first followup of sophomore participants in High School and Beyond Survey (HSB), U. S. Department of Education, National Center for Education Statistics. Data for 1972 seniors are drawn from base-year of the National Longitudinal Study of the High School Class of 1972 (NLS), U. S. Department of Education, National Center for Education Statistics.

(a) This can be interpreted as follows : "In 1982 the general education track participation rate for American Indian students was 62 percent higher than (or 1.62 times) the general track participation rate for white students."

(b) Insufficient sample sizes

*Represents significant difference from the white population at or beyond the 0.05 level.

African American Students

The top panel of Table 1 shows that 36 percent of African American high school seniors in 1982 were enrolled in academic programs (as compared to 41 percent of White seniors), 25 percent were in general education programs (versus 30 percent of White seniors), and 39 percent were enrolled in vocational education programs (versus 29 percent of White seniors). Thus, compared to Whites in 1982, African American students were significantly overrepresented in the vocational education track and significantly underrepresented in the academic and general program tracks: African American students participated in the vocational track at a rate 34 percent higher than (or 1.34 times) the rate for White students. In contrast, the participation rate in academic programs among African American students was 88 percent of (or 12 percent below) the rate for Whites, and, in the general track, the African American student participation rate was 84 percent of (or 16 percent below) the rate for White students.

The bottom panel of Table 1 shows that in 1972, 33 percent of African American high school seniors were enrolled in academic programs (as compared to 52 percent of White seniors), 34 percent were in general education programs (versus 28 percent of White seniors), and 33 percent were enrolled in vocational education programs (versus 19 percent of White seniors). Thus, compared to Whites, African American students in 1972 were significantly overrepresented in the general and vocational education tracks and significantly underrepresented in the academic program track. African American students participated in the vocational track at a rate 71 percent higher than (or 1.71 times) the rate for White students and in the general track at a rate 20 percent higher than (or 1.20 times) the rate for White students; in contrast, the participation rate in academic programs among African American students was only 63 percent of (or 37 percent below) the rate for Whites.

Hispanic Students

The top panel of Table 1 shows that in 1982, 26 percent of

Hispanic high school seniors in 1982 were enrolled in academic programs (compared to 41 percent of White seniors), 30 percent were in general education programs (versus the same proportion—30 percent—of White seniors), and 44 percent were enrolled in vocational education programs (versus 29 percent of White seniors). Thus, compared to whites, Hispanic students in 1982 were significantly overrepresented in the vocational education track and significantly underrepresented in the academic program track. Hispanic students were in the vocational track at a rate 52 percent higher than (or 1.52 times) the rate for White students; in contrast, the participation rate in academic programs among Hispanic students was only 65 percent of (or 35 percent below) the rate for Whites.

Because these are nationally representative samples, we can compare the data and talk about "trends" that have occurred.

The bottom panel of Table 1 shows that in 1972, 28 percent of Hispanic high school seniors were enrolled in academic programs (as compared to 52 percent of White seniors), 42 percent were in general education programs (versus 28 percent of White seniors), and 29 percent were enrolled in vocational education programs (versus 19 percent of White seniors). Thus, compared to Whites, Hispanic students in 1972 were significantly overrepresented in the general and vocational education tracks and significantly underrepresented in the academic program track. Hispanic students participated in the vocational track at a rate 52 percent higher than (or 1.52 times) the rate for White students, and in the general track at a rate 50 percent higher than (or 1.50 times) the rate for White students; in contrast, the participation rate in academic programs among Hispanic students was only 54 percent of (or 46 percent below) the rate for Whites.

Trends Over 10 Years
The NLS data provide a snapshot of the status of program tracking for a nationally representative sample in 1972; the HSB data provide a snapshot of the status of program tracking for a nationally representative sample in 1982.

Because these are nationally representative samples, we can compare the data and talk about "trends" that have occurred. We have no way of knowing, however, the real progression of any changes that have taken place—whether changes occurred gradually over the time period or perhaps took place abruptly during a shorter time within the overall time period, or even whether changes occurred in one direction consistently or moved back and forth in various directions.

> The actual percents of African American and Hispanic seniors in the academic track in 1972 and 1982 show clearly that they achieved no real gain in movement into the academic track.

The major trend over the 1972-1982 period for both African American and Hispanic students was to continue, compared to Whites, to be overrepresented in vocational education tracks and underrepresented in academic tracks.

The magnitude of the underrepresentation of both groups compared to Whites in academic tracks had diminished by 1982—African American representation was 88 percent of the White rate in 1982 compared to 63 percent of the White rate in 1972; Hispanic representation was 65 percent of the White rate in 1982 compared to 54 percent of the White rate in 1972.

On the surface, this looks as if African American students, especially, have made substantial gains in representation in the academic track in their senior year of high school. And they have, compared to White representation, but the gain from 63 percent to 88 percent of the White rate was due mainly to a decrease in White students in the academic track (from 52.5 percent in 1972 to 40.9 percent in 1982). The same is true for the Hispanic gain from 54 percent of the White rate in 1972 to 65 percent in 1982—the gain is mostly accounted for by the decrease in White students in academic tracks from 1972 to 1982.

The actual percents of African American and Hispanic seniors in the academic track in 1972 and 1982 show clearly that, although these subgroups achieved increased

parity with White students, they achieved no real gain in
movement into the academic track. The percent of Hispanic students in the academic track, in fact, decreased
from 28.1 to 26.5, while the percent of African American
students in the academic track increased slightly—from
33.0 to 35.9. If the percent of White students in the academic track had stayed the same from 1972 to 1982, the
African American student rate of representation compared
to Whites would be only 68 percent in 1982, compared to
65 percent in 1972. Similarly, the rate of Hispanic student
representation compared to Whites would be only 50
percent in 1982, compared to 54 percent in 1972. What
these figures clearly show is that movement toward parity
with White students by African American and Hispanic
students from 1972 to 1982 does not reflect that more of
these students moved into the academic track in that ten-
year period; it mostly reflects the fact that White students
shifted in substantial numbers from academic tracks to
vocational and especially general tracks from 1972 to 1982.

We will look briefly at the trends in representation in
the vocational and general tracks from 1972 to 1982. Both
African American and Hispanic students continued to be
overrepresented in the vocational track in 1982 compared
to Whites, and both had substantial increases in the
percent of students actually in vocational education
programs—African Americans increasing from 33.1
percent in 1972 to 38.7 percent in 1982, and Hispanics
increasing from 29.5 percent in 1972 to 43.9 percent in
1982. The Hispanic students, despite their large actual
increase in the percent of students in the vocational track,
remained at the same parity level with Whites as in 1972
(represented at a rate 1.52 times that of White students)
because White students also increased their actual percent
participation in the vocational track from 19.4 to 28.9
percent during the ten-year period. Similarly, although
African American students gained in parity with White
students, going from a rate of 1.71 times to a rate of 1.34
times that of White students, this gain came about because
of the influx of a larger percent of White students in

vocational tracks, not because the African American students decreased their own percentage in the vocational track.

Both African American and Hispanic students decreased their actual percent of participation in the general track from 1972 to 1982, and both went from being overrepresented in the general track compared to Whites (1.2 percent and 1.5 percent of the White rate, respectively) to being slightly underrepresented in the general track compared to Whites (.84 and .98 percent of the White rate, respectively). Again, the move from over- to underrepresentation was influenced by an increased percentage of Whites moving into the general track (28.2 percent in 1972 to 30.2 percent in 1982), but this time much of the shift was accounted for by actual movement out of the general track by the African American and Hispanic students.

Little change occurred from 1972 to 1982 in the percentage of African Americans and Hispanics in academic tracks.

The data in Table 1 alone are insufficient to interpret the trends that we've reported. We can note that little change occurred from 1972 to 1982 in the percentage of African Americans and Hispanics in academic tracks. Both these population subgroups remain underrepresented compared to Whites in the track that leads to further education and better career opportunities. Also, both these groups increased their rates of participation in vocational education tracks substantially from 1972 to 1982, and both remain heavily overrepresented compared to Whites in the track that, in theory, leads to employment directly out of high school.

We can comment on our findings regarding participation in the general track, which is acknowledged by most educators as being basically a "holding track" for students who otherwise would drop out. The substantial decrease in the percentage of African American and Hispanic students in the general track is a positive change only if the vocational track, where most of them went, does indeed provide worthwhile programs that lead to the acquisition of worthwhile and marketable skills and entrance into meaningful employment. At the same time, the fact that few of these students moved into the academic track is disquieting. It is very possible that the change out of the general track occurred because some high schools serving African Americans and Hispanics simply eliminated the general track. The question then becomes whether the vocational track into which these students moved was broadened and expanded to provide them with a strong practical education, or whether it simply became the new holding arena.

American Indian and Asian Students

The top panel of Table 1 show that 19 percent of American Indian high school seniors in 1982 were enrolled in academic programs (as compared to 41 percent of White seniors), 49 percent were in general education programs (versus 30 percent of White seniors), and 32 percent were enrolled in vocational education programs (versus 29 percent of White seniors). Thus, compared to Whites, American Indian students in 1982 were significantly overrepresented in the general education track and significantly underrepresented in the academic program track. American Indian students participated in the general track at a rate 62 percent higher than (or 1.62 times) the rate for White students; in contrast, the participation rate in academic programs among American Indian students was only 46 percent of (or 54 percent below) the rate for Whites.

In the top panel of Table 1, the data show that 58 percent of 1982 Asian high school seniors were enrolled in academic programs (as compared to 41 percent of White seniors), 22 percent were in general education programs (versus 30 percent of White seniors), and 20 percent were enrolled in vocational education programs (versus 29 percent of White seniors). Thus, compared to Whites in 1982, Asian students were significantly underrepresented in the general and vocational education tracks and significantly overrepresented in the academic program track. Asian students participated in the academic track at a rate

42 percent higher than (or 1.42 times) the rate for White students; in contrast, the Asian participation rate in general education programs was only 74 percent of (or 26 percent below) the rate for Whites, and in vocational education programs the participation rate was only 68 percent of (or 32 percent below) the rates for Whites.

These distributions of program placements have implications for students' access to "learning opportunities" as reflected in specific course enrollment patterns.

ABILITY GROUPED CLASS ASSIGNMENT AND CURRICULUM TRACKING

Our next sets of data pertain to the assignment of students to classes according to ability. Elementary school students often are assigned to high, average, or low achieving self-contained classes on the basis of some combination of a composite achievement measure, IQ scores, and/or teacher judgment, and remain with the same ability-grouped classes for all academic subjects. In junior high and middle schools, ability grouped class assignment may take the form of block scheduling, where students are assigned to one class by ability and travel together from subject to subject, or students may be assigned by ability to each subject separately. High school students are usually assigned to academic, vocational, or general program tracks, but then also assigned to separate ability grouped courses within the curriculum tracks (e.g., Honors or Advanced Placement, regular, and remedial courses).

Tables 2–7 report the prevalence of ability-grouped class and course assignment for African American, Hispanic, American Indian, Asian, and White students at various grade levels based on multiple data sets. The Johns Hopkins University National Survey of Middle Grades asked principals whether they assign students to homogeneous groups on the basis of ability or achievement. Their responses, as presented in Table 2, reveal several important differences in homogeneous grouping practices by subject and by school ethnic composition and "average" student ability.

Table 2

Patterns of Homogeneous Ability Grouped Class Assignment in Public
Schools Serving Early Adolescents by Selected Student Characteristics

	All Students	English	Mathematics	Reading	Science	Social Studies
All Schools						
All Homogeneous Classes	22.0	25.0	39.3	29.6	6.5	4.7
< 20% Minority	20.0	25.2	40.6	30.1	5.9	4.3
> 20% Minority	26.8	24.4	35.4	28.0	7.0	5.2
Schools where "typical" entering student is :						
Below Average						
All Homogeneous Classes	24.0	21.8	40.0	23.5	7.1	6.0
< 20% Minority	23.5	20.8	39.9	23.2	6.8	5.8
> 20% Minority	28.0	25.1	38.0	24.2	6.2	6.4
Average						
All Homogeneous Classes	20.2	30.0	40.7	35.2	5.2	2.6
< 20% Minority	17.6	32.2	43.1	37.5	5.5	2.5
> 20% Minority	28.0	23.5	32.8	27.4	3.3	2.4
Above Average						
All Homogeneous Classes	21.4	22.5	35.9	30.0	7.7	6.0
< 20% Minority	15.5	18.9	35.0	30.3	4.1	4.5
> 20% Minority	25.2	24.9	36.3	29.9	9.6	6.7

Source : Johns Hopkins University 1988 National Survey of Middle Grades Principals

Table 2 shows, for grade seven students, the percent
of schools that use all homogenous grouping by subject.
Analyses reported elsewhere reveal that roughly two-thirds
of the schools report using at least some between-class
ability grouping (Braddock 1990; Epstein & Mac Iver,
1990). Across all types of schools, mathematics, reading
and then English are the subject most often grouped by
ability. Table 2 shows that the use of between-class grouping to create "all" classes homogeneous in ability is quite

common in grade 7; roughly one of five schools report that their seventh grade classes are ability grouped for *each* subject. Interestingly, the practice of homogeneous ability grouping for all subjects is more often found in schools with sizable (more than 20%) enrollments of African American and Hispanic students. As the bottom three panels of Table 2 show, this relationship between full scale ability grouping and ethnic concentration holds even when schools are disaggregated in terms of principal reports of "average" student ability.

> Nearly all (92 percent) report the use of between-class ability grouping in some subjects.

The National Longitudinal Study of the High School Class of 1972 (NLS) also asked principals whether they assign students to homogeneous groups on the basis of ability or achievement. Principal responses to this question in the NLS survey are presented in Table 3.

Table 3 shows the percent of high schools that use homogenous grouping in all or some of their classes. Nearly all (92 percent) report the use of between-class ability grouping in some subjects. Where ability grouping is used, it typically applies to all students (57 percent). However, the use of ability grouping to create "all" homogeneous classes is somewhat more common for high ability students (8 percent) than for low ability students (5 percent).

Table 4 shows patterns of course tracking in high schools by subject. In grade 12, English (59 percent), mathematics/science (42 percent), and social studies (39 percent) are the subjects in which students are most often grouped by ability. English more often segregates students into a larger number of groups (12 percent report five or more ability levels) than other academic subjects.

Thus Table 3 and 4 show concurrently that course tracking—between-class ability grouping—is a prevalent grouping method in high schools and especially in major subjects. Patterns of course tracking by race-ethnic student subgroups (see Table 5) reveal some strikingly dissimilar distributions among Whites and African

Table 3

Patterns of Course Tracking in Public Comprehensive High Schools for Different Types of Students and Schools

	All Subjects		Some Subjects	
School Uses Between-Classes Ability Grouping	7.9		92.1	

	All Students	High Ability Students Only	Low Ability Students Only	No Students
School Uses Between-Classes Ability Grouping (where applicable)	57.5	8.4	4.7	29.4

Source : National Longitudinal Study of High School Class of 1972

Table 4

Patterns of Course Tracking in Public Comprehensive High Schools by Subject

	Subjects			
Tracking Patterns	English Language	Science/ Mathematics	Social Studies	Vocational Courses
School Uses Between-Class Ability Grouping	59.1	42.3	39.4	6.2
Number of Ability Groups (where applicable)				
Two	20.2	41.7	34.8	59.4
Three	46.2	40.0	41.4	12.2
Four	21.1	11.9	16.2	19.7
Five or more	12.5	6.4	7.6	8.7

Source : National Longitudinal Study of High School Class of 1972

Americans. The top panel of Table 5 shows that only 34 percent of the African American high school seniors who were enrolled in academic programs (compared to 39 percent of White seniors) were in their school's top math/science classes.

Similar patterns among African American and White seniors are found in the top English (30 vs 36 percent) and social studies (37 vs 43 percent) classes of their schools. African Americans and Whites in the general education and in vocational education programs show few striking differences in top class participation patterns except for English in general education (6 vs 14 percent) and science/math in vocational education (12 vs 18 percent). Thus, overall differences between Whites and African American student participation rates in top classes across core academic subjects are primarily linked to academic college preparatory programs.

HONORS AND REMEDIAL GROUP COURSE PLACEMENTS

How do student placements in "low track" remedial and special education courses versus "high track" honors courses differ by students' race-ethnic status? Based on data from High School and Beyond, Table 6 presents a summary of multiple regression analyses showing the effect of race-ethnicity on placement in special education courses and placement in remedial courses in English and mathematics of 1982 high school seniors with controls for sex, high school demographics—region, urbanicity, and size of 12th grade class.

Table 6 shows that, compared to White high school seniors, African American seniors are significantly over-represented in both remedial English (b=.071) and remedial mathematics (b=.128) courses. These effects are net of statistical controls for sex, track placement, and school demographics—size, region, and urbanicity.

American Indian seniors are also significantly over-represented in remedial English (b=.077) and remedial mathematics (b=.151) courses, compared to White high school seniors.

Table 5

Patterns of Course Tracking in Public Comprehensive High Schools by Subject Areas and Student Ethnicity

| Subject and Ability Group | High School Program | | | | | | | | | | | |
| | General | | | Academic | | | Vocational | | | Totals | | |
	African American	Hispanic	White	African American	Hispanic	White	African American	Hispanic	White	African American	Hispanic	White
Science/Mathematics												
Top Class	15.0	16.0	14.0	34.1	44.6	39.3	12.4	5.9	18.3	23.6	26.0	32.3
Second	55.3	59.0	58.5	40.5	47.8	49.6	49.6	39.5	56.2	47.0	50.2	52.1
Third	20.4	22.1	16.6	23.7	6.9	10.2	29.8	39.4	15.6	24.0	19.6	11.9
Fourth	4.7	1.1	5.9	1.7	0.8	0.5	4.2	11.6	4.1	3.3	2.8	1.9
Fifth or Below	4.6	1.9	5.1	--	--	0.4	4.0	3.6	5.8	2.2	1.3	1.8
Mean	2.31	2.16	2.32	1.93	1.64	1.73	2.42	2.71	2.23	2.15	2.05	1.90
S.D.	1.03	0.85	1.04	0.80	0.65	0.71	1.03	1.01	0.99	0.95	0.89	0.86
English/Language												
Top Class	6.0	9.0	13.7	30.9	38.3	36.1	9.2	4.4	9.8	15.4	16.7	24.8
Second	47.2	48.7	54.8	42.5	47.4	50.1	49.6	43.4	50.0	46.5	47.7	51.5
Third	33.3	34.1	25.1	22.5	12.9	11.4	30.7	39.3	27.4	28.6	28.5	18.1
Fourth	9.3	4.4	3.3	3.3	--	1.6	7.9	7.8	10.3	7.1	3.8	3.9
Fifth or Below	4.3	3.7	3.1	0.7	1.4	0.8	2.6	5.1	2.5	2.5	3.3	1.7
Mean	2.60	2.47	2.29	2.00	1.79	1.82	2.47	2.67	2.46	2.35	2.31	2.07
S.D.	0.93	0.92	0.92	0.85	0.77	0.80	0.92	0.94	0.91	0.93	0.95	0.90
Social Studies												
Top Class	13.8	12.6	17.7	36.9	47.6	43.1	11.1	11.4	12.8	22.3	22.1	30.3
Second	52.0	57.7	48.2	44.6	43.4	46.6	54.9	57.1	56.6	50.0	52.9	49.2
Third	26.1	28.0	26.6	17.3	9.0	9.9	27.9	25.7	20.5	22.7	22.6	16.3
Fourth	6.0	1.1	4.3	0.6	--	--	4.1	5.9	7.5	3.7	2.0	2.6
Fifth or Below	2.0	0.6	3.2	0.5	--	0.4	1.9	--	2.5	1.4	0.3	1.6
Mean	2.30	2.20	2.29	1.83	1.61	1.68	2.32	2.26	2.31	2.12	2.05	1.97
S.D.	0.86	0.72	0.98	0.77	0.65	0.71	0.83	0.74	0.91	0.84	0.76	0.88

Source: National Longitudinal Study of the High School Class of 1972

Table 6

Effects[1] of Race-Ethnic Status on Special Education and
Remedial English and Mathematics Course Placements among
1982 High School Seniors, Controlling for Students'
Background and School Demographic Factors

Race-Ethnic Group

Course Placement	African American	Hispanic	American Indian	Asian
Special Education	0.006	0.014*	0.008	-0.011
Remedial English	0.071***	0.063 ***	0.077*	0.038
Remedial Mathematics	0.128***	0.131***	0.151***	0.018

Source : High School and Beyond

(1) Effects are unstandardized partial regression coefficients derived from multiple regression analyses where course placement is regressed on race-ethnic group with controls for students' sex, curriculum track placement and school demographic characteristics (region, urbanicity, and size).

*   denotes direct effect is significant at 0.05 level
**   denotes direct effect is significant at 0.01 level
*** denotes direct effect is significant at 0.001 level

In addition, Table 6 shows that, compared to White high school seniors, Hispanic seniors are significantly overrepresented in remedial English (b=.063), remedial mathematics (b=.131), and special education (b=.014) courses.

In contrast, Asian seniors are not significantly overrepresented in remedial English (b=.038), remedial mathematics (b=.018), or special education (b=.014) courses, compared to White high school seniors.

Table 7 presents a summary of multiple regression analyses showing the effect of race-ethnicity placement in honors (English and mathematics) courses for 1982 high school seniors with controls for sex, high school track placement, and school demographics—region, urbanicity, and size of 12th grade class.

Table 7

Effects[1] of Race-Ethnic Status on Honors English and
Mathematics Course Placements among
1982 High School Seniors, Controlling for Students'
Background and School Demographic Factors

Race-Ethnic Group

Course Placement	African American	Hispanic	American Indian	Asian
Honors English	-0.052***	-0.031**	-0.001	0.039
Honors Mathematics	-0.031**	-0.032**	0.008	0.123***

Source : High School and Beyond

(1) Effects are unstandardized partial regression coefficients derived from multiple regression analyses where course placement is regressed on race-ethnic group with controls for students' sex, curriculum track placement and school demographic characteristics (region, urbanicity, and size).

*   denotes direct effect is significant at 0.05 level
**   denotes direct effect is significant at 0.01 level
*** denotes direct effect is significant at 0.001 level

Table 7 shows that, compared to White high school seniors, African American seniors are significantly underrepresented in both honors English (b=−.052) and honors mathematics (b=−.031) courses. Hispanic seniors, also, are significantly underrepresented in both honors English (b=−.031) and honors mathematics (b=−.032) courses.

In contrast to other race-ethnic subgroups, Asian seniors are significantly overrepresented in honors mathematics (b=.123), and are neither over- nor underrepresented in honors English (b=.039) courses, compared to White high school seniors.

American Indian seniors are neither over- nor underrepresented in honors English (b=.001) or honors mathematics (b=.008) courses, compared to White high school seniors.

These race-ethnicity effects are net of statistical controls for sex, track placement, and school demographics—size, region, and urbanicity. The unstandardized regression coefficients shown in Table 7 indicate that the negative effect on honors English course placements of race-ethnicity is somewhat stronger for African Americans than for Hispanics, while race-ethnicity has an equal depressing effect on honors mathematics course placements for both groups.

> The maldistributions of programs and ability group placements that we have detailed in Tables 1-7 have obvious implications for students' access to "learning opportunities."

However, the strongest net effect observed in these analyses is the positive effect on honors mathematics placement of race-ethnicity for Asian students.

The maldistributions of programs and ability group placements that we have detailed in Tables 1-7 have obvious implications for students' access to "learning opportunities." Our next analyses examine the connections between this restricted access in high school and adult literacy outcomes.

TRACKING AND LITERACY

Despite some variations among race-ethnic subgroups and across different literacy domains, young adult literacy is strongly affected by high school curriculum track placements. This generalization holds even when levels of educational attainment and key social background factors are statistically controlled.

Table 8 presents results from regression analyses based on the recent National Assessment of Educational Progress (NAEP) Young Adult Literacy Survey. These analyses compare the effects of high school curriculum track placement for African American, Hispanic, Asian and White students on three major dimensions of adult literacy:

Prose — skills and strategies needed to understand and use information from sources that are often found in the home or community, e.g., a newspaper editorial;

Table 8

Effects[1] of High School Curriculum Track Placement on Three Dimensions of Young Adult Literacy by Ethnic Subgroup with Controls[2]

Curriculum Effects (with and without controls)	Prose				Document				Computational			
	White	African American	Hispanic American	Asian American	White	African American	Hispanic American	Asian American	White	African American	Hispanic American	Asian American
TRACK (unadjusted)												
Metric	21.24	14.44	25.03	30.93	20.08	21.34	23.04	35.32	11.92	21.90	19.92	13.67
t statistic	24.12**	5.90***	5.99**	6.42***	22.70***	8.33***	4.42***	6.07***	12.93***	7.97***	4.34***	3.08**
Multiple R(2)	0.11	0.05	0.09	0.24	0.10	0.09	0.05	0.22	0.03	0.08	0.05	0.07
TRACK (+) (Social Background)												
Metric	14.37	7.01	16.29	28.13	14.46	15.65	11.26	29.48	6.93	14.91	11.15	12.41
t statistic	16.33***	2.69**	3.99***	5.37***	15.98***	5.54***	2.23*	4.85***	7.25***	4.97***	2.44**	2.55**
Multiple R(2)	0.23	0.19	0.32	0.28	0.18	0.17	0.30	0.32	0.10	0.18	0.26	0.11
TRACK (+) (Social Background + Education Level)												
Metric	5.64	-0.92	1.72	20.99	6.79	9.63	-5.12	22.08	0.48	9.30	-2.13	6.57
t statistic	6.76***	0.40	0.54	3.83***	7.66***	3.54***	1.22	3.44***	0.50	3.17**	0.53	1.28
Multiple R(2)	0.38	0.40	0.62	0.34	0.30	0.28	0.56	0.37	0.18	0.26	0.48	0.16

Adult Literacy Domains

Source: National Assessment of Educational Progress 1986 Young Adult Literacy Survey

(1) Effects are unstandardized partial regression coefficients derived from multiple regression analyses where literacy outcomes are regressed on track placement with controls.

(2) Controls include respondents' education level, sex, age, parent education, region, and county of birth

(a) The unstandardized partial regression coefficient can be interpreted as follows: Among Asian American young adults, academic track participants score roughly 21 points higher on the prose domain of the NAEP literacy assessment battery than Asian American non-academic track participants, net of controls for educational attainment, sex, age, parents' education, region, and county of birth.

* p < 0.05   ** p < 0.01   *** p < 0.001

Document — skills and strategies required to locate and use information contained in nontextual materials, including graphs, charts, indexes, tables, schedules and the like; and

Computational — skills and knowledge needed to apply arithmetic operations in addition, subtraction, multiplication, and division (singly or sequentially) in combination with printed materials in tasks such as balancing a checkbook or completing an order form.

These analyses show that high school tracking alone (top panel) can be a substantial and statistically significant determinant of young adult literacy. For prose literacy skills, high school tracking accounts for between five percent (for African Americans) and twenty-four percent (for Asian Americans) of the total variation in young adult proficiency. A similar range of effects is observed for document literacy skills where high school track placement accounts for from five percent (for Hispanics) to twenty-two percent (for Asian Americans) of the variance in young adult proficiency levels.

In contrast, although still statistically significant, the explanatory power of high school tracking is substantially less for computational or quantitative literacy skills, accounting for as little as three percent of the variance in young adult proficiency among Whites and a high of only eight percent among African Americans.

The middle and bottom panels of Table 8 show that, in general, high school tracking continues to exhibit a significant effect on young adult literacy proficiency even when social background and educational attainment indicators are statistically taken into account.

Among White and Asian American young adults, the net effect of high school tracking after controlling for social background and educational attainment remains substantial and significant for both prose and document literacy skills, but not for computational literacy skills. In contrast, among African American young adults, the net effect of high school tracking washes away and is not significant for prose literacy but remains significant and quite substantial for both document and computational literacy skill domains.

For Hispanic young adults, educational attainment appears to wash away any influence of high school tracking on all three literacy domains. (The illogic of this finding indicates that it is probably an artifact of the data, and further study is required.)

Overall, it appears that high school track effects on young adult literacy are stronger for Asian Americans and African Americans than they are for Whites, with Asian Americans exhibiting the strongest effect among the ethnic subgroups examined.

> High school track effects on young adult literacy are stronger for Asian Americans and African Americans than they are for Whites.

The net effects of track placement on young adult literacy shown in the bottom panel of Table 8 indicate that tracking exhibits a substantially stronger influence among African Americans than among Whites on two of the three literacy domains examined here—document and computation skills.

For document literacy skills the net effect of high school track placement is about forty percent greater among African Americans while the net track effect on computational literacy skills is nearly twenty times that observed for tracking on the quantitative proficiency of White young adults. For Asian American young adults, the magnitude of the track net effect exceeds that of Whites across all three literacy domains by an even greater margin, although among both groups it is statistically significant only for prose and document literacy.

Our findings on the relationship between curriculum tracking and young adult literacy skills show clearly that placement in the academic track as opposed to placement in general and vocational tracks has substantial positive effects on prose, document, and computational literacy for young adults, while placement in general and vocational tracks has substantial negative effects on these literary measures. In general, because these effects remain after we control for educational attainment and social background, we can say with some confidence that the tracking itself, over and above other factors, is responsible for a significant portion of the disparate outcomes among White, Asian American, and African American groups.

To some degree this statement applies to the disparate outcomes for Hispanic young adults also, based on the fact that the effects remain significant for Hispanics after we control for social background, although not when we control for educational attainment as well.

IMPLICATIONS OF TRACKING FOR RACE/ETHNIC STUDENTS

Our findings on the maldistributions of groups of race/ethnic students in curriculum tracks and ability groups, and the effects of placement in those tracks and groups, have many policy implications for equity and excellence in the American educational system.

First, our clear findings on the effects of curriculum tracking and ability grouping indicate the need for change. There may have been a time when curriculum tracking in schools did actually coincide with the needs of the society and the economy outside of schools—that is, a number of academically proficient students were needed to pursue further education and careers that depended upon that education, while a number of non-academically oriented students were needed to enter the workforce directly and perform the important and even well-paying jobs that required less education. This situation has changed dramatically, but curriculum tracking still exists.

The effects of tracking and ability grouping are especially negative for American Indian sub-groups. This is no new concern. The historic ineffectiveness of American schooling for this disadvantaged population is well documented, and a significant amount of federal funds has been and is being directed toward this population, with few results so far. We badly need an accounting and synthesis of the educational programs that have been developed in our attempts to improve education for American[s] that will provide some basis for identifying and further developing programs that are actually effective.

The effects of curriculum tracking and ability grouping are also especially negative for African American and Hispanic subgroups. For both of these subgroups, our analyses show no real movement out of general and vocational track programs into academic programs over a ten-year period. Students in these two subgroups constitute our largest minority populations and the future economical health of the country depends upon their access to a high quality education.

Our findings of large positive effects of tracking for Asian Americans should be viewed cautiously—too many of the implications are negative. The national media report that the success of Asian American students in our curriculum-tracked schools is creating social backlash against this population that bodes ill for the successful integration of Asian American children into the fabric of American society. At the same time, the overall success of Asian American students in tracked American high schools obscures the fact that some Asian American subgroups are as educationally disadvantaged as the African American, Hispanic and American Indian subgroups.

> The effects of curriculum tracking and ability grouping are also especially negative for African American and Hispanic subgroups.

Finally, there are negative implications of our findings for White majority students. The decrease of White students in the academic track between 1972 and 1982 (from 52.5 to 40.9 percent, coupled with the increase in the general and vocational tracks (from 28.2 to 30.2 and from 19.4 to 28.9, respectively), could easily be viewed as a major shift from being advantaged to being less advantaged or even disadvantaged in terms of educational opportunities to learn.

ALTERNATIVES TO TRACKING AND ABILITY GROUPING

The maldistributions and their effects on adult literacy outcomes presented in this paper make clear that if schools are to meet the requirements of our economy for a more highly skilled future workforce (especially in light of changing demographics) public schools must provide more equitable access to "learning opportunities" which cultivate reasoning, inference, and critical thinking.

Accomplishing this important shift in educational policy will require major school restructuring efforts that encourage effective alternatives to tracking and between-class ability grouping.

Tracking is intended to match the curriculum with students' actual current competencies and to reduce the range within a class so the group lessons can meet the needs of all the students enrolled.

But, tracking is often done by using one general test (such as an IQ test or composite achievement result) and students remain in the same groups for all subjects. Tracking (or between-class grouping), which earlier had occurred mainly in secondary grades, now is very often found in elementary grades (in which within-class grouping used to be the main approach). For example, if there are three grade-four classes, these classes are now often organized as 4-1, 4-2, 4-3, ranked by a test score (see McPartland, Coldiron & Braddock, 1987).

Tracking poses several dangers:

1. **Inappropriate placement.** One test often fails to pick up the variety of individual student strengths and weaknesses across different subjects. For example, a student may be behind in reading, ahead in math.

2. **Differential resource allocation.** The low tracks often get the poorest resources, especially the least experienced or least expert teachers, due to seniority regulations and many teachers' preferences for the top classes.

3. **Differential teacher behavior.** Low tracks are often accompanied by low expectations. Teachers and students think the lowest classes are for "dummies" and there is little push to work very hard at demanding learning tasks. Sometimes there is even a policy of low grades in low tracks (no A's).

4. **Restricted learning opportunities.** There may be a cumulative process by which things get worse over the grades for students in the lowest tracks. Early low-track

placement means poorer resources and expectations which produce lower learning rates for the next class assignments, and so on. Thus small initial differences get magnified.

Whatever their achievement effects may be, ability grouping plans in all forms are being questioned by many educators, who feel uncomfortable making decisions about elementary-aged students that could have long-term effects on their self-esteem and life chances.

> **Ability grouping plans in all forms are being questioned by many educators.**

In desegregated schools, the possibility that ability grouping may create racially identifiable groups or classes is of great concern (Epstein, 1985). For these and other reasons, several alternatives to ability grouping have been proposed.

Effective and innovative responses to student diversity do not just happen. Educators and researchers agree that substantial investments by school systems in staff training may be required to substantially alter current patterns of ability grouping and tracking. Thus if educators are to ensure equal educational opportunities and to provide *every* student with *opportunities to learn* to their fullest potential, it is necessary to know more about both how to deal with student diversity and how to train teachers to do so.

An appealing alternative to ability grouping proposed by Oakes (1985) and Newman & Thompson (1987), among others, involves cooperative learning instructional methods in which students work in small, mixed-ability learning teams. Research on cooperative learning has found that when the cooperative groups are rewarded based on the learning of all group members, students learn consistently more than do students in traditional methods (Slavin, 1983).

Thus cooperative learning offers a plausible alternative to ability grouping which takes student diversity as a valued resource to be used in the classroom rather than a

problem to be solved. However, research has not specifically compared cooperative learning to ability grouping.

Braddock & McPartland (1990) describe several
other possibilities. Flexible grouping processes offer other
alternatives to tracking. These processes include tracking
only in math and/or English but not in other subjects,
using appropriate *subject-matter tests* to make student
placements in the selected subjects; making all groups as
heterogeneous as possible, even in tracked classes; and
covering basic subjects (such as Algebra) at all levels. If
there are nine sections in 9th grade math, for example,
these sections can be subsumed under two or three broad
groups, so there will be less stigma.

There are more ambitious alternatives—such as
replacing tracking entirely in elementary and middle
grades with the use of within-class grouping plus cooperative learning methods, or with the use of competency-
based curriculum in multi-grade groupings, as in the
Joplin Plan.

Looking at the evdience, this is not a yes-no question
of whether to favor or oppose tracking or between-class
ability grouping—it is an issue of considering and evaluating *alternative instructional approaches* to each as primary
ways to deal with student diversity.

REFERENCES

Braddock, J. H. II. (1990). Tracking the middle grades: National
    patterns and trends. *Phi Delta Kappan*, February, 445–49.

Braddock, J. H. II and McPartland, J. M. (1990). Alternatives to
    tracking on the agenda for restructuring schools. *Educational
    Leadership* (in press).

College Entrance Examination Board. (1985). *Equality and Excellence:
    The Educational Status of Black Americans.* New York.

Epstein, J. L. (1985). After the bus arrives: Resegregation in desegre-
    gated schools. *Journal of Social Issues, 41*(3):23–44.

Epstein, J. S. & Mac Iver, D. J. (1990). *Education in the middle grades:
    Overview of a national survey of practices and trends.* Baltimore,
    MD: Report No. 45, Center for Research on Elementary and
    Middle Schools, The Johns Hopkins University.

Findley, W. G. & Bryan, M. (1971). *Ability grouping: 1970 status, impact, and alternatives.* Athens, GA: Center for Educational Improvement, University of Georgia. (ERIC Document Reproduction Service No. ED 060-595).

Gamoran, A. (1987). The stratification of high school learning opportunities. *Review of Educational Research, 43*, 163–179.

Good, T., & Marshall, S. (1984). Do students learn more in heterogeneous or homogeneous groups? In P. Peterson & L. Cherry Wilkinson, *Student diversity and the organization, process, and use of instructional groups in the classroom.* New York: Academic Press.

Hobson v. Hansen, 269 F. Supp. 401 (1967).

McPartland, J., Coldiron, J. R. & Braddock, J. H. II (1987). *School structures and classroom practices in elementary, middle, and secondary schools.* Baltimore, MD: Johns Hopkins University, Report No. 14 Center for Research on Elementary and Middle Schools.

National Education Association (1968). *Ability grouping research summary.* Washington, DC: National Education Association.

Newmann, F. M. & Thompson, J. (1987). Effects of cooperative learning on achievement in secondary schools: A summary of research. Madison, WI: University of Wisconsin, National Center on Effective Secondary Schools.

Oakes, J. (1985). *Keeping track: How schools structure inequality.* New Haven, CT: Yale University Press.

Oakes, J. (1983). Limiting opportunity: Student race and curricular differences in secondary vocational education. *American Journal of Education.* (May):328–355.

Slavin, R. E. (1989). *Effects of ability grouping on Black, Hispanic, and White students.* Baltimore, MD: Johns Hopkins University, Center for Research on Effective Schooling for Disadvantaged Students.

Slavin, R. E. (1987). Ability grouping and student achievement in elementary schools: A best evidence synthesis. *Review of Educational Research, 57*, 213–236.

Slavin, R. E. (1983). *Cooperative Learning.* New York: Longman.

U.S. Department of Education v. Dillon County School District No. 1. (1986). Initial decision in compliance proceeding under Title VI of the Civil Rights Act of 1964, 42 U.S.C. Sec. 200d *et seq.*

Wilson, B,. & Schmits, D. (1978). What's new in ability grouping? *Phi Delta Kappan, 60*, 535–536.

Classroom Opportunities
Curriculum Goals and Instruction

by Jeannie Oakes

with Tor Ormseth, Robert Bell, Patricia Camp

T
hus far, we have considered the distribution of opportunities that create boundaries around what students
can learn in science and mathematics—extensiveness,
content, and rigor of school programs; access of students
judged to be of different abilities to science and mathematics courses; allocation of well-qualified teachers; and
the availability of important enabling
instructional resources. In each case, we
have found distressing patterns of fewer
opportunities for students who typically
exhibit patterns of low achievement and
minimal participation in science and
mathematics—low income, African-
American, Hispanic, and inner-city
students. In this section, we step inside
classrooms to examine whether schools
and classes of different types also differ
in the curricular goals teachers set for
their students and in the type of instruction they provide,
and explore the implications of differences for students'
learning opportunities.

> We have found dis-
> tressing patterns of
> fewer opportunities for
> students who typically
> exhibit patterns of low
> achievement and
> minimal participation
> in science and
> mathematics.

CURRICULUM GOALS AND EXPECTATIONS

Some case-study research suggests that even when course
titles are the same, the curriculum taught in predominantly poor and minority schools is essentially different

Excerpted from *Multiplying Inequalities: The Effects of Race, Social
Class, and Tracking on Opportunities to Learn Mathematics and Science,*
by Jeannie Oakes, from the RAND Corporation, July 1990 p. 80–101.
Reprinted with permission.

from that taught in predominantly white middle- and upper-class schools. These differences suggest that advantaged, white children are more likely to be exposed to essential concepts (as opposed to isolated facts) and to be taught that academic knowledge is relevant to their future lives (Anyon, 1981; Carnoy and Levin, 1986; Hanson, in press). For the most part, however, these issues have received little research attention.

In contrast, there is considerable evidence of differences in the opportunities to learn science and mathematics content in different classrooms within the same school: On average, high-ability groups in elementary schools progress further in a school curriculum over the course of the year (Rist, 1973; Hanson and Schultz, 1978; Barr and Dreeben, 1983; Rowan and Miracle, 1983; Gamoran, 1986). While we know of no systematic studies of content differences in ability-grouped science and mathematics instruction at the elementary level, low-ability reading groups have been shown to spend more time on decoding activities, whereas in high-ability groups more emphasis is placed on the meanings of stories (Alpert, 1974; Hiebert, 1983). High-ability-group students do more silent reading and are interrupted less often when reading aloud (Allington, 1980; Eder, 1981). The high-ability-group advantage is presumably cumulative over the years, and as a result, students with a history of placement in high-ability groups cover considerably more material—and distinctively different material—in elementary school.

> White children are more likely to be exposed to essential concepts and to be taught that academic knowledge is relevant to their future lives.

Differences in pace and quantity of coverage have also been detected at junior and senior high school levels (Ball, 1981; McKnight et al., 1987; Metz, 1978; Page, 1984). McKnight et al. (1987) used data from the SIMS to examine differences in content for eighth graders enrolled in different types of mathematics classes (e.g., remedial, typical, honors, or algebra). Not only did the lower-level courses provide students with access to fewer mathematics topics and skills, students in lower-level classes in the United States had much narrower curriculum opportunities than their counterparts in many other nations (see Kifer, in press). Not surprisingly, the lack of opportunity to learn various topics was reflected in these students' performance on test items.

Low-track classes not only typically offer a limited array of topics and skills, they consistently emphasize *less-demanding* topics and skills, whereas high-track classes typically include more complex material and more difficult thinking and problem-solving tasks (Burgess, 1983, 1984; Hargreaves, 1967; Metz, 1978; Nystrand and Gamoran, 1988; Oakes, 1985; Powell, Farrar, and Cohen, 1985; Sanders, Stone, and LaFollette, 1987).

In an earlier study of 300 junior and senior high school English and mathematics classes, quantitative and qualitative analyses of data from teacher and student questionnaires, teacher interviews, classroom observations, and content analyses of curriculum packages revealed that high-track students were more often presented with traditional academic topics and intellectually challenging skills (Oakes, 1985). Additionally, teachers in high-track classes more often cited having students learn to be competent and autonomous thinkers as among their most important curricular goals. Teachers of low-track classes more often emphasized basic literacy and computation skills and presented topics commonly associated with everyday life and work. Their important curricular goals focused on conformity to rules and expectations.

CURRICULAR EMPHASIS ACROSS SCHOOLS AND CLASSROOMS

The NSSME data provide useful information about the importance teachers place on central goals of science and mathematics education and about how their expectations vary for different groups of students.

Teachers were asked to rate, on a scale from "none" to "very heavy," the emphasis they placed in a particular class on having students achieve the following objectives:

- Become interested in science/mathematics.
- Learn basic science concepts (science only).
- Know mathematical facts, principles, algorithms, or procedures (mathematics only).

- Prepare for further study in science/mathematics.
- Develop inquiry skills.
- Develop a systematic approach to solving problems.
- Learn to communicate ideas in science/mathematics effectively.
- Become aware of the importance of science/mathematics in daily life.
- Learn about the applications of science/mathematics in technology.
- Learn about the career relevance of science/mathematics.
- Learn about the history of science/mathematics.
- Develop awareness of safety issues in the lab (science only).
- Develop skill in laboratory techniques.

Because both school and classroom characteristics can affect students' access to science and mathematics courses, it is important to understand the emphasis teachers place on various curriculum objectives both at schools of different types and in classes of different track levels. Then, to evaluate the relative influence of the school and the classes a student is enrolled in within the school, we must compare the emphasis in classes of the same ability levels in different types of schools.

Elementary Schools. At the elementary school level, about the only differences we found were in the emphasis teachers placed on developing awareness of safety issues in the science laboratory. Teachers in inner-city and rural schools reported emphasizing laboratory safety more than teachers in other urban and suburban settings. There were no school-level differences related to the racial or socioeconomic makeup of the school population.[1]

However, across the sample of elementary schools, we found considerable differences in teachers' emphasis on various objectives in classes that differed in ability level. Table 1 shows the strength and direction of these differences.[2]

In many respects, teachers have considerably higher expectations for students in high-ability classes. They

Table 1
Elementary Teachers' Curricular Objectives:
Relationship to Class Ability Level

Objectives Showing No Significant Positive Relationship with Class Ability Level	Objectives Showing Significant Positive Relationship with High Class Ability Level
Math, facts and principles	Interest*
Math, computations	Science, basic concepts**
Importance in life	Preparation for further study**
Technology applications	Inquiry skills**
History	Problem-solving approach **
Career relevance	Communicate ideas **
Science, lab safety	
Science, lab technique	

NOTE: * = significant at 0.05 level; ** = significant at 0.01 level

clearly place more emphasis on some goals that have been widely heralded as critical, not only for future scientists, but for scientifically literate citizens and productive workers in an increasingly technological economy. Such goals as interest in science and mathematics, inquiry skills, and problem-solving are believed to promote essential adult knowledge and competencies; indeed, many science educators suggest that they constitute the core of science and mathematics education.[3] Moreover, teachers place greater emphasis on preparing high-track students for further study in science and mathematics—a goal that might be seen as equally important for the low-track students who are at risk for continuing low achievement and nonparticipation in science and mathematics courses in later grades.

Compounding this unequal access to some important curricular goals, students in low-ability classes are not receiving correspondingly greater emphasis on other curriculum objectives. Teachers of low-ability classes simply seem to set their sights lower than teachers of classes at other track levels.

Secondary Schools. At the secondary level, there are both school and classroom differences in the emphasis teachers place on various objectives. Teachers at high-SES schools emphasize preparing students for further study in mathematics and science, developing inquiry skills and laboratory skills, and acquiring a systematic approach to solving problems.[4] Teachers at lower-SES schools emphasize becoming aware of the importance of science and mathematics in daily life and recognizing the career relevance of these subjects.[5]

We found racial composition to have relatively little effect on teachers' curriculum objectives. At predominantly white schools, teachers place more emphasis on learning basic science concepts; at predominantly minority schools, they place more emphasis on becoming aware of the importance of science and mathematics in daily life.[6]

There are far more differences among classes than among schools. As Table 2 illustrates, teachers' emphasis on curriculum objectives differs considerably with the ability composition of their classes. Students in low-track or disproportionately minority classes are disadvantaged in the degree to which teachers emphasize *most* curriculum objectives. Teachers of low-track classes were found to give less emphasis to every curriculum objective except becoming aware of the importance of science and mathematics and performing computations. As at the elementary level, these differences distance students in low-ability classes from some of the most important goals of science and mathematics. Moreover, there is a certain irony to the greater emphasis teachers of low-ability classes place on developing an appreciation of the importance of science and mathematics in daily life. While few would question the importance of this goal, teachers behave as if they believe that this is all low-track students can do. One might speculate that teachers of low-ability classes work for student appreciation rather than helping their students become knowledgeable and competent.

These track-level differences reveal important nationwide differences in the types of goals teachers emphasize

Table 2

Secondary Teachers' Curricular Objectives:
Relationship to Class Ability Level

Objectives Showing Significant *Negative* Relationship with High Class Ability Level	Objectives Showing No Significant Monotonic Relationship with Class Ability	Objectives Showing Significant *Positive* Relationship with High Class Ability Level
Importance in daily life** Math, computations**	Career Relevance	Interest* Science, basic concepts** Math, facts and principles** Preparation for further study Inquiry skills** Problem-solving approach** Communicate ideas** Technology applications** History** Science, lab safety* Science, lab techniques**

Note: * = significant at 0.05 level; ** = significant at 0.01 level

and their expectations for different groups of students. However, because of the uneven distribution of track levels among different types of schools, it is important to understand whether low-track classes receive different curricular emphasis partly because they tend to be at schools that emphasize different objectives. In fact, school differences do not appear to account for the ability-level differences noted above. With the influence of school-SES differences accounted for, ability-group differences in teachers' emphasis on preparing students for further study remain.[7] The same is true for developing inquiry skills,[8] laboratory techniques,[9] and a systematic approach to problem solving.[10] However, there is an interesting interaction between school type and track level on some objectives. At the lowest-SES schools, teachers of low-ability classes placed somewhat greater emphasis on inquiry skills and laboratory techniques than did teachers of average classes. In all cases, however, teachers of these two types of classes placed less importance on these objectives than did teachers of high-ability classes.

School differences did not affect the greater emphasis in low-track classes on appreciating the importance of science and mathematics in daily life, but low-SES schools' greater emphasis on the career relevance of these subjects is responsible for ability-group differences. That is, this objective appeared to receive greater emphasis across the sample of low-track classes because it was given greater weight in low-SES schools, and low-track classes were found in far greater numbers in these schools. Thus, track level alone did not produce these differences. Once the differences among schools of different racial compositions were taken into account, ability-group differences in the emphasis placed on learning basic science concepts disappeared. Low-track classes received greater emphasis because there are disproportionately more of them in high-minority schools that place more emphasis on this objective in all types of classes.

Most striking, however, is the finding that teachers of classes at the *same track levels* in very *different types of schools* appear to place similar emphasis on various curriculum objectives.

As shown in Table 3, even when the most widely different school types are compared, the curricular emphasis in classes at various ability levels are more alike than they are different.[11]

The similarities are particularly noticeable among low-track science and mathematics classes. On only two curricular objectives did teachers of low-ability classes in low-SES, predominantly minority, urban schools deviate from their counterparts in high-SES, predominantly white, suburban schools. The curricular focus in high-ability classes was also quite similar across school types. The teachers of these classes in the widely different schools differed on only one objective rated high by more than half of the science teachers and about half of the mathematics teachers: The goal of having students become aware of the importance of science and mathematics in

Table 3

Secondary Teachers' Curricular Objectives in High- and Low-Ability Classses in Schools of Different Types

More Emphasis in Disadvantaged Schools than In Advantaged Schools*	More Emphasisi in No Significant Differences	More Emphasis in Advantaged Schools than in Disadvantaged Schools*
	Low-Ability Classes	
Inquiry skills* History**	Interest Science, basic concepts Math, facts Preparation for further study Problem-solving approach Communicate ideas Importance in daily life Technology applications Career relevance Science, lab safety Science, lab techniques	
	High-Ability Classes	
Importance in daily life** Technology niques** applications** Career Relevance History**	Interest Science, basdic concepts Math, facts Preparation for further study Inquiry skills Problem-solving approach Communicate ideas	Science, lab safety** Scinece, lab tech-

NOTE:* = significant at 0.05 level;** = significant at 0.01 level.
*Disadvantaged schools are low-SES, inner-city or urban, and 50-100% minority schools; advantaged schools are high-SES, suburban, and 0-50% minority schools.

daily life was considered more important in schools serving disadvantaged, minority students.

While school characteristics do influence the curriculum emphases at secondary schools, considerably greater differences result from the judgments educators make about the abilities of their students and the types of class groupings they form. While the NSSME data do not permit causal inferences, school differences appear to stem largely from the disproportionate number of students at high-SES, white schools who are judged to be able learners and the disproportionate number at low-SES, minority schools who are judged to be less able. However, high- and low-track students are generally thought to need much the same curricular focus regardless of where they go to school. The one exception is the more applied and historical curriculum that is offered to low-track students in low-SES, minority schools—a difference that may result from having a less-qualified staff and fewer instructional resources.

LEARNING APPROACHES AND ACTIVITIES
The types of instructional activities that take place in classrooms are useful indicators of *how* teachers go about engaging students in learning. We know of no prior research that has examined differences in instructional practices at the school level or among ability-grouped science and mathematics classes at the elementary level, although considerable case-study and some survey research has investigated the variation in instructional activities with the track level of secondary school classrooms.

Evidence from both American and British ethnographers indicates that teachers describe their expectations for high- and low-track students' classroom participation in different terms (Hargreaves, 1967; Lacey, 1970; Rosenbaum, 1976; Metz, 1978; Ball, 1981; Schwartz, 1981). Hargreaves, for example, found a high-track blackboard with the sign, "We must always remember to behave as an A class," whereas a teacher of a low-ability-level class remarked, "You just can't afford to trust that lot." Such comments seem to be typical of many schools.[12]

Not surprisingly, these differences parallel differences in teaching practices. High-track teachers report spending more time preparing for class, and they appear to be more enthusiastic and more willing to push their students to work harder (Rosenbaum, 1976; Metz, 1978; Schwartz, 1981; Oakes, 1985). Instruction in low tracks, on the other hand, has been characterized as oversimplified, repetitive, and fragmented. Observers report that teachers of low-track classes use recitation and worksheets to break topics down into minute bits of information, causing lessons to lack overall coherence (Hargreaves, 1967; Keddie, 1971; Metz, 1978; Oakes, 1985; Page, 1987a). Low-track assignments require more rote memory and less critical thinking than work in high-track classes (Hargreaves, 1967; Oakes 1985). In high-track classes, teachers sometimes pursue serious understanding of complex themes; in low-track classes, instruction is often limited to basic, surface-level understanding of simplified materials (Keddie, 1971; Oakes, 1985; Page, 1987a, 1987b). Even when ostensibly similar materials are used, low-track classes "caricature" other classes in their abbreviated discussions and simplification of ideas. Page (1987b:21) quoted one teacher as saying, "In this particular ninth grade history class, we're less concerned about history and more concerned about improving your reading skills." Thus, students find the "main idea" of a paragraph about the American Revolution, but they do not discuss the implications of the idea itself.

> **Instruction in low tracks has been characterized as oversimplified, repetitive, and fragmented.**

Using national data, Vanfossen, Jones, and Spade (1987) found that college-track students were more likely than others to describe their teachers as patient, respectful, clear in their presentations, and enjoying their work. In earlier work, we found that the use of time also varied by track: In high-track classes, more time and emphasis were devoted to learning activities, and less to behavior management; high-track students also spent slightly more time on-task and were expected to spend more time on homework (Oakes, 1985). In another study, Gamoran (1987) found that high-ability classes were characterized by more open-ended questions, more higher-order cognitive tasks, and more student control over work.

Thus there is strong and consistent evidence of differences in the implementation of curriculum across tracked classes. Reports of fragmentation and rote tasks in low-track classes indicate a consistent pattern of low-quality instruction. This probably also relates to teacher ability and qualifications. Less-qualified teachers have a more limited instructional repertoire and tend to rely on worksheets more often. However, many of the criticisms that have been leveled at low-track classes have also been listed as concerns for the average American classroom. Not only low-track, but also regular classes are described as lifeless, emotionally flat, having fragmented curricula, and including little critical thinking or cognitive challenge (Goodlad, 1984; Powell, Farrar, and Cohen, 1985). Consequently, these differences must be seen within the context of across-the-board classroom instruction that is not very engaging (Gamoran and Berends, 1987).

The NSSME data provide additional insights into how schools and classes enrolling different groups of students vary in the learning activities they provide. The data include the percentages of teachers who used particular types of activities in the last science and/or mathematics lesson and the percentages of class time teachers say students spend on these activities.[13]

DO LEARNING ACTIVITIES DIFFER AMONG ELEMENTARY SCHOOLS AND CLASSES?
Elementary teachers were asked which of the following activities they included in the last science or mathematics lesson they taught:

- Lecture
- Discussion
- Student use of computers
- Student use of hands-on materials
- Students doing seatwork assigned from textbook
- Students completing supplemental worksheets

Those reporting on science were also asked whether the following additional activities were included in their most recent lesson:

- Teacher demonstration
- Students working in small groups

Teachers reporting about mathematics lessons were also asked about the following activities:

- Student use of calculators
- Tests or quizzes

Teachers at all types of schools reported using basically similar activities in their lessons. Perhaps the most important difference was that a larger proportion of teachers at high-poverty schools used tests or quizzes in their mathematics lessons.[14] Test use also differed among schools of different racial composition, with predominantly minority schools using tests most often.[15] Elementary schools of different types diverged on only one other instructional activity, discussion. A slightly greater proportion of teachers at high-minority schools said that discussion was a part of their most recent lesson.[16]

In addition to reporting the types of learning activities included in their most recent lesson, teachers also indicated how much time they spent on learning activities, daily routines, interruptions, and other noninstructional activities.[17] Science teachers also estimated the time spent on:

- Teacher lecturing
- Students working with hands-on, manipulative, or laboratory materials
- Students reading about science
- Students taking tests or quizzes
- Other science instructional activities

In contrast, mathematics teachers also estimated the time spent in various types of instructional groupings:

- Teacher working with entire class as a group (e.g., lecture, test, etc.)
- Teacher working with small groups of students
- Teacher supervising students working on individual activities

Although we found few differences in the total amount of time spent on instruction,[18] science teachers at high-minority schools assigned students only about half as much hands-on and laboratory work as teachers at schools with predominantly white enrollments,[19] and those in predominantly minority schools spent twice the time on tests.[20] Also, mathematics teachers at predominantly minority schools had students spend more time working in small groups than did teachers at majority-white schools.[21] While greater amounts of small-group time may appear to provide students greater opportunities for active, engaged learning interaction, in most cases, small-group work actually decreases the amount of instructional time individual students spend with teachers, since the teacher can work with only one group at a time. Individual students, although grouped, often work alone at seatwork while they are waiting for their group's turn with the teacher. Moreover, these findings may well reflect the slightly smaller percentage of homogeneous ability classes in predominantly minority schools, noted in Section II. The greater percentage of class time spent in small groups in these schools probably represents more within-class ability grouping for mathematics instruction.

> These findings suggest that students in less-advantaged schools have less access to active, engaging learning activities.

School location was not a factor in either the distribution of types of activities or the way time was spent.

We found no differences in the *types* of activities that elementary teachers of high-, average-, and low-track classes included in science and mathematics lessons. However, we did find some small differences in their *allocation of class time*; for example, low-track classes spent the most time in class routines.[22] These differences largely reflect the larger number of low-ability classes in low-SES schools, where routines generally consume more time. Even when we controlled for school differences, however, we found that students in low- and average-ability science classes spent less time on testing[23] and more time on reading than high-ability groups did.[24]

Low-track mathematics classes spent considerably less time than did average- and high-track groups in whole class instruction[25] and considerably more time working with the teacher in small groups.[26] However, once again, these differences are largely a reflection of school differences, although the greater time low-ability classes spend in small groups is not entirely explained by the greater small-group time spent in high-minority schools, where disproportionate percentages of low-ability classes are found.

In summary, we find that teachers in high-minority elementary schools less often involve students in hands-on or laboratory activities. And students in such schools spend more lesson time on routines, testing, and working in small groups than do students in other types of schools. Together, these findings suggest that students in less-advantaged schools have less access to active, engaging learning activities. Track-level differences suggest additional instructional disadvantages for students in low-track classes at these and other types of schools, who spend less time than their peers in other classes actively engaged with the teacher in science and mathematics lessons. In racially mixed schools, because of the placement of large numbers of minority students in low-ability classes, these class-level differences have a disproportionate effect on the opportunities of minority students.

DO LEARNING ACTIVITIES DIFFER IN SECONDARY SCHOOLS AND CLASSES?

There is little school-related variation in the types of activities secondary teachers include in their lessons. Neither the composition of the student body nor the location of the school has a noticeable effect on the strategies teachers use in science and mathematics classes. In all types of schools, most teachers lecture and few use computers,[27] and most activities specifically related to science or mathematics classes—such as teacher demon-

strations,[28] small-group science activities,[29] or the use
of calculators in mathematics—are similar across
school types.[30]

However, the differences we do find are telling. For
example, the percentage of teachers who ask their students
to do seatwork is strikingly higher at schools with large
concentrations of low-income students—65 percent,
compared with 48 percent of teachers at low-poverty/high-
wealth schools.[31] Also, nearly half of the teachers in inner-
city schools said that they used worksheets in their last
lesson, compared with about a third of the teachers in
other types of communities,[32] and nearly twice the
percentage of teachers in high-minority schools said that
their last lesson included a test.[33] The use of hands-on
laboratory activities also differed at schools of different
SES levels, and seatwork differed with school location.
However, the direction and meaning of these relationships
are muddy.[34]

There is also considerable divergence in *how much
time students spend on different types of activities* at different types of schools. The higher the minority population at
schools, the more time teachers spend on daily routines,
interruptions, and noninstructional activities, although the
size of these differences is small (ranging from 13 percent
at schools with minority populations greater than 90
percent to 11 percent at schools with 90 percent or more
white populations).[35] More significant, science teachers in
schools with higher concentrations of low-income and
minority students have their students spend more time
reading than do teachers in other schools. Students in the
lowest-SES schools spent 14 percent of their class time
reading, while those in the high-wealth schools spent only
4 percent. Consistent with this pattern, students in inner-
city schools spent more time reading in science classes
than did students in other communities.[36] Additional
science time spent on reading may come at the expense of
instruction delivered directly by the teacher; teachers at
the highest-SES schools spent 43 percent of their time
lecturing, while those at the lowest-SES schools spent only
33 percent.[37]

Mathematics teachers in high-poverty and majority-minority schools also have their students spend somewhat more time working alone and less time working with the whole class than do teachers with more-advantaged students. Students in high-poverty schools spent, on average, 53 percent of their class time working with the whole class (e.g., listening to teachers' lectures) and 24 percent working alone; students in high-wealth schools spent 60 and 21 percent of their class time, respectively, in these ways.[38]

> The pattern of more isolated, routine activities in low-track classes is clear.

Overall, then, while there are more similarities than differences in science and mathematics instruction in various types of schools, the pattern of differences is revealing. Students at higher-income and majority-white schools spend more instructional time on whole-class activities and less time working alone, i.e., reading or doing worksheets, than do those at lower-SES, high-minority schools

THE LINKS BETWEEN TRACKING AND CLASSROOM ACTIVITIES

Far more striking than the differences between schools of various types are the differences among tracks within schools. Here, too, the differences in how time is spent are greater than the differences in the types of activities teachers include. But, taken together, the differences reveal quite distinct patterns of students in low-track classes spending more time on routine, less engaging, perhaps even less instructional activities. Table 4 shows that although teachers of the three class levels include most types of instructional activities at the same rates, the pattern of more isolated, routine activities in low-track classes is clear. Students in these classes are more often given seatwork, worksheets, and tests.

Table 5 shows how time is divided into classes of different track levels. Students in high-track science classes are advantaged by spending less class time on routines and reading and more time on hands-on activities and receiv-

Table 4

**Percentages of Secondary Teachers Including Various Instructional Activities
in Last Science or Mathematics Lesson, by Class Ability Level**

Instructional Activity	Class Type			Significance of Differences	
	Low	Average	High	F	P<
All classes					
Lecture	89	85	88	2.25	**
Discusssion	88	86	85	1.45	**
Seatwork	63	61	52	10.20	0.001
Worksheets	43	37	29	16.11	0.001
Small groups	41	37	40	1.17	**
Hands-on	23	26	27	1.08	**
Test or quiz	21	18	16	3.07	0.05
Calulators	13	12	25	29.02	0.001
Computers	8	5	6	2.47	**
Science classes					
Demonstration	46	39	46	3.36	0.05

NOTE: ** = not significant

ing instruction from teachers. Students in high-ability mathematics classes spend more time on whole-group instruction and less time working alone.

Considerable literature suggests that the instructional patterns we have observed reflect an overemphasis on control processes and a concomitant de-emphasis on educative processes in lower-track classes. In an earlier study where similar instructional differences were found, teachers spent more time disciplining than teaching in lower-track classes (Oakes, 1985). These classes focused on passive drill and practice with trivial bits of information, whereas the upper-track classes included more imaginative, engaging assignments. Other studies describe a similar balance between education and order in high-, average-, and low-track classes, both in the United States and in other industrialized nations, and at the elementary as well as the secondary school level (e.g., Ball, 1981; Eder, 1981; Goodlad, 1984; Hargreaves, 1967; Page, 1987a;

Table 5

Percentages of Time Spent On Various Instructional Activities
In Secondary Science and Mathematics Lessons,
By Class Ability Level

	Class Type			Significance of Difference	
Instructional Activity	Low	Average	High	F	P<
All classes					
Routine	12	12	10	14.08	0.001
Science classes					
Lecture	36	36	41	4.98	0.01
Hands-on	20	20	26	5.85	0.01
Reading	12	10	5	22.58	0.001
Test or quiz	7	7	6	0.26	**
Other activities	13	14	12	0.96	**
Mathematics classes					
Class-lecture,test,etc.	48	55	59	18.71	0.001
Small groups	10	9	10	0.65	**
Individual	29	25	20	14.57	0.001

NOTE: ** = not significant

Powell et al, 1985; Schwartz, 1981). These findings, combined with evidence that active learning strategies are most likely to promote student achievement in science and mathematics (Bredderman, 1983), suggest that the instructional patterns observed in the NSSME data restrict opportunities to learn in low-ability classes.

The track-level differences remain, even when we control for instructional differences among different types of schools. With the effect of school location accounted for, low-ability groups were found to do seatwork as a part of their lessons far more often than students in other track levels.[39] With school differences in racial composition accounted for, low- and average-ability classes were more often made to complete worksheets,[40] and more teachers of low-ability classes gave tests and quizzes.[41]

Ability-group differences in how class time is spent also remain when school characteristics are controlled. The high-track advantage in the smaller amount of time

Table 6

Percentage of Time Spent on Various Instructional Activities in High- and
Low-ability Classes in Secondary Schools of Different Types

Instructional Activity	Low-Ability Classes in Low-SES, Minority Urban Schools	High Ability Classes In High-SES, White High-SES, White Suburban Schools
All classes		
Routine	17	9
Science classes		
Lecture	28	51
Hands-on	20	26
Reading	21	1
Test or quiz	10	4
Mathematics classes		
Class-lecture, test, etc.	46	63
Small groups	7	8
Individual	26	20

spent on routines remained,[42] as did the greater exposure
to teacher-led instruction in these classes.[43] Clear instructional disadvantages for low-track classes also remained
after we accounted for school differences. Students in low-
track classes across all school types spent greater amounts
of their science class time reading.[44] Similarly, low-ability
groups spent more time working alone in mathematics
and less time doing whole-class activities.[45]

The combined effect of being in a low-track class in a
low-SES high-minority, inner-city school is that lessons
tend to be considerably more passive than those in higher
tracks at any school. The contrasts shown in Table 6
between the most extreme cases—low-track classes in
high-poverty, minority, inner-city schools and high-ability
classes in high-wealth, white, suburban schools—are
particularly striking.

DO EXPECTATIONS ABOUT HOMEWORK DIFFER AMONG SCHOOLS AND CLASS TYPES?

Finally, we examined how expectations about homework—the instructional time students spend outside of school—differ among schools and classes of different types. We first considered the percentage of teachers who assign homework as a part of their science and mathematics lessons. Then we compared the amount of time teachers in different settings expect students to spend doing homework.

> Teachers of classes at all levels were equally inclined to assign homework, but teachers of high-ability classes assigned considerably more homework than other teachers.

Among elementary schools, neither the concentration of low-income students nor the location of schools made any difference in whether teachers assigned homework or how much time they expected students to spend on it. However, while about a third of the elementary teachers at mixed-race and all-white schools included homework as a part of their science and mathematics lessons, 54 percent of those in schools with predominantly minority enrollments assigned homework.[46] We also found large differences in the time teachers expect students to spend on their homework. While teachers in schools with predominantly white populations expected students to spend about 8 minutes on an average day, teachers in high-minority elementary schools expected students to spend twice that much—16 minutes per day.[47] Within elementary schools, the track level of classes made no difference in whether or not teachers assigned homework, but the class ability level did relate to the amount of homework assigned. Teachers in high-track classes assigned students an average of 14 minutes per day, slightly more than the 13 minutes assigned to low-track classes. Teachers assigned average-track classes somewhat less homework, an average of about 10 minutes.[48]

At the secondary level, school type made no difference in the percentage of teachers assigning homework (63 percent across the sampled teachers) or in the amount of time students were expected to spend on homework (an average of 27 minutes per day). Teachers of classes at all levels were equally inclined to assign homework, but teachers of high-ability classes assigned considerably more homework than other teachers. High-ability classes were assigned an average of 33 minutes of homework per day; average-ability classes, 26 minutes; and low-ability classes, 24 minutes.[49]

> Schools with large concentrations of low-income and minority students offer fewer classroom conditions that are likely to promote active engagement in mathematics and science learning.

The fact that students in low-track classes were expected to spend less time on their homework than other students points to a fundamental irony found in earlier studies of track-level differences in homework (Oakes, 1985). That is, those students who probably need to spend the most time engaged in learning activities to overcome their current deficiencies in science and mathematics are the ones of whom less out-of-school learning time is expected. In contrast, the students who achieve most easily in these subjects are expected to spend the most time learning at home. Thus, teachers have unequal expectations about homework that are likely to further distance high- and low-track students' learning.

SUMMARY

This section has examined two central dimensions of classroom learning opportunities: the curriculum goals that teachers emphasize and the instructional strategies they use to achieve them. Once again, we find patterns that suggest that disadvantaged, minority, inner-city students have more-limited learning opportunities than their more-advantaged, white peers. In the elementary years, differences in curricular goals and instruction are small, but not unimportant. In high-minority elementary schools, there are some small exceptions to the patterns, including higher teacher expectations concerning the amount of homework assigned to students. We must caution, however, that at the elementary level, our measures of opportunity are few and gross in nature, and more work needs to done on measuring what goes on at this level. It is also possible that the increased investment in instructional time and homework may be having perverse, unintended effects: The additional time may not in fact impart the types of knowledge that encourage participation at a later stage in students' academic careers. The evidence from recent achievement assessments appears to bear this out. Finally, there may be processes at work in middle schools or in the early high school years that undo gains at the elementary level. Our data show that the differences in curricular and instructional opportunities—as in the areas investigated in earlier sections of this report—grow considerably wider in secondary schools.

Again, we find evidence of a double disadvantage for low-income and minority students, particularly in secondary schools. Teachers in schools serving large proportions of these students place somewhat less emphasis on such essential curriculum goals as developing inquiry and problem-solving skills. Moreover, teachers in low-ability classes (where disproportionate percentages of minority students in mixed schools are found) place less emphasis on nearly the entire range of curricular goals.

Schools with large concentrations of low-income and minority students offer fewer classroom conditions that are likely to promote active engagement in mathematics and science learning—such as opportunities for hands-on activities and time working with the teacher. These differences are also compounded by differences in the experiences of students classified as high-, average-, and low-ability. The latter group are disadvantaged in their access to engaging classroom experiences and in their teachers' expectations for out-of-school learning. Because low-income and minority students are disproportionately assigned to low-ability classes, these track-related differences further disadvantage these groups. Thus, our evidence suggests that unequal access to science and mathematics curriculum goals is further exacerbated by discrepancies in instructional conditions in schools and classrooms. Together, the data reveal striking differences in classroom opportunities.

NOTES

1. Where curriculum objectives (or other classroom-level-dependent variables) were analyzed with respect to school characteristics, teachers' responses were averaged within each school and the class weights were summed. In these cases, the number of observations was equal to the number of schools, not the number of teachers surveyed.

2. The analysis of track level applies only to classrooms with homogeneous grouping; mixed-ability classes were omitted. Class weights were used to provide nationally representative information about differences among classes at different ability levels. Within each category of the respective independent variables, we calculated the teachers' mean response, but because of the difficulty of interpreting the questionnaire's Likert scale responses in absolute terms, we focused primarily on the relative differences in emphasis between categories.

3. See, for example, Bybee et al., 1989; Champagne and Hornig, 1987.

4. For preparing students for further study in mathematics and science, $F = 3.63$, $P<0.05$; for developing inquiry skills, $F = 4.73$, $P<0.01$; for laboratory skills, $F = 4.32$, $P<0.01$; for acquiring a systematic approach to solving problems, $F = 6.45$, $P<0.01$.

5. For students becoming aware of the importance of science and mathematics in daily life, $F = 5.97$, $P<0.01$; for the career relevance of these subjects, $F = 4.48$, $P<0.01$.

6. For basic science concepts, $F = 3.11$, $P<0.05$; for becoming aware of the importance of science and mathematics, $F = 3.07$, $P<.05$.

7. $F = 95.47$, $P<0.01$.

8. $F = 27.83$, $P<0.01$.

9. $F = 20.01$, $P<0.01$.

10. $F = 19.91$, $P<0.01$.

11. For these analyses we used two groups of schools: The first included those with at least 30 percent of the students from families that were unemployed or on welfare, those with minority populations exceeding 50 percent, and those located in inner-city or other urban neighborhoods. The second group included those in which at least 30 percent of the students had parents in professional or managerial occupations, those with white populations exceeding 50 percent, and those located in suburban neighborhoods.

12. We are grateful to Reba Page for reminding us of this study.

13. Teachers were asked to report the instructional activities that took place during the last science or mathematics lesson they taught. While data about a single lesson cannot provide a full picture of time use and activities in any one class, the weighted data can be aggregated to provide representative descriptions for various types of schools (as defined by SES, racial/ethnic composition, and locale). The data also reveal patterns of time use and learning activities among classes of various types (e.g., ability levels).

However, the data are limited in that the types of activities listed (e.g., lecture, seatwork, quiz) are *gross* categories, the specific nature of which may differ considerably from class to class. Therefore, analyses of these data cannot begin to portray the subtle differences in the activities or in the teacher-student interactions that take place during instruction—subtleties that can make a tremendous difference in the quality of the instructional opportunities made available to students.

14. Twenty-three percent, as compared with 17 and 15 percent ($F = 2.90$, $P<0.05$). Because teacher reports were aggregated at the school level, these percentages represent the average percentages of teachers within schools of each type.

15. Twenty-five percent of the teachers in high-minority schools and 29 percent of those in schools with between 50 and 90 percent minority populations reported that they used tests or quizzes, compared with 18 and 19 percent, respectively, in majority white and 90 percent or more white schools ($F = 2.94$, $P,0.05$).

16. Teachers at high-minority schools included discussion somewhat more often (96 percent) than did teachers at other majority-minority schools (88 percent), majority-white schools (85 percent), or perdominantly white schools (90 percent) ($F=3.23$, $P<0.05$).

17. Teachers were asked to report the number of total minutes spent on the last lesson and then divide those minutes among the list of activities.

18. For example, teachers at high-poverty and low-poverty schools spent slightly more time on routines and other noninstructional activities (12 and 11 percent of lesson time, respectively) than did those at moderate-poverty and high-wealth schools (9 percent each) ($F = 4.24$, $P<0.01$).

19. Twenty-four percent at schools with between 50 and 100 percent minority; 30 percent at schools with 50 to 90 percent white students; and 48 percent at schools with more than 90 percent white students ($F = 2.89$, $P<0.05$).

20. Twelve percent at each of the predominantly minority school types, compared with 6 percent at each of the two types of majority-white schools ($F = 3.44$, $P<0.05$).

21. Twenty-two and 26 percent for schools with minority populations greater than 90 percent and 50 to 90 percent, respectively. This compares with 17 percent in schools with between 50 and 90 percent white students and 19 percent for schools with more than 90 percent white students ($F = 3.25$, $P<0.05$).

22. Teachers of elementary low-track classes said they spent slightly more time on classroom routines (11 percent) than did teachers of average- (9 percent) or high-track groups (10 percent) ($F = 2.93$, $P<0.05$).

23. Five and 7 percent, compared with 12 percent for high-track classes ($F = 3.79$, $P<0.05$).

24. Eighteen percent for low-ability, 22 percent for average-ability, and 13 percent for high-ability groups ($F = 5$, $P<0.05$).

25. Thirty-five percent, compared with 45 and 47 percent ($F = 8.04$, $P<0.01$).

26. $F = 2.96$, $P<0.05$.

27. For example, 87 percent of all secondary teachers said they lectured during their last lesson; 85 percent said they included discussion; and only 6 percent reported using computers.

28. Reported by 44 percent of the science teachers.
29. Thirty-seven percent.
30. Twenty-one percent.
31. $F = 6.98$, $P<0.01$.
32. Forty-seven percent of the teachers in inner-city schools, compared with 37 percent of suburban teachers, 35 percent of rural, and 31 percent of other urban ($F = 4.47$, $P<0.01$).
33. Thirty-one and 26 percent in high-minority and majority-minority schools, compared with 21 percent and 16 percent in majority-white and nearly all-white schools ($F = 6.20$, $P<0.01$).
34. High-poverty and high-wealth schools had the lowest percentages of teachers who said that hands-on or laboratory activities were part of their most recent lesson (24 and 25 percent, respectively); 33 percent of teachers at moderate-poverty and 28 percent at low-poverty schools reported using such activities ($f = 3.85$, $P<0.01$). Inner-city and suburban schools had the fewest teachers indicating that their students did seatwork (53 percent at each type of school, compared with 61 and 63 percent, respectively, at rural and other urban schools) ($F = 5.99$, $P<0.01$). However, the low incidence of seatwork in inner-city schools may be accounted for by the greater use of worksheets, as noted above.
35. $F = 3.03$, $P<0.05$.
36. For reading and SES, $F = 10.61$, $P<0.01$; for reading and racial composition, $F = 8.52$, $P<0.01$; for reading and school location, $F = 7.60$, $P<0.01$.
37. For lecturing and SES, $F = 3.11$, $P<0.05$; for lecturing and racial composition, $F = 2.75$, $P<0.05$.
38. For SES and individual activities, $F = 3.18$, $P<0.05$; for SES and whole-class activities, $F = 4.05$, $P<0.01$; for racial composition, $F = 4.20$, $P<0.01$.
39. An average of 63 percent of the lesson time in low-ability classes was spent on seatwork, compared with 45 percent in high-ability classes ($F = 12.44$, $P<0.01$).
40. The contrasts between low- and high-track classes and between average- and high-track classes were both significant at the 0.01 level.
41. Overall ability-group differences were significant at the 0.05 level, $F = 3.04$.
42. For location and time on routines, $F = 13.77$, $P<0.01$; for racial composition and routines, $F = 8.48$, $P<0.02$.
43. $F = 6.78$, $P<0.01$.
44. For SES and reading, $F = 18.96$, $P<0.01$; for racial composition and reading, $F = 12.07$, $P<0.01$; for school location and reading, $F = 18.17$, $P<0.01$.
45. For racial composition and working alone, $F = 3.94$, $P<0.05$; for SES and whole-class activity, $F = 9.25$, $P<0.01$; for SES and working alone, $F = 8.27$, $P<0.01$; for SES and class activities, $F = 10.74$, $P<0.01$.
46. $F = 2.85$, $P<0.05$.
47. $F = 9.13$, $P<0.01$.
48. $F = 8.95$, $P<0.01$.
49. $F = 80.09$, $P<0.01$.

[Editor's note: For references please refer to *Multiplying Inequalities: The effects of race, social class, and tracking on opportunities to learn mathematics and science* by J. Oakes, with T. Ormseth, R. Bell, and P. Camp. (R-3928-NSF) Published by RAND Corporation, 1700 Main St., P.O. Box 2138, Santa Monica, CA 90406-2138.]

On the Wrong Track?

by Daniel Gursky

Defenders of tracking say it is the only way a teacher can deal effectively with diversity in the classroom. But a growing number of minority parents say it permanently condemns their children to an inferior education. Their protests could make ability grouping a major civil rights issue in the 1990s.

When George Frey set out to reform the student tracking system in the San Diego schools, he started something he didn't expect—a heated, often nasty, controversy.

To Frey, it all seemed pretty straightforward. As a high school principal, he had seen that students tracked into remedial courses were flunking the lowest-level math classes his school offered, so he figured it could do no harm to enroll them in higher level, more stimulating courses such as algebra. He did and found that most of these low-achieving students performed just as well in the tougher classes, and some performed better. But when he became an assistant superintendent in San Diego and tried to make similar changes in the entire school system, he ran head-on into vigorous opposition from some of the community's more outspoken, influential members—the predominantly white, middle-class parents of high-achieving students.

One of the changes Frey hoped to make was to de-emphasize ability grouping. He planned to eliminate remedial classes and place more minority students in

> When George Frey set out to reform the student tracking system in the San Diego schools, he started something he didn't expect—a heated, often nasty, controversy.

From *Teacher Magazine*, May 1990, p. 42–51. Reprinted with permission.

mixed-ability classes. But many parents of students in the honors tracks took strong exception. "If tracking is abolished," the mother of a gifted student wrote to district officials, "bright and highly motivated children who now respond to the rousing of their creativity will probably lose their incentive to do more than is required of them, or they may become too bored to participate."

After months of intense, sometimes harsh, debate, San Diego implemented a core curriculum for all students in 1987. But advocates for gifted students convinced the district to preserve the high-track programs. Instead of eliminating them, Frey says, the district has attempted, with some success, to increase the number of minority students in the honors courses.

San Diego is certainly not the only city where tracking has flared tempers and raised angry voices. Conflicts have been played out across the country as schools and districts struggle to promote educational equality and improve academic performance. In Selma, Ala., a dispute over tracking recently erupted into one of the most tense and widely reported racial confrontations since the landmark civil rights marches there 25 years ago. At issue in Selma was the future of a black superintendent who tried to change a tracking system he said relegated a disproportionate number of black students to the low-track classes. After the superintendent's contract was not renewed, protesters—mainly black students and parents—closed the schools for a week; tensions continued to simmer even after students returned to heavily guarded schools.

The Selma protesters see tracking very differently from the outraged parents in San Diego. Their criticisms are shared by a growing number of people who denounce tracking for what they say are its damaging effects on students unfortunate enough to be placed in the low tracks. They also maintain that tracking permanently condemns many students—a disproportionate number of whom are minorities—to an inferior education, both in what and how they are taught. As one group recently put it, tracking "effectively seals the child's fate, sometimes for life." Their protests could make tracking one of the central civil rights issues of the 1990s.

Although much of the headline-making controversy over tracking has been fueled by factions outside of the school, teachers find themselves at the center of the issue, and they are far from united. One National Education Association official calls tracking "probably the most professionally divisive issue in the association." Those who teach specialized groups of gifted or learning-disabled students have an extra stake in the grouping process. But for most teachers, the issue boils down to how to give slower students the extra attention they need without short-changing the more able students who may lose interest. For every teacher who believes in tracking, there's one who views it as harmful.

> Civil rights activists, decrying the overrepresentation of minorities in low-level classes and their underrepresentation in honors courses, say tracking produces resegregation even in 'integrated' schools.

Still, tracking is by far the most widely used method for dealing with student diversity, particularly in secondary schools. But more and more districts, schools, and individual teachers are trying to loosen or eliminate the practice. Not surprisingly, they have found that simply abandoning tracking is not enough. Managing a more diverse group of pupils in mixed groupings requires innovative approaches such as cooperative learning, small-group work, peer tutoring, and team teaching. In effect, they say, doing away with tracking requires rethinking the way we educate children.

Critics of tracking cite history and research on current education practice to support their arguments. Jeannie Oakes, an associate professor in the graduate school of education at the University of California at Los Angeles and author of *Keeping Track: How Schools Structure Inequality*, traces tracking's advent to the turn of the century. At that time, Oakes says, most children in public schools were from upper-middle-class families, but large numbers of black and working-class students were starting to enter the schools as a result of compulsory schooling laws and rising immigration. Tracking became standard practice in response to the influx of lower-class students. Separate curricula were developed for the relatively small percentage of students destined for higher education and for the masses who went on to menial industrial jobs.

Although the world outside of schools has changed, tracking remains, Oakes argues, because society still expects its schools to sort students and prepare them for different roles as adults. "The idea of grouping makes sense," she concedes. "But we're not very good at sorting kids into homogeneous groups. Instruction is aimed at one level in a classroom that is really full of very diverse kinds of kids. Tracking masks the diversity of classrooms and fools teachers into believing that the same lesson plan works for all kids."

> Tracking masks the diversity of classrooms and fools teachers into believing that the same lesson plan works for all kids.

Oakes has examined the skills and content that are taught in various tracks. In math and science classes—disciplines that typically use the most rigid tracking—she has found obvious inequities in the education each group receives. The high-track students tend to learn concepts, reasoning ability, and the sort of critical-thinking skills necessary to succeed in college and beyond. Low-level classes, by contrast, focus much more on simple skills, facts, and memorization, which leave the students unprepared for either higher education or fulfilling, well-paid jobs.

Vocational classes are seen as one possible alternative to remedial academic tracks, but they, too, receive less-than-favorable reviews from Oakes and other opponents of tracking. "Lots of times, in lots of schools," she says, "vocational education is used as a dumping ground. The classes are for kids who are seen as not capable of making it in more challenging courses." Oakes cites data indicating that, except for students who take a lot of practical business courses in high school (girls preparing to become secretaries, for example), most students in vocational tracks aren't even prepared for entry-level jobs after graduation. In California, she adds, there's evidence that vocational-track students don't fare any better after high school than their peers who dropped out.

Well before the racial tensions in the Selma schools hit the headlines, some educators and civil rights activists were decrying the overrepresentation of blacks, Hispanics, and Native Americans in these low-level remedial and vocational classes, and the corresponding lack of minority students in the college-prep honors tracks. These inequalities, they assert, produce a form of resegregation, even in schools with seemingly mixed student populations.

One group, Quality Education for Minorities, has made the elimination of tracking a significant piece of its ambitious reform agenda for the nation's schools. The group's recent, widely publicized report, *Education That Works: An Action Plan for Educating Minorities*, paints a grim picture of the effects of tracking on some students: "In the first few days of school, judgments are made about children in the classroom. . . . In most school systems in our nation, this decision effectively seals the child's fate, sometimes for life. Students classified as slow almost never catch up, and school rapidly becomes a forum for failure, not an arena for success. By the time these children are in middle school, tracking intensifies and options begin to close.

"Minority children are more likely to be placed in nonacademic tracks because they do not fit the stereotypical, middle-class images our present educational system holds up as ideals."

Project director Shirley McBay says that even the youngest children understand when they've been placed in a low-level group. "The students internalize that and start to think they're something less than others," says McBay, who is dean of student affairs at the Massachusetts Institute of Technology. "It affects their self-esteem and confidence."

Across the Charles River from McBay and MIT, a children's advocacy group has looked at the effects of tracking in one city school system. The Massachusetts Advocacy Center's year-long study of the Boston public schools concludes that "tracking is harmful to kids' achievement," says Ann Wheelock, a policy analyst for the center.

"We saw a funny cycle emerging," Wheelock explains. "Kids are labeled as unready, and then they are given a curriculum that is pretty impoverished, so they never get ready. They get this kind of education all the time, and they simply never become ready for anything more challenging or more educational. They fall further and further behind, and then they don't score at grade level.

> Critics of tracking also argue that special-education and remedial academic programs can lock students into those tracks.

Critics of tracking also argue that special-education and remedial academic programs can lock students into those tracks. "Everybody wants the classes to work those kids out of special education," says Jeffrey Schneider, a program development specialist for the National Education Association. "But the reality is that once students are placed in special education, they tend to stay there until the end. All placement is supposed to be designed to meet the skill needs of students at a given time. If that placement becomes destiny, you've got a real problem."

Widely unequal distribution of wealth and resources can create a form of tracking between schools within districts, as well. Schneider uses math classes to illustrate this point. Poor schools with high concentrations of minority students, he says, tend to have one or two 9th grade algebra classes and only one high school calculus class, if that. A wealthy neighboring school, however, might have enough of these high-level math classes to accommodate four or five time as many students. The same holds true for advanced science courses such as chemistry and biology. And, as Oakes has pointed out, with many academic subjects organized around a strict sequence of classes, if a student doesn't complete algebra or basic physical science by 9th grade, it's unlikely he or she will finish high school with the academic background needed to enter college as a math or science major.

The arguments for tracking are certainly more subtle today than they were 90 years ago, but efficiency still overshadows equality. Tracking proponents say that it is easier to teach relatively homogeneous classes and unrealistic to expect everyone to master the same curriculum, and that students feel more comfortable and learn better when they're grouped with peers of similar abilities. They say tracking enables teachers to tailor instruction to the needs of respective groups of students.

Some of the strongest support for ability grouping comes from the Council for Exceptional Children, a 55,000-member advocacy organization for both special-education and gifted-and-talented programs. Fred Weintraub, CEC's communications director, is fond of making his case by drawing analogies. He compares the main body of American education to a railroad, with a limited number of cars, destinations, and departure times. Special education, on the other hand, more resembles trucking, with a much wider array of services to reach every part of the system.

"Children differ in both what they need to learn and how they learn," he says. "Any educational system that fails to recognize that will serve some children well and some children poorly. If you have a system with one curriculum, one track that everyone is on, that's fine for the kid who can make it on that track."

But what about the 5-year-old who reads *The New York Times* and does advanced math? Weintraub asks. "I would suggest that the local kindergarten is not a valuable learning program for that child," he says. "We clearly believe that there are kids who require a different curriculum."

The CEC also contends that students at the other end of the spectrum—those with learning disabilities—can benefit most from the targeted programs of special education. But Weintraub says special education is usually relegated to the "oh, by the way" part of the system; it has rarely even been mentioned in the major reports that have flooded education during the past decade. "After reading those reports," he says, "you'd basically conclude that these kids do not exist," when in fact, they make up 15 or 16 percent of the total school population.

Neither the NEA nor the American Federation of Teachers, the nation's two major teachers' unions, has voiced an official position on tracking. But the fate of an antitracking resolution presented at the NEA's annual convention a few years ago shows how contentious the issue can be among teachers. Former NEA president Mary Hatwood Futrell often criticized tracking and questioned its benefits for students, so when the resolution condemning tracking came before the union's Representative Assembly, there was widespread speculation that the measure would pass. Instead, the NEA's Schneider says, it was soundly defeated, largely because of opposition from special-education teachers. The vote led Futrell to appoint an executive committee task force to take a closer look at tracking and prepare a final report that will be presented at the group's convention this summer.

Based on his experience with that task force, Schneider offers this somewhat informal assessment of teachers' opinions on the issue: "Our figures show that about one-third of the teachers like academic tracking for one reason or another, one-third dislike it intensely, and the other third find it useful but don't like it."

Likewise at the AFT, tracking is a topic of spirited and seemingly endless discussion and disagreement, says Pat Daly, an AFT vice president. "You can find as many studies that support it as oppose it," he notes. "But I think the trend is definitely in the direction of not tracking."

Still, as the NEA figures suggest, a large percentage of teachers endorse the philosophy and practice of tracking. Many would likely agree with Charles Nevi, director of curriculum and instruction for the Puyallup (Wash.) School District, when he says that "tracking can be made to work."

Unfortunately, he adds, it has become such a "loaded term" that many people are quick to oppose tracking without really examining the issue objectively. "Sometimes, what is traditionally called tracking is a reasonable option," Nevi maintains. "If it's done as a means of empowering students, as a means of teaching them information and skills they can use, then it's not inherently bad.

"When you take large numbers of students and organize them for instruction, you have to group them on some basis. And there are times when the groupings themselves lead to improved instruction. They enable us to provide programs that are more appropriate.

Catherine Schwartz, who has taught in Howell, Mich., for 30 years, believes mixed groups can work with younger students. But by the time they get to her high school writing-composition classes, she's a firm believer in tracking.

"I am totally opposed to heterogeneous grouping in 11th and 12th grade," says Schwartz. "The needs of the college-prep students are not met, and the needs of the average and low students are not met; nobody's needs are met. They should be tracked so they feel comfortable with a group that is like they are. I know a lot of what I say flies in the face of a lot of Ph.D. researchers, but I'm a classroom teacher and I know what works."

'I am totally opposed to heterogeneous grouping in 11th and 12th grade…. What I say flies in the face of a lot of Ph.D. researchers, but I'm a classroom teacher and I know what works.'

All the participants in the debate over the relative merits of tracking and mixed-ability classes can find research studies to back their arguments. But most recent research does show that heterogeneous classes can benefit all students, particularly the slower learners. These studies, however, also come with a caveat: It is not enough simply to eliminate tracking. Lumping students of all abilities together in one lecture-oriented class won't work; teachers must adopt new methods of instruction and flexible curricula to cope with these more diverse groups of students.

"The studies seem to show that [heterogeneous grouping] doesn't harm the higher-ability kids, and it may help students of lower ability," the AFT's Daly says. "But at the same time, from the teachers' point of view, unless you have some understanding or training in how to do it, it's not easy to balance high- and low-ability students with traditional forms of teaching."

Even when there's agreement that tracking harms some students, there's no clear consensus on what should replace it.

Daly, who taught social studies for 30 years, knows what it is like to go from tracked classes to heterogeneous grouping. The social studies department at his Dearborn, Mich., high school eliminated tracking when he was there. "It required you to learn how to do some things differently, to get students to help one another," he says. "But I didn't find that to be a handicap. On balance, I found it to be a more positive experience."

Large public school districts are starting to follow the lead of Dearborn and the many other districts that have experimented with mixed groupings on a small scale. Denver and Orlando are among the urban districts that have joined San Diego in moving away from rigid tracking. Denver plans to eliminate remedial classes at all grade levels and place those students in regular classrooms. In Orlando, many of the changes focus on the middle schools, which are now structured around mixed-ability groups of 120 students who work with an interdisciplinary team of four teachers in English, math, science, and social studies.

"This has allowed us to work without having to label groups of kids as slow achievers," says David Sojourner, an associate superintendent for the Orange County, Fla., school system, which includes the city of Orlando. "If anything, kids who are labeled as slow live up to those expectations. But if you expect them to be successful, they pretty much live up to those expectations."

One of the largest experiments at the elementary school level is the Accelerated Schools Program, led by

Henry Levin, a Stanford University education professor. Some 40 elementary schools nationwide, primarily in urban areas, are implementing sweeping changes aimed at bringing all students up to grade level by the 6th grade so that they can compete equally with their peers for the rest of their school careers. The project staff hopes to extend its efforts into middle schools in the next few years, according to project coordinator Wendy Hopfenberg.

She says the accelerated program combines a relevant, challenging, interdisciplinary curriculum; instructional changes, such as cooperative learning and peer tutoring; and a school-management plan that gives teachers a central role in decision making.

The growing number of schools that are attempting different ways of grouping students adds credibility to Daly's belief that one day rigid tracking will be "a relic of the past." But the arguments over the issue probably won't go away anytime soon: Even when there's agreement that tracking harms some students, there's no clear consensus on what should replace it.

Although some teachers are starting to change their own grouping practices, it's not easy for them to think about alternatives. "They are part of the same process that everyone is part of," says Schneider of the NEA. "Teachers, like everyone else, are going to have a great deal of difficulty giving up the ability-grouping process that's been around them forever. Whether they like it or dislike it, it's one that they understand, that they know how to deal with."

In the end, he maintains, the focus will have to be local if schools are going to better serve the entire spectrum of students. "Can we devise an educational system which effectively meets the needs of students, assuming that all students are special and have special needs?" he asks. "Can it take all students as far as they need to go in order to productively meet their own needs and the needs of society? That's the challenge, and the changes will have to take place one school at a time."

Tracking and Ability Grouping: What About the Gifted?

If tracking and ability grouping are so detrimental, is there anyone who supports these practices? Often, the most vocal arguments in support of tracking and grouping practices come from the advocates for the gifted, those that benefit most by the sorting system. Parents of gifted children tend to worry that the progress of their children's learning may be somehow slowed when they work with students from medium- and low-achievement levels.

The authors suggest that tracking and ability grouping do *not* benefit gifted students. In fact, they consider these practices to be major stumbling blocks to substantive school renewal as well.

In this section, Robert Slavin presents an analysis of the tracking research as it relates to arguments about the gifted child. Contrary to popular belief, he finds the evidence does not prove that tracking and ability grouping are beneficial for high-ability students. Slavin suggests cooperative learning as a more effective alternative.

Concurring with Slavin are David and Roger Johnson. These authors agree that cooperative learning is a much more beneficial way to positively impact the achievement of all students, including the gifted. According to the Johnsons, "when you are really serious about high-ability and gifted students mastering and retaining assigned material, cooperation is the instructional method of choice." In this in-depth article, the Johnsons use research on cooperative learning to ask and answer a host of questions about its effect on gifted students.

Are Cooperative Learning and "Untracking" Harmful to the Gifted?

by Robert E. Slavin

I find no evidence ... that ability grouping is worthwhile for high achievers and find much to recommend cooperative programs for these (and other) students.

In the past few years there has been remarkably rapid development in American education on two distinct but related fronts. One is the adoption of various forms of cooperative learning, and the other is the search for alternatives to traditional tracking and ability-grouping practices. Cooperative learning and "untracking" have completely different rationales, research bases, and political and practical implications. Cooperative learning can work within a completely tracked school, and untracking by no means requires cooperative learning. Yet the two movements have become intertwined in the minds of educators because cooperative learning is often offered as one means of teaching the very heterogeneous classes created by untracking and because of a widespread assumption that if homogeneous large groups are bad, then heterogeneous small groups must be good. Perhaps I have contributed to the confusion by having written in support of both practices (see, for example, Slavin 1988 and 1991).

> In education, there is no fundamental change that does not generate enemies.

From *Educational Leadership*, vol. 48, no. 6, p. 68–71, March 1991. Reprinted with permission.

In education, there is no fundamental change that does not generate enemies. In the case of both untracking and cooperative learning, opposition is now developing among members of the same group: researchers, educators, and parents concerned about the education of gifted children. For example, recently in *ASCD Update*, cooperative learning was cited by several researchers and educators involved in gifted education as having a detrimental effect on the gifted, both in that the cooperative learning movement has often led to abandonment of separate gifted programs and in that gifted students "report feeling used, resentful, and frustrated by group work with students of lower ability" (Willis 1990, p. 8). And in this issue of *Educational Leadership*, Susan Allan writes that "gifted and high-ability children show positive academic effects from some forms of homogeneous grouping."

The questions of untracking and cooperative learning for the gifted are important for others besides the five percent (or so) of students who are identified as academically gifted, because arguments about the gifted are often used to defeat attempts to reduce or eliminate tracking with the remaining 95 percent of students.

What is the evidence on ability grouping and cooperative learning for gifted or other high-ability students? In this article I discuss the research and the logic around these issues of programming for very able students.

IS UNTRACKING BAD FOR HIGH ACHIEVERS?

Leaving aside the question of cooperative learning or other instructional strategies, it is important to understand what has been found in the research on ability grouping in general. Susan Allan correctly observes that the popular press has distorted the research, making ability grouping appear disastrous for the achievement of all students. She is also correct in noting that different ability grouping practices have different achievement effects (see Slavin 1988). However, I strongly disagree with her conclusion that ability grouping is beneficial to high achievers and her implication that it is therefore a desirable practice.

First, let me make a critical distinction between "high achievers" and the "gifted." In most studies, high achievers are the top 33 percent of students; "gifted" are more often the top 3-5 percent. These are very different groups, and I will address them separately.

Is ability grouping beneficial for high-ability students? My reviews of research on between-class ability grouping (tracking) found it was not. In elementary studies I found a median effect size for high achievers of +.04, which is trivially different from zero (Slavin 1987).[1] In secondary schools, the effect was +.01 (Slavin 1990a). Kulik and Kulik (1987) obtained medians of +.10 in elementary, +.09 in secondary schools—higher than mine, but still very small. Most reviewers consider an effect size less than +.20 to be educationally insignificant. In almost every study I reviewed, the achievement differences between ability-grouped and heterogeneous placement were not statistically significant for high achievers. The possibility that the failure to find educationally meaningful effects could be due to ceiling effects on standardized tests is remote; standardized tests are certainly designed to adequately measure the achievement of the top 33 percent of students.

> Is ability grouping beneficial for high-ability students? My reviews of research on between-class ability grouping (tracking) found it was not.

Now let's consider the gifted, the top 3-5 percent of students. Gifted programs fall into two categories, *enrichment* and *acceleration*. In acceleration programs, students either skip a grade or take courses not usually offered at their grade level (for example, Algebra I in 7th grade). When acceleration involves only one subject, that subject is almost always mathematics. All other gifted programs, which do not involve skipping grades or courses, are called "enrichment."

Research on *acceleration* does favor the practice (see Kulik and Kulik 1984), although this research is difficult to interpret. If one student takes Algebra I and a similar student takes Math 7, the Algebra I student will obviously do better on an algebra test. Still, studies of this type find that the accelerated students do almost as well as non-accelerated students on, say, tests of Math 7, so the extra algebra learning is probably a real benefit.

Research on *enrichment* programs, which are far more common in practice, is, to put it mildly, a mess. Most such studies compare students assigned to a gifted program to students who were not so assigned, often to students who were *rejected* from the same programs! Such studies usually control statistically for IQ or prior achievement, but these controls are inadequate. Imagine two students with IQs of 130, one assigned to a gifted program, the other rejected. Can they be considered equivalent? Of course not—the rejected student was probably lower in motivation, actual achievement, or other factors highly relevant to the student's likely progress (see Slavin 1984). A study by Howell (1962), included in the Kulik and Kulik (1982, 1987) meta-analyses, compared students in gifted classes to those rejected for the same program, controlling for nothing. The only study I know of that randomly assigned gifted students to gifted (enrichment) or heterogeneous classes (Mikkelson 1962) found small differences favoring *heterogeneous* placement. Reviewers of the literature on effects of gifted programs (for example, Fox 1979) have generally concluded that while acceleration programs do enhance achievement, enrichment programs do not. Even if enrichment programs were ultimately found to be effective for gifted students, this would still leave open the possibility that they would be just as effective for *all* students (Slavin 1990b).

> Nearly all researchers would agree that the achievement effects of between-class ability grouping (tracking) for all students are small to nil.

Leaving aside for a moment the special case of acceleration, nearly all researchers would agree that the achievement effects of between-class ability grouping (tracking) for all students are small to nil. What does this say to the practitioner? Since arguments for ability grouping depend entirely on the belief that grouping increases achievement, the absence of such evidence undermines any rationale for the practice. The harm done by ability groups, I believe, lies not primarily in effects on achievement but in other impacts on low and average achievers. For example, low-track students are more likely to be delinquent or to drop out of school than similar low achievers not in the low track (Wiatrowski et al. 1982). Perhaps most important, tracking works against our national ideology that all are created equal and our desire to be one nation. The fact that African-American, Hispanic, and low socioeconomic students in general wind up so often in the low tracks is repugnant on its face. Why would we want to organize our schools this way if we have no evidence that it helps students learn?

I do believe that schools must recognize individual differences and allow all students to reach their full potential, and they can do this by using flexible within-class grouping strategies and other instructional techniques and other instructional techniques without turning to across-the-board between-class grouping (see Slavin et al. 1989). In some cases (mostly mathematics), acceleration may be justified for extremely able students. But the great majority of students can and should learn together.

IS COOPERATIVE LEARNING BAD FOR HIGH ACHIEVERS?

In research on cooperative learning, we have routinely analyzed achievement outcomes according to students' pretest scores. Those in the top third, middle third, and low third have all gained consistently, relative to similar students in control classes, as long as the cooperative learning program in use provides group goals and individual accountability (see Slavin 1991). High achievers gain from cooperative learning in part because their peers encourage them to learn (it benefits the group) and because, as any teacher knows, we learn best by describing our current state of knowledge to others (see Webb 1985).

In preparation for writing this article, I asked my colleague, Robert Stevens, to run some additional analyses on a study he is doing in two suburban elementary

Figure 1: Difference in Effect Sizes Between High Achievers in Two
Cooperative and Two Control Schools

Measure	Top 33%	Top 10%	Top 5%
Reading Vocabulary	+.42	+.65	+.32
Reading Comprehension	+.53	+.68	+.96
Language Mechanics	+.28	+.11	−.14
Language Expression	+.28	+.48	+.17
Math Computation	+.63	+.59	+.62
Math Concepts & Applications	+.28	+.32	+.19

Note: These data are from Point Pleasant and Overlook Elementary Schools
and two matched comparison schools in Anne Arundel County, Maryland, a
Baltimore suburb.

schools. The two schools have been using cooperative
learning in all academic subjects for many years, in which
all forms of between-class ability grouping are avoided and
in which special education teachers team with regular
classroom teachers to teach classes containing both
academically handicapped and non-handicapped students.
Stevens' analyses focused on three definitions of high
ability: top 33 percent, top 10 percent, and top 5 percent.
The results for grades 2-5 on standardized tests are summarized in Figure 1.

Figure 1 shows that even the very highest achieving
students benefited from cooperative learning in comparison to similar students in the two control schools. The
only exception was on Language Mechanics, probably
because the writing process approach we use does not
emphasize mechanics out of the context of writing. It is
important to note that the Stevens study does not involve
run-of-the-mill cooperative learning in reading, writing/
language arts, or mathematics, but uses Cooperative
Integrated Reading and Composition or CIRC (Stevens et
al. 1987) and Team Assisted Individualization (TAI)
Mathematics (Slavin 1985) (also see Slavin et al. 1989/90).

These programs incorporate flexible grouping within the class and therefore differentiate instruction for students of different achievement levels. Still, no separate grouping or special program was needed to substantially accelerate the achievement of even the highest achievers (and of other students as well).

Many of the concerns expressed about high achievers in cooperative learning are based either on misconceptions or on experience with inappropriate forms of cooperative learning. First, many educators and parents worry that high achievers will be used as "junior teachers" instead of being able to move ahead on their own material. This is a confusion of cooperative learning with peer tutoring; in all cooperative methods, students are learning material that is new to all of them. A related concern is that high achievers will be held back waiting for their groupmates. This is perhaps a concern about untracking, but not about cooperative learning. In cooperative learning students are typically exposed to the same content they would have seen anyway; and in forms of cooperative learning such as CIRC and TAI, they may progress far more rapidly than they otherwise would have. Sometimes parents are concerned when their youngsters' grades are made dependent on those of their groupmates. This does happen in some forms of cooperative learning, but I am personally very opposed to the practice. Certificates or other recognition work just as well, and grades can and should be given based on individual performance.

NO EVIDENCE IN FAVOR OF TRACKING

My personal philosophy of education is that all students should be helped to achieve their full potential. I am in favor of potential. I am in favor of acceleration programs (especially in mathematics) for the gifted, and I believe in differentiating instruction *within* heterogeneous classes to meet the needs of students above (and below) the class average in performance. But I see no evidence or logic to support separate enrichment programs for gifted students. Enrichment is appropriate for *all* students. I see little evidence at all for separate tracks for high achievers. The burden of proof for the antidemocratic, antiegalitarian practice of ability grouping must be on those who would group, and no one who reads this literature could responsibly conclude that this requirement has been met. The likely impact of untracking *per se* on the achievement of high achievers is no impact at all—these students will do well wherever they are. However, with the use of effective cooperative learning programs, especially those that differentiate instruction within the class, high achievers are likely to benefit in achievement, even the very top-achieving 5 percent. Educators of the gifted should be in the forefront of the cooperative learning movement, insisting on the use of forms of cooperative learning known to benefit gifted and other able students. If these methods also happen to be good for average and below average students, so much the better!

Author's note: This article was written under a grant from the Office of Education Research and Improvement, U. S. Department of Education (No. OERI-R-117-R90002). However, any opinions expressed are mine and do not represent OERI positions or policies.

NOTES

1. In this case, an "effect size" is the difference between ability grouped and ungrouped students on achievement tests divided by the test's standard deviation. Effect sizes between -.20 and +.20 are generally considered to indicate no meaningful differences.

REFERENCES

Fox, L. H. (1979). Programs for the gifted and talented: An overview. In *The gifted and talented: their education and development*, pp. 104–126, edited by A. H. Passow. Chicago: University of Chicago Press.

Howell, W. (1962). Grouping of talented students leads to better academic achievement in secondary school. *Bulletin of the NASSP*, 46: 67–73.

Kulik, C-L., & Kulik, J. A. (1982). Effects of ability grouping on secondary school students: A meta-analysis of evaluation findings. *American Educational Research Journal*, 19: 415–428.

Kulik, C-L., & Kulik, J. A. (1984). Effects of accelerated instruction on students. *Review of Educational Research* 54:409–425.

Kulik, C-L., & Kulik, J. A. (1987). Effects of ability grouping on student achievement. *Equity and Excellence* 23:22–30.

Mikkelson, J. E. (1962). An experimental study of selective grouping and acceleration in junior high school mathematics. Doctoral dissertation, University of Minnesota.

Slavin, R. E. (1984). Meta-analysis in education: How has it been used? *Educational Researcher*, 13(8): 6–15, 24–27.

Slavin, R. E. (1985). Team-Assisted Individualization: Combining cooperative learning and individualized instruction in mathematics. In *Learning to cooperate, Cooperating to learn*, pp. 177–209, edited by R. E. Slavin, S. Sharan, S. Kagan, R. Hertz-Lazarowitz, C. Webb, and R. Schmuck. New York: Plenum.

Slavin, R. E. (1987). Ability grouping and student achievement in elementary schools: A best-evidence synthesis. *Review of Educational Research*, 57: 293–336.

Slavin, R. E. (1988). Synthesis of research on grouping in elementary and secondary schools. *Educational Leadership*, 46(1): 67–77.

Slavin, R. E. (1990a). Achievement effects of ability grouping in secondary schools: A best-evidence synthesis. *Review of Educational Research*, 60(3): 471–499.

Slavin, R. E. (1990b). Ability grouping, cooperative learning, and the gifted. *Journal for the Education of the Gifted*, 14: 3–8.

Slavin, R. E. (1991). Synthesis of research on cooperative learning. *Educational Leadership*, 48(5): 63–74.

Slavin, R. E., Madden, N. A., & Stevens, R. J. (1989/90). Cooperative learning models for the 3 R's. *Educational Leadership*, 47(4): 22–28.

Slavin, R. E., Braddock, J. H., Hall, C., & Petza, R. J. (1989). *Alternatives to ability grouping*. Baltimore, MD: Johns Hopkins University, Center for Research on Effective Schooling for Disadvantaged Students.

Stevens, R. J., Madden, N. A., Slavin, R. E., & Farnish, A. M. (1987). Cooperative integrated reading and composition: Two field experiments. *Reading Research Quarterly*, 22: 433–454.

Webb, N. (1985). Student interaction and learning in small groups: A research summary. In *Learning to cooperate, cooperating to learn*, pp. 147–172, edited by R. E. Slavin, S. Sharan, S. Kagan, R. Hertz-Lazarowitz, C. Webb, and R. Schmuck. New York: Plenum.

Wiatrowski, M., Hansell, S., Massey, C. R., & Wilson, D. L. (1982). Curriculum tracking and delinquency. *American Sociological Review*, 47: 151–160.

Willis, S. (1990). Cooperative learning fallout. ASCD *Update*, 32(8): 6, 8.

What to Say to People Concerned with the Education of High Ability and Gifted Students

by David W. Johnson and Roger T. Johnson

You can always tell when it is coming. A parent, colleague, administrator, or school board member stands up with a shrug and a smile and you brace yourself to hear the question once again: "I am an advocate of cooperative learning, but is not the academic progress of high-achieving and gifted students slowed down when they work with medium- and low-achieving classmates?"

A concern that all educators hold in common is how to challenge the academic capabilities of **all** students and maximize their intellectual development. This includes the high-ability and gifted as well as under-achieving students. When considering how to intellectually challenge high ability (the academically top 33 percent) and gifted (the academically top 5 percent) students, cooperative learning has to be considered. For the rest of this article the term high-ability will be used to subsume gifted. There are often uncomfortable anxieties about (a) all accelerated work will be dropped and (b) the possibility that brighter students will be "held back" when they work in a cooperative group with middle- and low-achieving peers. It is often difficult to calm these anxieties. Reassurances rarely work. When doubters are rational, referring them to the research will help.

> A concern all educators hold in common is how to challenge the academic capabilities of *all* students and maximize their intellectual development.

From the Cooperative Learning Center, January 1991, University of Minnesota. Reprinted with permission.

In order to discuss the issue of whether or not high-ability and gifted students should learn in cooperative groups it must first be noted that:

• High-achieving students should not *always* work in cooperative groups (see Johnson & Johnson, 1991). There are times when high-ability and gifted students should work alone, individualistically, in isolation from all other students. There are times when gifted students should compete to see who is best.

• When high-achieving and gifted students do work in cooperative groups the groups should not always be heterogeneous. There are times when gifted students should be segregated for fast-paced accelerated work.

• Well-structured cooperative learning groups are quite different from traditional classroom grouping and poorly structured cooperative groups (Johnson, Johnson, & Holubec, 1990). To be most effective, cooperation must be structured so that group members (a) believe that they are responsible for and benefit from each other's learning, (b) promote each other's learning face-to-face by helping, sharing, assisting, and encouraging, (c) are accountable to do their fair share of the work, (d) utilize the required leadership, communication, decision-making, trust-building, and conflict resolution skills required for the group to ensure the success of each member, and (e) regularly process how effectively [each] is functioning. In this article it is assumed that cooperative groups are structured to include these five essential elements.

For many reasons, however, high-achieving and gifted students should learn the majority of the time in well-structured cooperative learning groups. And frequently they should work with a wide variety of peers. Not because of ideology or philosophy, but because of hard-headed pragmatism. The education of high-achieving and gifted students should not be conducted on the basis of personal preference or folklore. It should be based on what has been empirically demonstrated to be effective by research and evaluation.

There are at least five outcomes of interest to educators involved in the education of high-ability and gifted students. They are:

- The mastery and retention of assigned material.
- The use of higher-level reasoning strategies.
- The valuing of their abilities and seeing their achievement as positive (i.e., academic self-esteem).
- Being accepted, appreciated, supported, and liked by their classmates (i.e., peer acceptance).
- The development and refinement of leadership skills, problem-solving procedures, the constructive resolution of conflicts, and other social competencies.

Over the past 15 years we have conducted nine studies examining the impact on high-ability and gifted students of learning individualistically, competitively, cooperatively in homogeneously high-ability groups, and cooperatively in academically heterogeneous groups. In these carefully controlled experimental studies, students were randomly assigned to conditions, teachers were rotated across conditions so each taught the same amount of time in each condition, the same curriculum materials were used in all conditions, and each condition was systematically observed daily to ensure it was being implemented appropriately. In most of the studies the impact of high-, medium-, and low-ability students were analyzed separately, allowing us to make conclusions about the impact of cooperative learning on each ability level. In a few of the studies only high-ability students were included.

> Cooperative learning is a beneficial and benign instructional method that has numerous benefits on students' achievement, relationships with classmates, and psychological adjustment.

Cooperative learning is a beneficial and benign instructional method that has numerous benefits on students' achievement, relationships with classmates, and psychological adjustment. Still, many people are concerned about its impact on high-ability and gifted students. A brief review of what we know empirically may be helpful. Here are the questions and the answers that current research now indicates.

Do high-ability and gifted students benefit academically from participating in cooperative learning groups? Yes. The purpose of a cooperative learning group is to make each member a stronger individual in his or her own right. This includes high-ability members. The discussion and exchange within the cooperative learning group needs to benefit the high-ability member as much as any other member. And when cooperative groups are carefully structured, it does. Consistently, the mastery and retention of assigned material by high-ability and gifted students has been found to be higher in cooperative than in competitive or individualistic learning situations. What they learn within the group discussion they demonstrated and used in subsequent situations when they worked individually. When you are really serious about high-ability and gifted students mastering and retaining assigned material, cooperation is the instructional method of choice.

Does learning cooperatively with medium- and low-achieving peers decrease critical thinking and higher-level reasoning? No. Just the opposite. High-ability and gifted students should not be burdened with long hours of drill and review and lower-level cognitive tasks. Their time should be spent primarily in conceptualizing, thinking critically, and developing higher-level reasoning strategies. Cooperative learning is the first step for doing so (Johnson, Johnson, & Holubec, 1990). Structured academic controversies are the second step (Johnson & Johnson, 1987). Many of our studies on cooperative learning have focused on quality of reasoning strategy, level of cognitive reasoning, and metacognitive strategies. When high-ability students were given tasks that could be solved by using either a higher-level or a lower-level reasoning strategy, they more frequently discovered and used the higher-level reasoning strategy when they learned cooperatively (as opposed to competitively or individualistically). In a study with Linda Skon (Skon, Johnson, & Johnson, 1981), students worked on a categorization and retrieval task that could' be completed using either a higher-level or a lower-level reasoning strategy. Eighty-nine percent of the subjects in the cooperative condition used the higher-level strategy and derived the correct answer, while less than one percent of the subjects in the competitive and individualistic conditions did so.

Are there academic advantages for high-ability and gifted students of working within heterogeneous cooperative learning groups? Usually Yes. In our studies we have consistently found that high-ability students who work cooperatively with medium- and low-ability students outperform and use higher-level reasoning strategies more frequently than do high-ability students who work competitively or individualistically. The results of our studies indicated that high-ability and gifted students working competitively or individualistically often learn material quickly but superficially while using lower-level reasoning strategies; when working in cooperative groups with medium- and low-achieving peers, however, they almost always discovered and used higher-level reasoning strategies and retained the material better. Pat Heller, one of our colleagues, in a study of how frequently students in physics classes use novice or expert reasoning strategies found that cooperative groups made up of high-, medium-, and low-achieving students discovered expert problem solutions while high-achievers used novice reasoning strategies when working by themselves. The conclusion from these and other studies seem clear. High-achievers gain academically from working cooperatively with a wide variety of students.

> Learning material with the expectation of teaching it to others results in learning it at a higher cognitive level.

Despite the clear evidence that high-achieving students benefit academically from working cooperatively with medium- and low-achieving classmates, many people still ask, "How can this be so?" To clarify, the dynamics within cooperative groups that cause this finding must be identified. The research points to several reasons. **First,** learning material with the expectation of teaching it to others results in learning it at a higher cognitive level than does learning material to pass a test. **Second,** explaining the material to others increases the level of one's achievement, increases the level of one's cognitive reasoning, and increases retention. **Third,** checking the explanations of others for accuracy tends to increase the gifted student's achievement. **Fourth,** cognitive growth requires social interaction and the collision of adverse opinion. It is primarily through discussing material being studied and problems being solved in ways that provide disagreement and intellectual arguments among group members that cognitive growth, critical thinking, and higher-level reasoning is achieved. Intellectual conflict can be promoted through the use of academic controversy. The procedures for structuring academic controversies are covered in our training on the creative use of conflict within classrooms and schools. **Finally,** viewing issues from a variety of perspectives promotes higher-level reasoning and general growth in cognitive reasoning. High-ability and gifted students gain cognitively and academically from working with a wide variety of peers who have different perspectives and take different approaches in solving problems and completing work.

Do low-achieving students contaminate the achievement of high-ability and gifted students? No. High-ability and gifted students tend to benefit academically from working with low- and medium-achieving peers. High-ability and gifted students initially explain the material being studied and how to complete the assignment. The cognitive restructuring and practice that occur during the giving of explanations facilitates a more thorough grasp of the material and its commitment to long-term memory. A series of research studies by Frank Murray, furthermore, indicated that while the nonconserver learns to conserve as a result of working with a conserver, the conserver does not "unlearn" conservation. Cognitive growth seems to be unidirectional. In other words, when students at different levels of cognitive development work together, truth wins out. Cognitive development is not reversed.

Would not the gifted student's achievement be higher if he or she worked only with other gifted students? Probably No, for several reasons. **First,** there is some evidence that fewer explanations take place within all gifted groups, which lowers the level of achievement and retention. **Second,** there may be less expectation that one will have to explain what one is learning to others. Studies have found that expecting to teach what one is learning to others (as opposed to learning it to pass a test) results in learning the material at a higher level of cognitive understanding. **Third**, the research by Frank Murray again is relevant. He found that a conserver who works with a conserver does not do any better on later conservation tasks than does a conserver who works with a nonconserver. An all-gifted group seems to have no advantage over heterogeneous groups in terms of level of cognitive reasoning. And sometimes it does less well!

Are there academic disadvantages of heterogeneous learning groups for gifted students? Perhaps. While the quality of learning is increased, the quantity may go down. Gifted students may produce less in terms of quantity as they spend more time in conceptualizing and cognitively networking what they are learning.

> Like everyone else, high-ability students seek social acceptance and psychological affiliation with their peers.

Many high-ability and gifted students fear peer rejection if they exert much effort to learn. Can cooperative learning help? Yes. In many cases high-ability students underachieve. Two hypotheses for such underachievement are a lack of academic self-esteem (students do not take pride in and value academic success) and peer rejection of high achievers. Being a high-ability student does not guarantee that the student will have high academic self-esteem. In many cases the self-esteem of high-ability students is assaulted by the social rejection of peers who label high-achievers "nerds." Peer pressure against excelling academically can exist. High-ability students who defy such peer pressures in effect make classmates look like losers in teachers' eyes. They set a standard of performance that serves to increase the effort classmates have to put into schoolwork. This is typically not appreciated. Often classmates in turn label high-achievers as losers in the peer social system by labeling them as "nerds" and "brains." If such labels are internalized by high-achieving students, their academic self-esteem suffers.

Like everyone else, high-ability students seek social acceptance and psychological affiliation with their peers. They struggle to develop and sustain high self-esteem based on their academic success. In order to raise the self-esteem of high-ability students it may first be necessary to increase the class cohesion and feelings of acceptance by peers.

The academic achievement of high-ability students can be valued by classmates when they have a stake in each other's success and benefit from each other's efforts. In our studies we found that when high-ability students work with cooperative learning groups with medium- and low-ability peers or other high-ability peers, the high-ability students (a) felt accepted, supported, and appreciated by their peers, (b) believed that class members liked and cared about each other, and (c) were proud of and positive about their academic abilities and achievement.

Does working in cooperative learning groups help provide the friendship, support, and social competencies high-ability and gifted students need to cope with stress? Typically yes. Like anyone else, high-ability and gifted students can feel isolated, lonely, and depressed. Their achievements can be seen as meaningless when parents get divorced, their peers reject them, or they are victims of crime. Anyone, no matter how intelligent or creative, can have such feelings. Recently in a Minnesota school district, a popular star athlete committed suicide. The note he left indicated feelings of loneliness, depression, and isolation. He is not unusual. Many students have the delusion that each person is separate and apart from all other individuals. A recent national survey reported that growing feelings of worthlessness and isolation led 30 percent of America's brightest teenagers to consider suicide, and 4 percent have tried it.

We are in an epidemic of depression and anxiety among our adolescents and young adults. And it seems to be spreading downward as more and more elementary school students are becoming depressed. The stark emptiness of the self and the vacuousness of "me" is revealed when students are faced with a personal crisis. What is denied is that personal well-being cannot exist without commitment to and responsibility for joint well-being.

A number of years ago, a speeding car carrying five teenagers slammed into a tree, killing three of them. It was not long before small, spontaneous memorials appeared at the tree. A yellow ribbon encircled its trunk. Flowers were placed nearby on the ground. There were a few good-bye signs. Such quiet testimonies send an important message: When it really matters, we are part of a community, not isolated individuals. We define ourselves in such moments as something larger than our individual selves—as friends, classmates, teammates, and neighbors.

It is easy to be concerned only with yourself. But when classmates commit suicide and when cars slam into trees killing classmates, the shock waves force us out of the shallowness of self into the comforting depth of community. An important advantage of placing high-ability and gifted students in cooperative learning groups and having them work together with a wide variety of peers to complete assignments is the sense of belonging, acceptance, and caring that results. In times of crisis, such community may mean the difference between isolated misery and deep personal talks with caring friends.

> Nothing motivates more than a sense of achieving a joint goal that is meaningful because it makes someone else's life better.

When gifted students are separated for enrichment, are there any guidelines to ensure that the learning experience is optimal? Yes. First, have the students learn in cooperative groups. Second, make the groups as heterogeneous as possible. Students can be gifted for many different reasons. Some students do well because they want to please adults, do everything right, and always work to complete extra-credit projects. Other students are gifted because they are creative risk-takers or because they are talented in a specific area, such as mathematics or writing. Within the limits imposed by the homogeneous situation, the cooperative learning groups should be as heterogeneous as possible. A student who is a creative risk-taker is a great learning partner for a student who wants to do everything right. Third, regularly structure academic controversies within the cooperative learning groups. The conceptual conflict resulting from being confronted with a variety of possible answers and points of view is essential for cognitive growth, critical thinking, and the development of higher-level reasoning strategies.

My child is very bright intellectually. But he/she is bored with and uninterested in school. What can be done? In order for students to exert long-term, hard, persistent efforts to learn they must believe that there is a good reason for doing so. While there is probably an intrinsic drive toward competence, for various reasons schools have a hard time tapping into that drive for most students. What a teacher of an undermotivated gifted student can do is structure learning situations cooperatively so that students are expected to contribute to other students' learning as well as their own. **Nothing motivates more than a sense of achieving a joint goal that is meaningful because it makes someone else's life better.** When making a choice between watching TV and doing homework, a student may be heard to say, "My group's counting on me. I have to do my homework."

What should the school do to make sure high-ability and gifted students have successful careers? Focus the gifted students on **mastery** (desire to tackle challenging tasks) and **hard work**, not on winning over others. Robert Helmreich and his colleagues at the University of Texas have studied competitiveness as a personality trait. They first determined that high achievers, such as scientists, MBA's, and pilots tend not to be very competitive individuals. High achievers in the real work of business, industry, and science tend to be low on competitiveness but high on the personality traits of wanting to take on challenging tasks and valuing hard work. They do not want to win over colleagues. The researchers found that competitiveness typically lowers job performance, as competitive individuals get so concerned about triumphing over colleagues that they ignore important aspects of their jobs, lack concentration and focus, lose sight of the "big picture" and overall goals, are very short-term oriented, and become distracted from the task at hand. Helmreich has not been able to identify a single professional arena where highly competitive individuals tend to be more successful. Similar studies of elementary, secondary, and college students (competitive students get lower grades) and of news reporters (competitiveness lowers job performance) found similar results.

REFERENCES

Gabbert, B., Johnson, D. W., & Johnson, R. (1986). Cooperative learning, group-to-individual transfer, process gain, and the acquisition of cognitive reasoning strategies. *Journal of Psychology, 120*, 265–278.

Heller, P., Keith, R., & Anderson, S. (1990). Group versus individual problem solving in a large introductory physics course. University of Minnesota, submitted for publication.

Helmreich, R., Sawin, L., & Carsrud, A. (1986). The honeymoon effect in job performance: Temporal increases in the predictive power of achievement motivation. *Journal of Applied Psychology, 71*, 185–188.

Johnson, D. W., & Johnson, R. (1987). *Creative conflict.* Edina, MN: Interaction Book Company.

Johnson, D. W., & Johnson, R. (1989). *Cooperation and competition: Theory and research.* Edina, MN: Interaction Book Company.

Johnson, D. W., & Johnson, R. (1991). *Learning together and alone: Cooperative, competitive, and individualistic learning.* Englewood Cliffs, NJ: Prentice-Hall.

Johnson, D. W., & Johnson, R., & Holubec, E. (1990). *Circles of learning.* Edina, MN: Interaction Book Company.

Johnson, D. W., Johnson, R., & Smith, K. (1982). Effects of cooperative and individualistic instruction in the achievement of handicapped, regular, and gifted students. *Journal of Social Psychology, 116*, 277–283.

Johnson, D. W., Johnson, R., Pierson, W., & Lyons, V. (1985). Controversy versus concurrence seeking in multi-grade and single-grade learning groups. *Journal of Research in Science Teaching, 22*, 197–205.

Johnson, D. W., Johnson, R., Roy, P., & Zaidman, B. (1985). Oral interaction in cooperative learning groups: Speaking, listening, and the nature of statements made by high-, medium-, and low-achieving students. *Journal of Psychology, 119*, 303–321.

Johnson, D. W., Skon, L., & Johnson, R. (1980). Effects of cooperative, competitive, and individualistic conditions on children's problem-solving performance. *American Educational Research Journal, 17*, 39–46.

Johnson, R., & Johnson, D. W. (1979). Type of task and student achievement and attitudes in interpersonal cooperation, competition, and individualization. *Journal of Social Psychology, 108*, 37–48.

Johnson, R., Johnson, D. W., & Taylor, B. (1991). Impact of cooperative and individualistic learning on high-ability students' achievement, self-esteem, and social acceptance. University of Minnesota. Manuscript submitted for publication.

Murray, F. (1983). Cognitive benefits of teaching on the teacher. Paper presented at American Educational Research Association Annual Meeting, Montreal, Quebec.

Skon, L., Johnson, D. W., & Johnson, R. (1981). Cooperative peer interaction versus individual competition and individualistic efforts: Effects on the acquisition of cognitive reasoning strategies. *Journal of Educational Psychology, 73*, 83–92.

Yager, S., Johnson, D. W., Johnson, R., & Snider, B. (1986). The impact of group processing on achievement in cooperative learning groups. *Journal of Social Psychology, 126*, 389–397.

Tracking and Ability Grouping: What Are the Alternatives?

Over the last twenty years there have been many attempts to address the issue of tracking and ability grouping in schools. In the late '70s, some high schools developed heterogeneous alternative programs that used internships, small-group study, individual learning contracts, and field studies to teach students of mixed ability. In the '80s, middle schools formed "houses" with heterogeneous mixes of students. All of these schools have demonstrated that the mixed-ability approach benefited not only the struggling and the average students, but also the best and the brightest.

Across the nation, schools are using new teaching methods with the goals of excellence and equity for all. Schools implementing the restructuring concepts of Sizer, Glasser, and Levin are finding ways to support student learning without tracks and ability groups. From this work, better ways to instruct students are emerging— methods that do not include sorting and separating to the advantage of a few.

This section introduces some of the programs that work without tracking and ability grouping. Adria Steinberg and Anne Wheelock describe one middle school where "every single kid gets to be bright every single day." They tell us of the successes of other middle schools that are trying to challenge a wide range of learners.

Offering encouraging news, Jeannie Oakes and Martin Lipton alert us to the fact that educators and policy makers are beginning to question the use of tracking and many are looking for alternatives. However, they caution, there may not be just *one* alternative that works for *all* schools. Instead, each school must assess its own situation to find the right alternative.

Effective alternatives to tracking such as cooperative learning, tutoring, and at-risk pull-out programs are outlined by the Center for Research on Elementary and Middle Schools. This report offers a convincing argument that effective instructional programs can "alleviate, for most at-risk students, the initial burden of poor academic performance early in their school careers."

According to Paul S. George, "parents of all students should be informed of the effects of tracking on the quality of the academic and social experiences of their children." His article clearly explains the problems of tracking, results of research on tracking, why it persists, and what can be done. He concludes that "tracking is an idea whose time has passed. But only the timely arrival of effective alternatives will permit educators to 'untrack' the schools."

After Tracking—What?
Middle Schools Find New Answers
by Adria Steinberg and Anne Wheelock

I f tracking would help us accomplish our goals at this school, then we would use it," says John D'Auria, principal of the Wellesley Middle School in Wellesley, Massachusetts. "But we believe in producing active learners, critical thinkers, and risk-takers, and tracking our students by ability quite simply doesn't allow us to achieve our goals."

Even a few years ago it would have seemed inconceivable to hear such a statement from the principal of a school in an upper-middle-class suburb. But today a growing number of educators question whether sorting students by ability is the best way to organize teaching and learning.

In some communities, this questioning has led to active attempts to try something different. Experiments in "untracking" can be found in urban, rural, and suburban middle-grade schools. A handful are more than five years into the process; most are at an earlier stage. Some are addressing the challenges of heterogeneity with home-grown curricula and approaches; others are adopting materials developed in university or laboratory settings.

> A seven-year plan calls for gradual elimination of bottom-level classes, beginning with math.

None would claim to have all the answers, but collectively they are tackling the key questions: What steps can be taken to reduce—and eventually eliminate—tracking? What values and goals should guide attempts to develop alternatives? What kinds of curricula

From *The Harvard Education Letter*, September/October 1992 (Vol. VIII, No. 5, 1–5). Reprinted with permission.

and instruction work best with heterogeneous groups? How can we ensure that less tracking results in more learning?

PLAN AHEAD

Crete-Monee Junior High in Crete, Illinois, is the result of the 1988 merger of two schools, one enrolling primarily white and the other primarily African-American students. With the stated goal of creating a climate of high expectations for all 700 students, the staff initiated efforts to reduce grouping within the building.

> **Staff members have begun to revise school routines that reinforce a "pecking order" among students.**

A seven-year plan calls for the gradual elimination of bottom-level classes, beginning with math offerings. The ultimate goal is heterogeneous classes in all academic subjects. Meanwhile, staff members have begun to revise school routines that reinforce a "pecking order" among students and to introduce changes designed to create a climate of high expectations.

The honor roll, for example, is no longer reserved for "straight A" students. To win academic honors, students and parents can sign a quarterly Academic Improvement Contract. Students agree to raise their average a minimum of one letter grade in two classes without letting other grades slip, to avoid missing more than three days of school, and to spend a stipulated amount of time on homework, which they can do with parental supervision or in the school homework center, open until 5:30 every day.

In Jericho, New York, the process of preparing for a new middle school began with study groups of parents and teachers carefully reviewing available research on the developmental needs of young adolescents. Convinced that academic tracking and competition on the playing fields were harming too many children, these groups made plans to pilot new approaches both inside and outside the classroom.

Four years into the process, the school fields as many teams as there are students who try out, and there is no longer an honors track in English or social studies. Instead of serving only selected students, the gifted and talented program now offers classroom enrichment projects for all.

For example, in studying Greek mythology, heterogeneous eighth-grade classes not only read and write myths but also express them in artistic and visual forms, such as by designing a Grecian urn. "Some of the most outstanding work comes from students who would never have been selected for gifted and talented or honors classes," notes the principal, Anna Hunderfund.

Initially, the kids—and their parents—were resistant to the changes. Heated meetings went on until 11 o'clock at night. The research was important, Hunderfund says, in convincing people to give the new plan a chance on a pilot basis. But, she adds, "It could never have happened without the full support of our superintendent, Bob Mannheim. If it doesn't happen politically, it doesn't happen educationally."

> Outstanding work comes from students who would never have been selected for gifted and talented or honors classes.

"TAKE IT TO HEART"

The stories of these two schools, in very different communities, illustrate a number of basic ingredients of recipes for detracking: a shared belief—among people at all levels of the hierarchy—that all students benefit from a challenging curriculum; a phase-in process allowing teachers, students, and parents time to prepare for heterogeneity; and a recognition that at stake are the very norms and assumptions that shape the culture of the school.

Most schools recognize that untracking requires more than simply regrouping students: the school must also adopt instructional, curricular, and organizational innovations to support heterogeneity. But the pace and order of such changes can vary. If untracking requires certain basic ingredients, each school combines these in different proportions, according to the taste of its school community, to create a flavor uniquely its own.

To students, the ultimate test of an experiment in untracking is whether the teachers "take it to heart." As one student at the Pioneer Valley Regional School (PVRS) in Greenfield, Massachusetts, sees it, "This heterogeneous grouping is a good thing. The only flaw is that the teachers have to really ... believe that all students are equal."

At the Wellesley Middle School, the faculty signaled its readiness to adopt more flexible grouping practices by generating the following list of core beliefs: (1) All students are capable of high achievement, not just our fastest and most confident learners. (2) Consistent effort leads to success. (3) You are not supposed to understand everything the first time around. (4) Mistakes help one to learn.

"The most important thing a principal can do to facilitate the initial steps in untracking," according to Anna Bernard, principal of Prescott Middle School in Baton Rouge, Louisiana, "is to communicate the belief that eliminating ability grouping is in the best interest of the students." But this does not mean that principals interested in reducing tracking must wait for philosophical agreement among the faculty. "You have to understand that different people have different comfort levels," says Sandra Caldwell, principal of the Middle School of the Kennebunks in Maine. "We don't expect everyone to do everything at the same time. We have always piloted with teachers who felt comfortable."

When pilot efforts are successful, broader acceptance follows. "When we opened," reports Mary Ellen Levin, principal of the Louis Armstrong School in New York City, "many of our teachers, veterans of the junior high schools in New York City, wanted homogeneous grouping. At this point, no one would hear of it. Even die-hards are converted."

CHANGING MINDS

Roger Genest, chairman of the English department at PVRS, readily admits to having been a "die-hard" himself. "Every member of the department except one was convinced it would not work in English. There was no way to detrack. Besides, we knew we had kids who go on to advanced placement. Why should we change?"

Not surprisingly, the push to eliminate tracking often begins with staff members who work with the lowest-achieving students. At PVRS the initial group included a guidance counselor and special education and remedial teachers—witness to "the fallout of the tracked program."

This ad hoc committee worked hard to convince others on the faculty of the need for change. "The committee kept putting research in our mailboxes," Genest recalls. "We believed a lot of things in the research but didn't think it had anything to do with teaching English. We thought the school was spending too much money as it was on kids at the lower end."

The committee churned up enough concern about tracking that a dozen faculty members signed up for a University of Massachusetts course on new models of teaching, offered at the school site. The turning point for Genest came when he decided to try out the new ideas with a pilot group of ninth graders from the honors, college, general, low, and special education tracks, and to videotape the class for the course.

Looking at the tapes, he noticed some "strange things": "The honors and college bound students were simply repeating material they already knew, parroting back what I had said. The general track students questioned them, forcing these 'academics' to clarify what they meant and put their ideas in terms everyone could understand."

His experiences with this group convinced Genest to move away from a teacher-centered classroom model and to adopt strategies, for example, from cooperative learning and peer teaching models. With his colleagues he began to develop thematic English courses and units with titles such as "War," "Dreams of the Depression," and "Who Am I?" After ninth grade, English courses at PVRS are not only mixed-level but multi-graded as well: tenth through twelfth graders select their courses on the basis of interest.

PVRS is in its eighth year of untracking, and Genest now counts himself a believer. "Education is what a student can do with the information, not how much information a student has. All our classes are academic now and the students receive every tool they need to get through."

LEVEL ONE FOR EVERYONE

Teachers and principals agree that the effort to reduce
tracking will fail without curricula that engage a wide
range of students. Fortunately, examples of such curricula,
emerging from both practice and research, are more and
more readily available (see Box: "Resources for Untracked
Classrooms").

Although no blueprint exists, curricula that work well
with heterogeneous groups tend to be thematic and
project-centered. Thus, for example, in one English
course, PVRS students begin by reading a book of oral
histories of war experiences and compiling their own
book, finding adults in the community with experiences to
share. Small groups of students, working cooperatively,
then specialize in particular wars. The wide selection of
novels, diaries, and histories available, as well as the many
dramatic films now on video, provide entry points for
students at all reading levels.

To ensure that students at lower levels keep up, a
number of middle schools have devised ways for them to
get extra help. Students can enroll in double periods for
particular subjects, or avail themselves of tutoring during
lunch or after school. At the Willard Junior High in
Berkeley, California, low-achieving students attend special
preparation sessions before their class begins a new unit
or project.

Another common feature of curricula for heterogeneous groups is the emphasis on having students create
products not just for grading by the teacher but also for
exhibiting to a wider audience. Students at Louis
Armstrong Middle School tape interviews with relatives
and neighbors and use these as the basis for dramatic
monologues, publications, readings, and a school exhibit.
In the PVRS course "Shakespeare and the Law" students
hold a trial in which Hamlet stands accused of murdering
Polonius. Defense and prosecution develop theories of
motive and come up with direct and circumstantial
evidence to make their case.

It is not always necessary to start from scratch in
developing new curricula and approaches. For example,

teachers at the Middle School of the Kennebunks use a curriculum known as Fundamental Approaches in Science Teaching (FAST) developed by the University of Hawaii's Curriculum Research and Development Group.

One favorite FAST project involves using the concepts of buoyancy, volume, mass, and density to design a model submarine. Rather than simply handing in their models to the teacher, students must demonstrate how well they work. The submarine must rest on top of the water in a fish tank for five seconds, submerge, rest on the bottom of the tank for a minute, and then rise to the surface—while the class watches, learning that there is more than one solution to such a complex problem.

> "Every single kid gets to be bright every single day."

Whether designing or adopting curricula, Kennebunks faculty members are clear about the goal. As Caldwell puts it, "In our middle school, every single kid gets to be bright every single day." What is less clear in many schools is how to create the time and support teachers need in order to develop or learn to use new curricula. In schools that are untracking, staff development and planning time are essential up-front costs with a long-term payoff.

Teachers also recommend two other ways to encourage risk-taking: allow for smaller class sizes at the beginning and suspend teacher evaluation during the first term of heterogeneous grouping. As Genest points out, the size of his first heterogeneous class was 16; several years later he was comfortable working with a group more than twice that size.

EVIDENCE GROWS

For every story of adventurous learning and exciting teaching, critics of heterogeneous grouping offer a story featuring a boring classroom where a teacher presents a watered-down curriculum to diverse learners. Some parents, especially those with high-achieving children, fear that their kids will be come sacrificial lambs on the altar of untracking (see "The Tracking Wars: Is Anyone Winning?" HEL, May/June 1992). One of the striking accomplishments of the schools featured here is that they have allayed such fears by showing parents that their children will continue to do high-quality academic work.

Some schools have also documented the results of their efforts, monitoring grades, test scores, course placement, attendance, discipline, and graduation rates. For example, Crete-Monee staff keep track of the number of students entering different course levels at the receiving high school. Since the number of tracks has declined, the number of eighth graders entering low-level language arts courses in high school has been cut by more than half.

Staff members at PVRS are able to point to a phenomenal rise in the percentage of students taking the SATs—from 22 percent in 1982 to 87 percent in 1991. Of recent graduates, 72 percent have gone on to four-year colleges.

In addition, when Genest first piloted a heterogeneous English class, he asked outside educators to read and assess papers written in this class and in his college-bound classes. Much to his surprise, members of the mixed-level class did as well as or better than their homogeneously grouped counterparts in five of six areas, including essay content, essay structure, and concepts of literature. A number of other middle schools, including Wellesley and Wayland in Massachusetts, have carried out similar comparisons with similar results.

Too often overlooked in the horror stories of "experimenting with our children" is the fact that many of the curricula and professional development programs that schools adopt are themselves based on research. Some, like the Program for Complex Instruction at Stanford University, have amassed impressive evaluative data on their effectiveness (see "Schools Where Kids Speak Spanish," HEL, November/December 1991).

More research is needed. There is still much to learn about what works in heterogeneous classes and how middle schools can most effectively encourage and challenge a wide range of learners. Meanwhile, the sense of renewal and energy in schools that are in the process of untracking continues to build the momentum for change. As one student sums it up, "It's a lot more fun to learn. I imagine it's a lot more fun to teach."

FOR MORE INFORMATION

Complex Instruction News. Published by the Program for Complex Instruction, Stanford University, CERAS Building, School of Education, Stanford, CA 94305.

Oakes, J., & Lipson, M. (February 1992). Detracking schools: Early lessons from the field. *Phi Delta Kappan*, 73, no. 6.

The pioneering practitioner: A journal on heterogeneous grouping, cooperative learning, and school change. Published biannually by Pioneers in Education, Inc., P.O. Box 46, Northfield, MA 01360.

Silvernail, D. L., & Capelluti, J. (Fall 1991). An examination of the relationship between middle level school teachers' grouping preferences and their sense of responsibility for student outcomes. Research in Middle Level Education, 15, no. 1

[Anne Wheelock's] new book, *Crossing the Tracks: How Untracking Can Save America's Schools* (New York: New Press, 1992), reports on a study of middle schools in the process of untracking. This study is the source for most of the school profiles and quotations in this article.

Detracking Schools: Early Lessons from the Field

by Jeannie Oakes and Martin Lipton

From individual anecdotes about and analyses of detracking projects, Ms. Oakes and Mr. Lipton conclude that a culture of detracking is more important than the specific strategy chosen.

During the past decade, research on tracking and ability-grouped class assignments has provided striking evidence that these practices have a negative impact on most children's school opportunities and outcomes. Moreover, the negative consequences of these practices disproportionately affect low-income, African-American, and Latino children.[1]

Increasingly, this research evidence is triggering responses from reform-minded policy makers and educators. The National Governors' Association has recommended detracking as part of its strategy for meeting the national education goals; the Carnegie Corporation endorses detracking in *Turning Points*, its report on reforms for the middle grades; and the College Board's report, *Access to Knowledge: An Agenda for Our Nation's Schools*, identifies tracking as a barrier in many students' paths to college. After vigorous discussion, the National Education Association resolved to eliminate tracking as it is now practiced. Across the country, local educators and policy

> Across the country, local educators and policy makers are questioning their own local practices, and many are moving toward alternatives.

From *Phi Delta Kappan*, vol. 73, no. 6, p. 448–454, February 1992. Reprinted with permission.

makers are questioning their own local practices, and many are moving toward alternatives.

While there has yet to be a comprehensive study of detracking,[2] the stories we've been told by those engaged in detracking projects, our informal observations in schools, and accounts reported in the media and by other analysts provide rich information about attempts to detrack. These individual anecdotes and analyses are of great interest to educators and policy makers who are contemplating detracking. But far more useful is the general lesson that can be drawn from them. This lesson is that a *culture of detracking* is more important than the specific alternative or implementation strategy chosen. While the particulars of detracking vary considerably from school to school, there appear to be commonalities in the cultures of schools that detrack successfully. These commonalities don't always take the same form, and they don't follow any particular sequence. But in some form, at some time, the following characteristics become part of the culture of "detracked" schools:

• recognition that tracking is supported by powerful norms that must be acknowledged and addressed as alternatives are created;

• willingness to broaden the reform agenda, so that changes in the tracking structure become part of a comprehensive set of changes in school practice;

• engagement in a process of inquiry and experimentation that is idiosyncratic, opportunistic, democratic, and politically sensitive;

• alterations in teachers' roles and responsibilities, including changes in the ways adults in the school work together; and

• persistence over the long haul that is sustained by risk-taking leaders who are clearly focused on scholarship and democratic values.

CONFRONTING POWERFUL NORMS
Schools that choose to undertake detracking may try jumping to agreement on new policies and practices. However, easy agreement usually proves elusive, and

successful schools move away rather quickly from an exclusively practical focus. Instead, they pay considerable attention to the philosophies, values, and beliefs that underlie their tracking practices and that make agreement about alternatives so difficult. We suspect that this happens because it becomes apparent that tracking makes perfectly good sense, given prevailing school norms, and that most of the proposed alternatives do not.

For example, tracking structures are firmly grounded in widespread and historically rooted beliefs about human capacity and about individual group differences. Tracking is also supported by outmoded conceptions that intelligence is global (i.e., a single entity that can be measured and reported as an IQ score), that is fixed quite early (either before birth or soon thereafter), and that learning is the accumulation of a sequence of knowledge and skills.

> **Alternatives to tracking begin to make sense when schools seriously entertain other conceptions of intelligence and learning.**

If the *capacity to learn* is understood as unalterable and the range in capacity among schoolchildren is perceived to be great, then tracking must appear sensible. In this view, schools accommodate differences by separating students according to their measured ability and by adapting curriculum and instruction accordingly. The fact that learning capacity seems to be unevenly distributed among groups—with disadvantaged members of minority groups exhibiting less capacity to learn—appears to be beyond the control of the school. Thus schools typically conclude that the disproportionate assignment of low-income and minority students to low-track classes is an appropriate, if regrettable, response.

Alternatives to tracking begin to make sense when schools seriously entertain other conceptions of intelligence and learning; when detracking is not merely a response to an abstract sense of fairness but is also a practical way to act on new knowledge about intelligence and learning. A number of educators have told us that their views have been dramatically altered by the work of Howard Gardner and of Robert Sternberg, both of whom argue compellingly that intelligence is multifaceted and developmental and that learning is a complex process of constructing meaning. Serious consideration of their work has enabled these educators to invest new meanings in such popular notions as "all children can learn," rather than simply to mouth them as meaningless, if well-intentioned, slogans. And when they no longer interpret such statements to mean that all children can achieve their very different "potentials," educators can let go of the belief that children of "like potentials" must be grouped together.

> **Detracking seems to involve a critical and unsettling rethinking of fundamental educational norms.**

These shifting conceptions of intelligence and learning have enabled a number of schools to support detracking by setting up heterogeneous classrooms in which instruction challenges the sense-making abilities of all capable (if different) children and in which differences become assets rather than liabilities. For example, Susan Benjamin of Highland Park (Illinois) High School described the values underlying untracked classrooms at her school. "In the English Department," Benjamin wrote in the March 1990 *English Journal*, "the basic philosophy is that diversity within the classroom enriches the learning environment."[3]

But powerful beliefs about the purposes of schooling also support tracking. For example, most Americans believe that schools should transmit the essential knowledge and values of the culture to all students as well as prepare a highly productive work force. While the first part of this belief argues for common schooling experiences, the second often provides a rationale for tracked schools with differentiated curricula that prepare students for different types of jobs. When schools explicitly acknowledge these seemingly contradictory purposes, they are likely to find that *all* students benefit from the diversity of learning experiences previously reserved either for college-bound or work-force-bound students.

Detracking, then, seems to involve a critical and unsettling rethinking of fundamental educational norms. This rethinking asks people to challenge their entrenched views of such matters as human capacities, individual and group differences, the purposes of schooling, and the ever-present tensions between the norms of competitive individualism and the more democratic norms of support and community. As Paula Hatfield of the J. A. Leonard Middle School in Old Town, Maine, observed, "Simply eliminating tracking will not cure all of the ills of schooling and society. However, it may set off a powerful synergistic reaction requiring other institutional changes, changes in how teachers teach, how students relate to each other, and how the school hierarchy operates. Most important, it may liberate students' and teachers' beliefs about who should and could achieve."[4]

CHANGE IS COMPREHENSIVE

Proposals for detracking often trigger the expectation that schools will simply mix their classes and then teach all children in the same way, at the same time. Of course, that has happened in some schools, and the "reform" has nearly always been frustrating, counterproductive, and short-lived. However, altered conceptions of students' learning capacity notwithstanding, most schools do not gloss over the fact that children are different and that they need opportunities to learn differently in heterogeneous schools and classrooms.

This realization almost inevitably leads to a much broader set of changes in school structures and practices. Most educators find that they must confront simultaneously the complex and often muddy interactions of the many dimensions of schooling: curriculum, teaching practices, the social organization of the classroom, responses to children's special needs, assessment, and much more. The following discussion illustrates how this can happen.[5]

Reconstructed curriculum. Most schools undergoing detracking redesign their curriculum around rich and complex ideas and steer away from a highly sequenced curriculum that focuses on discrete topics and skills. Educators at these schools don't assume that all children in heterogeneous classes will eventually know the same things (nor should they, given the many differences

among them), but they proceed on the assumption that all children can understand—and should be engaged in—the core ideas of the curriculum. Educators report that a rich, concept-based curriculum enables them to:
- frame learning tasks as complex problems,
- provide contexts that give meaning to facts,
- take informal knowledge seriously,
- allow for multiple right answers,
- promote socially constructed knowledge, and
- require long-term projects.

A curriculum so designed appears to be much more accommodating of differences in students' prior knowledge and skills. More practically, it permits educators to generate lessons that make it less likely that some students will be left behind or that others will be bored because the lessons have been watered down.

We find examples of such curricular shifts in a number of schools that are detracking For example, when the San Diego City Schools and the Denver Public Schools jettisoned their remedial classes in middle schools and high schools, the curriculum shifted from an emphasis on skills to an emphasis on contextual learning and problem solving. When Fox Lane High School in Bedford, New York, detracked its ninth grade, teachers formed interdisciplinary teams and organized the curriculum around such themes as the Cold War or the Middle East. They've also scheduled periods of flexible "team time" into the day, when students can work together on academic projects, use the library/media center resources, and meet with teachers for extra help.

At Pioneer Valley Regional School in Northfield, Massachusetts, the English Department chair reports that traditional approaches to curriculum and instruction needed to be revamped when classes became heterogeneous. He describes how neither teaching as he always had nor watering the down the curriculum worked with mixed groups of students. Consequently, the English Department decided to develop a new curriculum around themes. "The first year it bombed," he acknowledges. "We did not know what to do. We had always been the center of the class, made the decisions, told the kids how to look at material and judge its quality. The secret was to create a situation where everyone learned together, and no one dominated."[6]

Expanded instruction repertoire. It should come as no surprise that traditional, teacher-and-textbook-dominated instruction becomes inadequate when teachers design lessons intended to engage diverse groups of students in rich, complex ideas. Most educators look for alternative instructional strategies that depend less on students' similarities in prior achievement and that more easily accommodate multiple approaches to learning.

> Many educators have observed the positive effects on achievement when diverse groups of children work together on well-structured cooperative tasks.

That's why so many schools engaged in detracking turn to cooperative learning. Many educators have observed the positive effects on achievement when diverse groups of children work together on well-structured cooperative tasks, with even the strongest students making considerable intellectual gains.[7] Many are aware, too, of evidence that the status hierarchy related to levels of ability can also break down when teachers help students acquire the social skills for working together productively.[8] However, most detracking schools realize that cooperative groups alone can't provide the entire social, psychological, or intellectual context children require and that the effectiveness of cooperative learning can be limited if it is the only change in heterogeneous classrooms. Other strategies, such as long-term individual projects and classroom tasks that require active learning, are also well-suited to heterogeneous classrooms.

New provisions for special needs. One of the most logistically difficult and politically volatile aspects of tracking reform is whether and how heterogeneous schools and classrooms serve students with special needs—including those identified as having learning difficulties and those identified as intellectually gifted.

Schools that are detracking successfully make sure that the special needs of these children are addressed—even when they are members of heterogeneous classes.

Most parents of and advocates for learning-disabled students are eager to have them included in heterogeneous classrooms—as long as teachers are sensitive to their needs and have access to specialized help. And most of them find detracking with appropriate assistance a constructive response to the stigma and reduced opportunities that often accompany special education placements. For example, some schools schedule students' time with special education or Chapter 1 resource teachers after school; others team regular and special education teachers so that specialized help can be incorporated into the regular classroom. In some schools, students who are having difficulty keeping up in heterogeneous academic classes are enrolled in a support or booster class (taken in place of an elective) where they receive additional instruction; in others, peer- or cross-age tutoring programs offer after-school help. Some schools make reading assignments available on cassette tapes so that less accomplished readers can participate fully in academic coursework. Most schools find that once they accept the idea of providing extra help without tracking—once the norms change—devising specific strategies is quite easy.

> In some schools, students who are having difficulty keeping up in heterogeneous academic classes are enrolled in a support or booster class.

It is a far more difficult political problem to integrate students who've had access to gifted and talented programs or honors classes, partly because of the high status that accompanies these placements. Educators and parents are aware that these students have been advantaged educationally by these special programs, and, even if those advantages have been gained at the expense of other students, no one is eager to see any students wind up with less than they had before. Thus schools must develop heterogeneous classes that don't compromise the educational opportunities of gifted and talented students.

Many elementary and middle schools have taken the position that well-designed heterogeneous clases (built on the types of curriculum and instructional changes mentioned above) can meet the needs of most intellectually gifted students. But many schools also provide special activities for high achievers either within the regular classroom or after school. Most schools report success with this approach—but only after considerable time and work with parents.

Senior highs—particularly in districts where students have been tracked throughout elementary and middle school—have been less successful in detracking, especially in such highly sequenced subjects as mathematics. By the time students are in high school, the achievement and motivation gaps between the highest and lowest achievers have grown quite wide, and many teachers cannot envision a high-quality curriculum that could accommodate the range of student abilities, especially in mathematics and science. English and social studies teachers often seem less daunted, but even they find that their efforts to combine honors or gifted programs with regular classes—even regular college-preparatory classes— generate enormous resistance from parents.

> Schools developing alternatives to tracking often look for new assessment strategies.

In some districts, parents have used their political clout to halt any detracking efforts, and in others they have threatened to withdraw their children and enroll them in private schools. For both substantive and political reasons, many high schools choose to leave their honors and gifted programs in place, particularly for 11th- and 12-graders. However, some schools have adopted more of an "open admissions" policy, recruiting students with varying abilities into honors and advanced placement classes, rather than enforcing strict entry criteria.

Alternative assessment and grading practices. Traditional assessment strategies often have a profoundly negative impact on heterogeneous classes. When teachers routinely compare students with their peers and make those comparisons public (whether in as benign a way as posting charts with stars for every book read or in as crass a way as announcing test scores aloud), the status hierarchy of "ability" that detracking seeks to eliminate simply resurfaces within heterogeneous classes. In addition, public comparisons of students' performance lead many children to underrate their capacity for learning, and even very young students may come to believe that success or failure in school is beyond their control and so exert less effort and accomplish less.[9] This consequence—worrisome in any classroom—is particularly troubling in mixed-ability groups.

Not surprisingly, then, schools developing alternatives to tracking often look for new assessment strategies. Many eagerly await the refinement of technologies of portfolio assessments and structured observations of students engaged in tasks and experiments. Others are forging ahead and creating their own. For example, John Blaydes, principal of McGaugh Elementary School in Los Alamitos, California, engaged his staff in a process of obtaining more authentic assessments of children in detracked classes by having teachers try alternative types of testing, observe experiments, and collect portfolio samples. By these private and more personalized strategies, Blaydes and his teachers hope to develop the belief that hard work pays off and to prevent assessment from becoming the raw material for judgments about who is smart and who isn't.

Senior high schools face a tougher challenge as they confront normative grading practices held firmly in place by long-established traditions and by the admissions requirements of colleges and universities. In states in which grades are weighted according to the track level of academic classes, detracking threatens to deflate the grade-point averages of students who would ordinarily be in the highest tracks. For example, in California, guidance counselors are routinely told that students not taking honors classes are at a distinct disadvantage when they seek admission to the University of California.

Politically acceptable alternatives seem beyond the reach of most schools, in spite of many sensible proposals and some successful beginnings. Some schools, such as Parkway South High School in Manchester, Missouri, offer heterogeneous classes wherein students can choose to meet the standards for either an honors grade (additional research or advanced reading) or a regular grade. Others have made special arrangements with college admissions offices to allow alternative assessment information to supplement students' transcripts.

These few examples illustrate the point that successful detracking inevitably triggers many other changes. The reason is fairly clear; each current school structure and practice is consistent with and serves to hold others in place; changing any one—like tracking—invariably upsets the balance of the rest.

> One school's successful alternative or restructured practice can become another school's slick, packaged flash in the pan.

NURTURING INQUIRY

Attention to new norms, curriculum, instruction, assessment, and special needs constitute the "what" of detracking. We have also been able to observe some consistent patterns in the "how," the process of detracking.

Schools that have found some measure of success have proceeded in ways that are strategic, idiosyncratic, timely, and politically sensitive. In most places, educators, policy makers, and parents engage in difficult but fascinating inquiry into their own schools. They experiment with small-scale alternatives of their own design—moving and changing where they can, when they can, and with those who are eager to go along. This process is politically savvy in schools where not everyone favors detracking. But even in the unlikely event that everyone did favor detracking, schools could not simply replace tracking with a "correct" off-the-shelf alternative. This fact reflects an important lesson from the history of school improvement: one school's successful alternative or restructured practice can become another school's slick, packaged, and soon-to-be-abandoned flash in the pan.

An essential element of the process of detracking seems to be opening up a dialogue about tracking—both within and outside the school. Many districts and schools have convened task forces of interested members of the school community, including those vocal on both sides of the issue. Such task forces often read research on tracking, assess local practices, and explore alternatives. Schools often collect data about their own grouping structures and course placements and analyze these by race, socioeconomic background, language, gender, and special education status. Such data can form the basis for the discussion of such questions as, What are our school's grouping goals, and are they currently being met? What is the procedure for placing students in ability groups? Are there ample opportunities for interaction among students from different ability groups? What successful practices are employed within high-ability classes that can be replicated schoolwide?

For example, in 1984 the San Diego City Schools undertook a five-year study of their grouping practices and of the effects of tracking on educational opportunities. The data stimulated vigorous debate about the nature of the problem and ways to confront it. As in most school systems, the process was often uncomfortable, but it has led to a set of slow, incremental steps toward detracking.[10]

In Ann Arbor, Michigan, a 62-member task force that included parents, community representatives, teachers, and administrators spent two years reviewing the literature on tracking, collecting data about local practices, developing a board policy on ability grouping and tracking, and making recommendations for modifying existing practices. The participatory process educated decision makers, encouraged the thoughtful use of information, emphasized the importance of teacher judgment and reflection, and laid the groundwork for pilot projects and experiments. The policy that resulted from the efforts of the task force set guidelines and expectations for further decision making and created a five-year plan for detracking that wisely avoided rules, regulations, or specific prescriptions for change. The joint leadership provided by the superintendent, the board, and the task force helped establish communication, encouraged persistence when things got rough, and institutionalized the sharing of responsibility.[11]

In the Crete-Monee Central Unified School District in Crete, Illinois, progress toward alternatives occurred when teachers and administrators piloted alternatives to tracking and generated guidelines for new policies.[12] The following "insights" emerged:

- a proportion of teachers will maintain a "residual suspicion" of heterogeneous grouping;
- the curriculum is not set up to accommodate heterogeneous grouping;
- teachers must expand their perception of useful instructional strategies;
- unintended or covert tracking must be identified and anticipated;
- flexible skill-adjusted grouping and other potentially beneficial grouping practices "should be acknowledged and efforts taken to curtail any negative effects"; and
- teachers must receive appropriate training and preparation.

These aren't earth-shattering realizations. In some form or another they can be found in most research on educational change. Perhaps the only true surprise is that this knowledge was developed on site, "reinvented" by people who actually had to make use of the insights.

And it is important that productive inquiry and experimentation go beyond understanding the technology of tracking. As Ann Arbor's participatory process aptly demonstrates, successful efforts to create alternatives to tracking require careful attention to the prevailing norms and politics of the school and of the larger community.

"It takes a long time." Attitudes have to change, and that's not easy." "People feel threatened all over the place." We have yet to encounter an attempt to detrack a school or district that didn't generate comments such as these. "It's not a painless process," says Evrett Masters, principal of Pioneer Valley Regional School in Northfield, Massachusetts, in referring to his school's eight-year effort to move toward heterogeneous classes.

Yet Pioneer Valley School seems to have brought together the essential ingredients for genuine school change, including persistence over time and attention to the beliefs, politics, and technologies that seem to make for successful heterogeneous grouping. An ad hoc committee at Pioneer Valley drew attention to the problems generated by tracking. With the support of the chair of the school committee, workshops for teachers were held, and courses on new teaching styles and strategies were taught by unviersity faculty members. In the fall of 1990 the school sponsored its second conference on "Derailing the Tracked School" and shared its successes with other schools—even as it continues to struggle with its own thorny problems of heterogeneity.

> School systems must avoid dividing the tasks of inquiry and experimentation according to conventional notions of "who's good at what."

The primary lesson to be drawn from these experiences is that, if whole institutions can be said to learn new things, then schools must *make sense* of their own experinces and learn new ways through their own inquiry and investigation. To some degree, each detracking school reinvents the wheel.

CHANGES FOR TEACHERS

Perhaps most important, these promising moves toward detracking suggest that school systems must avoid dividing the tasks of inquiry and experimentation according to conventional notions of "who's good at what." Usually, inquiry into new policies and practices is thought to be the purview of the principal or the superintendent. These leaders are expected to read, discuss, and investigate research findings; to attend symposia on new topics; and so on. Conversely, teachers are expected to gain the technical competence to try out new teaching strategies— with little attention to theory and research.

Much is lost by this division of effort, and we doubt that detracking can succeed if the division persists. Where changes are occurring, site and district administrators take the time to become immersed in new practices and to become familiar with the new roles teachers will be asked to assume. When they do, administrators sense firsthand the full range of schoolwide changes that are needed to support new classroom practices, they can better explain and defend new practices to their communities, and they can more completely assess the effectiveness of those practices. Teachers, on the other hand, must be able to make sense out of the new practices and structures—not simply implement them. If teachers' roles are reduced to simply following new sets of teaching protocols or simply learning new classroom scripts, they are unlikely to be effective—if indeed they adopt the new practices at all.

The comprehensive changes that detracking requires almost always trigger significant changes in the ways teachers work together. In nearly every detracking school we've studied, teachers report that it's neither technically nor emotionally possible to undertake the shift to hetero-geneous grouping in isolation. Teaming is the most common solution we've encountered, although that does not always mean that teachers actually teach together.

Sometimes teaming means that teachers at a particu-lar grade level or teachers of a particular subject pool their resources to create new lessons for heterogeneous classes, try them out individually, and then assess and revise them collectively. In other cases, teachers have joined together in cross-disciplinary teams that share responsibility for a group of students for one or more years. This approach seems particularly useful among middle school teachers, who then are able to make decisions together about their students' academic and social needs. Of course, produc-tive cooperation imposes some special demands on the school schedule. Working together requires time, and at least some of that time must be available during the school day.

COMMITMENT OF LEADERS

Tracking is entrenched; sensible alternatives are complex, sometimes counter-intuitive, and often controversial. Even when alternatives emerge from an inclusive and democratic process of inquiry and experimentation, steering the process of detracking through the inevitably troubled waters of school and community politics calls for strong leaders who unequivocally and unambiguously—if gently—assert the research, theory, and democratic values that support detracking.

At schools we've watched struggle over tracking, we've heard leaders identify specific ways in which their efforts are thwarted by traditions that hold tracking in place. They have openly, often courageously, acknowledged that curricular, administrative, teaching, and other traditions are more powerful than the profession's best knowledge of how children actually learn and that sometimes these traditions run contrary to deeply held democratic values.

Sometimes commitment requires telling a truth that everybody already knows. For example, recently Steve Leonard, principal of Boston's Martin Luther King Middle School and a member of the Boston school system's task force reviewing tracking practices, told reporters, "I would like to be able to look every parent in the eye and say, 'If you put your child in the Boston public schools, we will do everything we can to ensure that your child has a successful academic experience.' Right now, I couldn't honestly do that."[13]

> Efforts to change a practice as deeply embedded as tracking necessarily address a broad array of normative and political concerns.

We've heard other district and site administrators insist that new knowledge about intelligence and learning form the basis of instructional decisions. They speak out for a curriculum that provides all students with access to the most valued knowledge, they support evaluation that isn't easily summed up in a single test score, and they tell parents of gifted children that their sons and daughters will be well-served in heterogeneous classrooms. We've heard other administrators state unequivocally that teachers must have dramatically altered working conditions (e.g., time, support resources, collegial work groups) if they are to make alternatives to tracking work.

Such assertions are a far cry from the pious and syrupy—if well-meant—statements of commitment to all children that garner widespread agreement and grace schools' mission statements. Confronting what's wrong with schools is a necessary—if risky—first step toward making changes. Successful leaders press their schools and communities to investigate, debate, and eventually move together toward practices that are consistent with research knowledge and democratic values. While these leaders are sensibly *strategic* as their schools implement new practices—perhaps taking step back for each two forward or settling for half a loaf rather than none—they do not compromise the knowledge and democratic values that guide their professional commitments to children. And, by the way, they nearly always report the process to be professionally and personally invigorating.

THE CENTRAL LESSON

Research on tracking documents the negative consequences that these practices have for most children. Moreover, the research implicates a broad, complex, and interacting set of school characteristics and beliefs that sustain these practices. It's not surprising, then, that efforts to change a practice as deeply embedded as tracking necessarily address a broad array of normative and political concerns, as well as technical matters.

The anecdotal data about detracking call attention to a set of early commonalities in the cultures of detracking schools, while confirming that there is no simple "detracking" formula. Alternatives and the specific ways in which schools go about detracking vary considerably. Like any other significant school reform, detracking is an extraordinarily difficult process that must fit the idiosyncrasies of local conditions.

Furthermore, while we have only a handful of completely detracked schools, partial solutions and compromises are springing up everywhere. Some of these efforts address fundamental tracking-related problems (e.g., enrolling low-achieving high school students in extra "booster" classes so that they can keep up in rigorous heterogeneous core courses); some represent politically viable first steps in a long-term reform process (e.g., piloting detracking in a single subject within a school). Others are far less promising (e.g., "detracking" except for honors and remedial classes). The latter effort is unlikely to alter tracking's negative consequences or to lead to more substantial reforms, since it maintains the norms and structures that foster tracking and does little more than reshuffle the status quo.

Perhaps the central lesson to be drawn from our observations is that successful models can give schoolpeople confidence about the possibility and direction for change. But, as useful as these examples might seem, we should hesitate to trumpet too loudly any one school's specific alternative or implementation process as a model for others to follow. Ultimately, each school must find its own way to create a *culture for detracking* that enables it to make sense of its own situation and create alternatives that fit.

NOTES

1. Gamoran, A., & Berends, M. (1987). The effects of stratification in secondary schools: Synthesis of survey and ethnographic research. *Review of Educational Research, 57*, p. 415–435; Oakes, J. (1985). *Keeping track: How schools structure inequality.* New Haven, CT: Yale University Press; idem. (1990). *Multiplying inequalities: The effects of race, social class, and tracking on opportunities to learn mathematics and science.* Santa Monica, CA: RAND Corporation; Oakes, J. et al. (in press). *Educational matchmaking: Toward a better understanding of high school curriculum and tracking decisions.* Santa Monica, CA: RAND Corporation; Slavin, R. (1989). Grouping for instruction in the elementary school, in idem, ed., *School and classroom organization.* (Hillsdale, NJ: Erlbaum; idem. (1990). Ability grouping and student achievement in secondary schools. *Review of educational research, 60*, p. 417–499; and idem, (March 1991). Are cooperative learning and "untracking" harmful to the gifted? *Educational Leadership,* p. 68–71.
2. Some preliminary work has been begun, however. In 1989 Robert Slavin and Jomills Braddock of the Center for Resarch on Effective Schooling for Disadvantaged Students conducted a survey of alternatives to tracking, and Anne Wheelock of the Massachusetts Advocacy Center has recently begun a project sponsored by the Edna McConnell Clark Foundation that will result in more comprehensive descriptions of detracked schools.
3. Tracking: What do you think? (March 1990). *English Journal,* p. 75.
4. Ibid.
5. For a more elaborate discussion of approaches to restructuring these and other domains of schooling, see Jeannie Oakes and Martin Lipton. (1990). *Making the best of schools: A handbook for parents, teachers, and policymakers.* New Haven, CT: Yale University Press.
6. Caldwell, J. (August 1990). A school on track without "tracking." *Boston Globe,* 5, p. 57.
7. Slavin, R. Ability Grouping…; and idem, Are cooperative learning and "untracking" harmful?

8. Cohen, Elizabeth. (1986). *Designing groupwork: Strategies for the heterogeneous classroom.* New York: Teachers College Press.
9. Stipek, D. (1986). Children's motivation to learn. In Tommy M. Tomlinson and Herbert J. Walberg, eds., *Academic work and educational excellence.* Berkeley, CA: McCutchan.
10. Frey, G. (1988). Equity in student placement in the San Diego Unified School District: The good, the bad, and the ugly, paper presented at the annual meeting of the American Educational Research Association, New Orleans; and Lytle, J. H. (1989). Minority student access to and preparation for higher education, preliminary report presented at the annual meeting of the Council for Great City Schools, Miami.
11. Doreen Poupard-Tice. (1988). Developing an instructional grouping policy: A participatory model, paper presented at the annual meeting of the American Educational Research Association. New Orleans.
12. Anderson, C. S., & Barr, R. (1990). Teacher response to proposed changes in grouping: Impact on policy and practice. In Reba Page and Linda Valli, eds. *Curriculum differentiation: Interpretative studies.* New York: Teachers College Press.
13. Ribudeneira, D. (October 1990). School chief picks panel on tracking, retention. *Boston Globe*, 12.

Research Identifies Effective Programs for Students At Risk of School Failure

by the Center for Research on Elementary and Middle Schools

A multitude of our nation's students are at risk. Of dropout, of pregnancy, of delinquency, of substance abuse, of unemployment and underemployment, of suicide, of school failure. At risk.

Programs abound in schools to address these students. Dropout prevention programs, sex education programs, delinquency prevention programs, vocational training programs, alternative school programs, counseling programs—each picks out a piece of the at-risk student problem.

The Center for Research on Elementary and Middle Schools works to address these immediate problems, but also sees clearly that a common thread winds its way through each— poor academic performance in school, usually from the early years onward.

Given this common thread, a scenario emerges. If schools could improve the academic performance of at-risk students beginning in the early years and continuing through the elementary grades, this improvement would have multiple positive effects on student dropout, delinquency, pregnancy, substance abuse, and other behaviors. Thus early improvement of

> If schools could improve the academic performance of at-risk students, this improvement would have multiple positive effects on student dropout, delinquency and other behaviors.

From the Center for Research on Elementary and Middle Schools, December 1987, The Johns Hopkins University. Reprinted with permission.

poor academic performance could greatly alleviate multiple aspects of the overall problem.

A two-step process could help schools improve the performance of at-risk students from the early grades on. First, identify programs in the early grades that have been rigorously evaluated and proved to be effective for at-risk students—programs that *improve the academic performance* of at-risk students.

Second, implement these programs as faithfully as possible in preschool, kindergarten, and each elementary grade level, so that at-risk students, at each level of their schooling, receive effective instruction day after day and year after year.

If we want to determine the results of these efforts, of course, we need to add a third step—extensive evaluation of the effects of the effective programs in widespread practice.

CREMS researchers have taken the first step. CREMS reviews of research have identified programs from preschool through elementary that offer strong evidence of effectiveness in improving the academic performance of at-risk students.

> CREMS reviews of research have identified programs from preschool through elementary that offer strong evidence of effectiveness in improving the academic performance of at-risk students.

EFFECTIVE PRE-SCHOOL PROGRAMS

CREMS researcher Nancy Karweit reaches a general conclusion in her examination of preschool effects—overall, preschool in itself improves the academic performance of at-risk children.

Karweit reviews existing studies of the short- and long-term effects of preschool attendance for at-risk students. She focuses on studies which evaluated programs for four-year-olds and which used an acceptable research design.

Her review concludes that preschool has robust effects on immediate tests of cognitive functioning, and has longer term effects on other variables related to school success—lower rates of grade repetition, referral to special education, and dropping out of high school. She finds inconsistent effects of preschool attendance on achievement in upper elementary school.

Karweit's research also addresses the question—are some specific kinds of preschool programs more effective than others for at-risk children? She examines three studies that compare the outcomes of different curricula. Two of the studies found no consistent differences due to participation in programs that differ in curricula.

The third study—the Curriculum Demonstration Program of High/Scope—compared the longitudinal effects of an academic preschool program, a cognitively oriented program, and a traditional nursery school program, along with a control group. Effects on student achievement and academic progress were found for all three types of programs, and no one program was significantly more effective than the other two.

This study also implied that the academic preschool program showed later links to increased delinquency. But this finding is not supported by other studies, Karweit notes, and the self-report delinquency scales that produced the finding are suspect.

Karweit's conclusion: The research finds that the preschool programs studied, in themselves, are effective for improving the academic performance of children at risk, as well as showing other benefits. But a major caveat accompanies this conclusion.

"The programs implemented in these studies shared some common features," Karweit says. "A small teacher-child ratio, for example, and sizable funding. We can't say that widespread implementation by schools of preschool programs that don't share these common characteristics will have the same effects. That's the question we now need to answer."

EFFECTIVE KINDERGARTEN PROGRAMS

A previous synthesis of research by Karweit established that full-day kindergarten programs, compared to half-day programs, improved the academic performance of students at risk. (See CREMS *Report*, June 1987). Now she has identified specific kindergarten programs that present convincing evidence that they improve the academic achievement of children who are at risk of school failure.

She defines a "program" as a set of procedures intended to be implemented as a total package and capable of being replicated by others, and she identifies six programs that present convincing evidence of effectiveness based on rigorous methodology.

Alphaphonics (Reading) and Astra's Magic Math— combines systematic, sequenced lessons into a gamelike format, provides abundant practice and repetition of presentation. Friendly visitors from outer space (Astro, in the Alphaphonics reading program, and Astra in the math program) leave a bag of lesson materials daily for the teacher and the children.

Make Every Child Capable of Achieving (MECCA)— provides daily observation, assessment, and planning for specialized teaching depending on children's needs. Provides additional activities based on a task analysis of the learning activity a child is having trouble with.

Project TALK—uses structured activities to foster language growth. Language specialist teaches specific expressive and receptive language lessons to the class twice a week; classroom teacher conducts follow-up lessons twice a week.

Multisensory Approach to Reading and Reading Readiness Program (MARC)—combines activities which emphasize knowledge through the senses with a systematic instructional delivery and management system. Increases readiness skills especially in letter recognition and auditory perception of beginning sounds.

First Level Mathematics—a diagnostic-prescriptive program that provides a sequential curriculum and management system. Uses concrete objects and physical operations, does not require children to display fine motor and visual skills.

Early Prevention of School Failure—creates individual profiles for children by screening for fine and gross motor, auditory, visual, and language skills. Provides additional pull-out instruction based on identified weaknesses; provides guides for direct modality instruction in each area.

EFFECTIVE ELEMENTARY SCHOOL PROGRAMS

Karweit's reviews of preschool and kindergarten research note that the effects on the academic performance of at-risk students wash out in elementary school. To maintain the improved performance and continue to increase learning, elementary schools must provide instructional programs that are effective for at-risk students.

> **The most cost-effective and efficient way would be through comprehensive classroom instructional programs that work for all students, including those at risk.**

This can be done in two ways— through effective pull-out programs, usually funded by Chapter 1, that concentrate on providing compensatory education services outside the classroom to at-risk students only, or through classroom instruction programs that are effective for all students.

The most cost-effective and efficient way, of course, would be through comprehensive classroom instructional programs that work for all students, including those at risk.

EFFECTIVE IN-CLASS ELEMENTARY PROGRAMS

Such elementary school classroom programs have been developed. CREMS researchers Robert Slavin and Nancy Madden review the evidence of effectiveness of in-class programs according to the following criteria:

- Programs had to have well-specified manuals, materials, and training procedures so they could be readily used;
- The evidence for effectiveness had to include effects on standardized reading and/or math scales in studies of at least a semester's duration;
- The program had to be compared to matched or randomized control groups, or report year-to-year gains of at least five normal curve equivalents (NCE's); and
- The program had to show that its evidence of

effectiveness applied to students eligible for
Chapter 1 services or other at-risk students.

Applying these stringent criteria, Slavin and Madden
identify sixteen programs in three categories that show
convincing evidence of effectiveness. The three categories
are continuous progress programs, individualized instruction programs, and cooperative learning programs.

Effective Continuous Progress Programs

These instructional programs share three common features. One, students proceed through a well-defined
hierarchy of skills, are tested at each level for their readiness to move on to the next skill, and receive further
instruction on a skill if they are not ready to move on.
Two, careful records are kept of each student's progress
through the curriculum, with the data used to make
grouping, remediation, and other decisions. Three, most
instruction is delivered by teachers to groups of students at
the same level.

The following programs all incorporate the above
three features in their instruction, and they provide strong
evidence of effectiveness based on comparisons using
random or matched control groups. Some distinguishing
features of each are noted.

Distar—provides teachers with specific scripts to use
in teaching reading and math and trains teachers in
specific methods. Uses direct instruction, rapid pace, high
frequency of student responses.

Utah System Approach to Individualized Learning
(U-SAIL)—while the teacher instructs skill-level
groups, other students work on independent, exploratory
activities.

PEGASUS—a classic continuous progress program.
Organizes the reading program into 17 levels spanning
grades K-8.

Exemplary Center for Reading Instruction (ECRI)—
students receive instruction in reading groups, then work
on materials at their own rates. Rapid instructional pace,
detailed instructions for teachers, frequent assessment of
student progress.

Project INSTRUCT—classic continuous progress. Students grouped according to skill levels; proceed through hierarchy of skills at their own rates.

Goal-Based Educational Management System (GEMS)—uses placement tests or pretests to place students in appropriate instruction groups; students proceed at their own rates through 200 skill levels covering grades K-12.

Early Childhood Preventative Curriculum (ECPC)— intended for use with high-risk first graders. An individu-

---

Effective Programs Offer Convincing Evidence

Any research synthesis that identifies specific projects or programs as effective can expect an immediate reaction. Why these projects and programs? What about Program X, currently being used in classrooms nationwide? What about Program Y, which has been written up in all the education publications?

The fact is, Program X and Program Y may very well be effective programs for students at risk—but they either haven't been evaluated to prove their effectiveness, or they have been evaluated but the results aren't convincing because the evaluation design was too weak. In short, no one is saying that Program X and Program Y are *not* effective—but convincing evaluative evidence is needed before anyone can say that they definitely *are* effective. CREMS researcher Robert Slavin notes in the Slavin/Madden review of in-class programs: "It is…likely that many programs excluded from this review will prove to be effective or could be modified to be effective."

And even when convincing evidence is available, there's still reason to hedge a little. Slavin cautions: "Even the carefully selected programs emphasized in this review could prove to be ineffective in later research." The reason: the evaluative data proving the effectiveness of the program could come from just one successful site, although the implementation of the program in other sites wasn't as successful.

The purpose of research synthesis is to sum up where we are now—what we know at the present time. We know from these CREMS syntheses that instructional programs and practices exist that can show convincing evidence of their ability to improve the academic performance of at-risk students in preschool, kindergarten, and elementary schools.

alized diagnostic-prescriptive program; most instruction given in small, skill-level groups.

Four other continuous progress models are identified by Slavin and Madden in their review. These, however, were evaluated using year-to-year gains on normal curve equivalents—evidence which is credible, but less convincing than using random or matched control groups. These programs are the Weslaco Individualized Reading and Language Arts Instruction and Staff Development Process (WILASD), Conceptually Oriented Mathematics Curriculum (COMP), Coordinated Learning Integration—Middlesex Basics (CLIMB), and Outcomes Driven Developmental Model (ODDM).

> The shared features of effective cooperative learning programs are that students work together on learning activities and receive recognition based on the performance of all team members.

Effective Individualized Instruction Programs

Three features distinguish individualized instruction programs. One, students work primarily on programmed or other individualized self-instructional materials. Two, teachers work mostly with individuals rather than groups of students. Three, as in continuous progress programs, careful records are kept of student progress through a structured, hierarchical set of learning objectives.

Slavin and Madden note that many continuous progress programs describe themselves as "individualized," but they do not use self-instructional materials. Also, the researchers caution that the three individualized programs which they identify as effective have *not* presented evidence of effectiveness specifically with at-risk students. The three programs are:

Matteson Four Dimensional Reading Program—students proceed at their own rates through individualized learning packets for 40-60% of the total reading period; some small- and large-group activities carried out during rest of period. Thus not a "pure" individualized model.

Andover's Individualized Reading System (AIRS)—delivers almost all language arts instruction through programmed self-instructional materials. Teachers, aides, and volunteers give one-to-one assistance as needed.

Systematic Teaching and Measuring Mathematics Program (STAMM)—fully individualized instructional program using self-instructional materials and one-to-one instruction by teachers and aides.

Effective Cooperative Learning Programs

The shared features of effective cooperative learning programs are that students work together on learning activities in structured teams and receive recognition based on the performance of all team members; teachers instruct students who are at the same level in a hierarchy of skills, students are assessed frequently, and corrective procedures are provided for students who do not meet a preset level of mastery.

Slavin and Madden identified two cooperative learning programs that presented convincing evidence of effectiveness for all students, including at-risk students.

Team-Accelerated Instruction (TAI)—teachers instruct students in skill-level groups on concepts of mathematics; students work in their cooperative teams on self-instructional materials.

Cooperative Integrated Reading and Composition (CIRC)—uses a combination of mixed-ability, cooperative work groups and skill-based reading groups to teach reading, language arts, and writing in the upper elementary grades. Teachers work with reading groups; students work in their teams on prescribed sets of activities.

EFFECTIVE PULL-OUT PROGRAMS FOR AT-RISK STUDENTS

Effective pull-out programs, according to many critics, is a contradiction in terms. But the "supplement, not supplant" regulations of Chapter 1 have made pull-out programs the most common method for using Chapter 1 funds to provide services to at-risk students—a situation that isn't likely to change until the Chapter 1 regulations change.

But Nancy Madden and Robert Slavin note what

Making Chapter 1 Make a Difference

"How can we bring about a state of affairs in which school districts are choosing from among proven programs, implementing those programs effectively, and producing measurable benefits for their at-risk students?"

Elementary School Program Director Robert Slavin asks this question and then discusses how Chapter 1 regulations, funding, and practices could be changed to accomplish this on a national scale.

1. Establish a valid list of effective programs for at-risk students. The CREMS research is a first step in this direction, but much remains to be done.

2. Provide resources to help districts adopt effective practices. For one example, establish state or regional Chapter 1 Effectiveness Centers, staffed by personnel trained in the various effective models and in the dissemination and implementation of successful practices.

3. Fund research and development of new effective models. Several groups of researchers and developers should be funded to follow a rational sequence of development, pilot-testing, small-scale evaluation, large-scale evaluation by developers, and large-scale evaluation by outside independent evaluators.

4. Establish independent evaluation centers. These centers would oversee and assist in independent evaluations of programs conducted by state and local evaluation agencies and conduct evaluations of their own. These evaluations would be essential to ensure the credibility of program effects.

To fund this sizable, long-term commitment to the creation of effective programs for at-risk students, Slavin notes that Chapter 1 is a $3.9 billion program; that none of this money is allocated to ensure that the programs it funds actually pay off in significant improvement of student achievement; and that one penny on the dollar would mean $39 million allocated to research and development of effective Chapter 1 programs.

REFERENCE
1. Slavin, Robert E. "Making Chapter 1 Make a Difference." *Phi Delta Kappan*, October 1987, pp. 110–119.

others have noted previously—that "the important issue is not the setting in which compensatory services are provided, but the quality of the programs provided in the setting."

Madden and Slavin find thirteen quality programs when they review the evidence of effectiveness of pull-out programs according to the same rigorous criteria used to identify effective in-class programs. Of these, six are tutoring programs, in which tutors work one-on-one with identified at-risk students; six are diagnostic-prescriptive programs, in which at-risk students are carefully assessed and instruction appropriate to their needs is given by a teacher outside the regular classroom; students; and two are computer-assisted instruction programs, in which students work on computers for at least part of their remedial reading or math time.

Among these three groups, the most powerful effects—the largest effect sizes—were found for the tutoring programs.

Effective Tutoring Programs

Training for Turnabout Volunteers (TTV)—uses volunteer junior high school students who take tutoring as an elective class to tutor low achieving first-through-sixth graders in reading and math. Allows underachievers who meet requirements to be tutors. Provides considerable initial and continuing training to tutors involving a structured curriculum.

School Volunteer Development Project—adult volunteers tutor underachieving students in grades one through six using a variety of materials for a half-hour a day, four-to-five days a week. Tutors receive training in tutoring skills and use of multimedia materials.

Success Controlled Optimal Reading Experience (SCORE)—uses highly programmed materials and structured tutoring session. Uses rapid drill and practice in list of words grouped to teach specific decoding skills. Tutees are tutored for 15 minutes a day until completion of program, usually four-to-six months.

Programmed Tutorial Reading—provides one-to-one tutoring by paraprofessionals to first graders in bottom quartile in reading. Uses highly structured tutoring process with programmed materials.

Wallach Tutorial Program—uses paraprofessionals to tutor children low in readiness skills for a half-hour per day on phoneme identification skills. Tutoring focuses on having tutees break up the sounds in words.

Prevention of Learning Disabilities—screens students for deficits in sensory skills related to reading at kindergarten or beginning first-grade level. Resource teacher tutors students one-to-one or in small groups of two-to-three, three-to-five times a week.

Diagnostic-Prescriptive Programs

Project Conquest—provides remedial services to groups of six students. Early in the year, students receive one-to-one tutoring until they acquire word perception skills. Students are carefully assessed by reading clinicians and given individual prescriptions.

Oklahoma City Chapter 1 Program—assesses student skills and learning styles and gives instruction appropriate to their needs either individually or in small groups. Uses some computer-assisted instruction.

Lincoln, Nebraska Chapter 1 Program—uses a diagnostic-prescriptive pull-out model with a computer management system that handles diagnostic tests, assigns students to the program, maintains coordination between the regular teacher and the Chapter 1 teacher, monitors student progress, and evaluates student success.

Diagnostic-Prescriptive Arithmetic Program—uses a math lab approach. Provides individualized and small group activities keyed to problems identified by the Stanford Diagnostic Mathematics Test.

Columbia, Missouri Chapter 1 Mathematics Program—emphasizes coordination of instruction between Chapter 1 and regular classroom teachers. These teachers exchange forms indicating objectives that students are working on, and time is set aside for teachers to meet.

Computer-Assisted Instruction

Computer Curriculum Corporation (CCC) Reading and Math Programs—use a mainframe with terminals linked to a central processing unit by telephone. The computer records student performance levels and progress and provides students with appropriate exercises.

The CCC curriculum itself has been evaluated for effectiveness. In addition, two programs that use the CCC curriculum also present convincing evidence—The Title I Mathematics Laboratory with Computer Assisted Instruction (math curriculum), and the Merrimack (Massachusetts) Education Center Program (reading).

Basic Literacy through Microcomputers—uses microcomputers or electric typewriters to supplement teacher instruction by having students practice applying phonics skills by typing words, sentences, and stories.

> The instructional programs are available right now for school districts to launch a long-term program that will improve the academic performance of most at-risk students.

TAKING THE RISK OUT OF AT-RISK

Karweit's reviews of preschool research found preschool, in general, to have short-term effects on achievement of at-risk children. Karweit also reviewed kindergarten research and identified specific kindergarten programs that presented strong evidence of their effectiveness. Slavin and Madden identified effective in-class elementary programs; Madden and Slavin identified effective elementary pull-out programs.

The findings of these reviews indicate that the instructional programs are available right now for school districts to launch a long-term program that will improve the academic performance of most at-risk students. Begin with preschool, follow-up with effective kindergarten programs, install effective in-class elementary programs, and, if Chapter 1 funding continues to demand pull-out programs, install pull-out programs that show convincing evidence of effectiveness.

In short, provide students who are at risk of school failure with effective instructional programs at every level from preschool through elementary school.

This scenario has the potential to alleviate, for most at-risk students, the initial burden of poor academic performance early in their school careers—the burden that shows up clearly as a risk factor in later delinquency, dropout, substance abuse, teen pregnancy, continued poor academic performance, unemployment, and other outcomes.

REFERENCES

Karweit, Nancy L. "Effective Kindergarten Programs and Practices for Students At Risk." Center for Research on Elementary and Middle Schools, The Johns Hopkins University, Report No. 21, November 1987, 40 pages, $3.60.

Karweit, Nancy L. "Effective Preschool Programs for Children At Risk." Center for Research on Elementary and Middle Schools, The Johns Hopkins University, Report No. 22, December 1987, 35 pages, $4.00.

Madden, Nancy A and Robert E. Slavin. "Effective Pull-Out Programs for Students At Risk." Center for Research on Elementary and Middle Schools, The Johns Hopkins University, Report No. 20, November 1987, 24 pages, $2.20.

Slavin, Robert E., and Nancy A. Madden. "Effective Classroom Programs for Students At Risk." Center for Research on Elementary and Middle Schools. The Johns Hopkins University, Report No. 19, November 1987, 38 pages, $3.50.

What's the Truth About Tracking and Ability Grouping Really?
An Explanation for Teachers and Parents

by Paul S. George

Faced with a dizzying array of differences among the students they attempt to teach, educators have struggled with ways to reduce these differences and make teaching more effective. One very common, and "common sense," way of dealing with these differences has been to divide students into class-size groups based on a measure of the students' perceived ability or prior achievement, and then design and deliver differentiated learning experiences to each group of students. This between-class ability grouping, commonly known as "tracking" has been practiced in virtually every school district in the nation sometime during the last 120 years. Some estimates indicate that as many as 85% of today's schools still group students for instruction in this way.

> The great preponderance of the evidence on tracking says "Don't do it." Still, the great majority of schools use it comprehensively throughout elementary, middle, and high school levels.

Not only is this practice widespread, it is a singularly controversial activity. In fact, the issue of the effectiveness of tracking and ability grouping may be the single most controversial and unresolved issue in American education today. In the last half-century, there have been over 700 studies on tracking and ability grouping, more than on any other topic in education. And rarely have educational research and common school district practices been at greater variance. The great preponderance of the

From University of Florida paper, 1988. Reprinted with permission.

evidence on tracking says "Don't do it." Still, the great majority of schools use it comprehensively throughout elementary, middle, and high school levels.

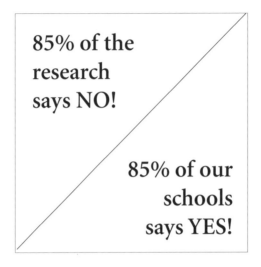

85% of the research says NO!

85% of our schools says YES!

PRETEST
Place a "T" in the space to the left of those statements you believe to be true, and an "F" for those you believe false.

____ 1. Tracking means dividing students into class-size groups based on a measure of the students' ability or prior achievement, arranging those groups in a hierarchical order, and then attempting to design and deliver differentiated learning experiences to each group.

____ 2. School practice is, for the most part, the exact opposite of what educational research says should be done about tracking and ability grouping.

____ 3. It is difficult to place students in between-class ability groups or tracks, accurately and fairly.

____ 4. Tracking frequently results in little, if any, academic achievement growth for all groups of students.

____ 5. Tracking may result in lower self-esteem for students in lower tracks.

____ 6. Tracking sometimes results in the over-representation of minority groups in the lower tracks.

___ 7. Many teachers strongly prefer to teach high-track classes.

___ 8. Prolonged exposure to low-track classes may adversely affect teachers' competencies.

___ 9. It may be more difficult for teachers to prepare for and instruct heterogeneously-grouped classes than homogeneously-grouped classes.

___ 10. The brightest and highest achieving students appear to do well regardless of the ways in which their classes are grouped.

Answers:

T (01) T (6) T (8) T (Z) T (9) T (S) T (Þ) T (Ɛ) T (Z) T (I)

THREE GOALS OF TRACKING

Tracking seems like such a sensible idea, since students come to teachers from such incredibly different points. Students seem widely differing in their ability to learn. They also appear different in their interest in learning, and in their willingness to behave in ways that are conducive to their learning and to the learning opportunities for other students. In fact, sometimes these differences seem to be the only things that students have in common!

• Identifying those differences and reducing such heterogeneity should, then, make it possible for teachers to target their instruction more accurately, and more fully meet students' needs. Teachers should be able to accomplish their tasks with greater efficiency and ease. New teachers, full of energy and enthusiasm, but less prepared to deal with the challenging curriculum of the advanced students, could become seasoned by beginning with classes of slower learners, requiring less content preparation. Experienced teachers, having put in their time as beginners, would be enthusiastic about teaching students who were exceptionally able and eager to learn.

• Students, in these circumstances, should learn better and feel more positive about themselves as a consequence of these groupings. Faster-learning students should profit from being pulled aside and would learn at much more rapid rates, being less bored than otherwise. Future leaders in science, government, and business require special handling and should learn more by being taught by teachers who had become experts in that area of content.

• Slower students, on the other hand, would be able to receive the extra help they need when they are in classes specially designed for them, taught by earnest and energetic young teachers. This would also lessen the sense of frustration and failure slower students feel when in class with brighter faster-learning students to whom they are often unfavorably compared.

The quest for a bias-free test continues.

Tracking, then, has three general goals. First, it is intended to raise the academic achievement of students above what it would be if those students were placed in heterogeneously grouped (mixed ability) classes. Second, it is aimed at helping students feel better about school, and themselves as learners. Third, teachers should be able to be more effective and enjoy teaching when students are grouped by ability between classes.

RESULTS OF RESEARCH ON TRACKING
Tracking does not appear to work out quite the way it is expected, at least not for the great majority of the students. Lets look at what we have learned about the practice of tracking.

Result #1: *Identification and placement of students into ability-grouped tracks is frequently difficult, if not impossible, to do accurately and fairly.*

Oakes (1985) identifies the serious deficiencies in the process which most schools use to identify and place students into tracks. First, educators and parents often are unaware that large differences on standardized test scores often do not equate to large absolute differences in what students know or are able to learn. When test designers build a standardized test, they must discard virtually every item that all students know, since these items fail to discriminate among test takers.

That is, a test that is going to be used to divide students into subgroups, on the basis of the differences in what they know, cannot include large numbers of items that all students know; the test has to include mostly those items that many students get wrong. What if a geography test, for example, were to discard 400 items that all students would get correct and include 100 items that many students would get wrong. Would it be fair to design classroom learning groups on the basis of the 20% of the test items that students did not know, instead of the 80% of the items that they all knew correctly? Probably not, since they have more knowledge in common than they do not.

Most educators are also familiar with the social and cultural problems of tests and related grouping decisions. The quest for a bias-free test continues. Teachers and counselors, it appears, are often unable to free themselves of perceptions which lead them to assign students to ability-grouped classes on the basis of social criteria which may have only a small relationship to ability. Misbehavior, lack of motivation, or low test scores may, for example, be completely unrelated to ability.

Sometimes parents' and students' decisions and choices regarding tracks and courses are uninformed and easily manipulated by well-meaning professionals. The result of this, and the other problems with identification of ability levels, is that students may be frequently misplaced.

Result #2: *Tracking and ability grouping do not result in consistently higher academic achievement for most students.*

Two recent comprehensive reviews of research on the effects of tracking on academic achievement point out that the expected benefits in elementary and secondary levels simply do not materialize. Slavin (1987) concludes that tracking in the elementary school has few, if any, benefits for student achievement. At the secondary level, when

differences occur, the results are favorable only to the
students in the highest tracks (Gamoran and Berends,
1987). Tracking for college bound students sometimes
appears to produce higher academic achievement for those
students, but lower achievement for students assigned to
other groups from which college bound students have
been withdrawn. For the most part, however, the research
indicates that, even at the high school level:

> ...bright students are not held back when they are in
> mixed classrooms. And we can be quite certain that
> the deficiencies of lower students are not more easily
> remediated when they are grouped together. And,
> given the evidence, we are unable to support the
> general belief that students learn best when they are
> grouped together with others like themselves (Oakes,
> 1985, 8).

Result #3: *Tracking produces no positive results in personal
or social effects.*

If the academic gains from tracking are negligible, we
could hope that the affective outcomes are positive enough
to justify the practice. Unfortunately, this does [not]
appear to be the case. The weight of the research evidence
indicates that the effect of tracking on individuals and
classroom groups, affectively, is often powerfully negative,
especially for students in low tracks.

It seems that the very act of collecting students of
perceived common ability levels in discrete classroom-size
groups may destroy the very benefits which were assumed
to emerge from the practice. In low tracks, a social labeling
process stymies progress toward improved self-esteem
which might otherwise result. As the students pass year
after year in low tracks, increasingly unsuccessful and
negative students begin to form a "critical mass of discour-
agement" which may transform the classroom climate into
one of hostility, little group cohesiveness, less trust, and
more teacher punitiveness.

Students in the low tracks resent their status, respond
defensively, and refuse to engage in the very academic

efforts which might bring them more success! Teachers, accurately perceiving the student negativity and hostility, frequently respond in ways which increase the force of those factors. Good and Brophy (1987) summarize:

> Even if teachers assigned to low-track classes do not have undesirable attitudes and expectations, they will find it difficult to establish effective learning environments in these classes because of the defeatism, alienation, and flat-out resistance they are likely to encounter there (407).

In the area of classroom climate, there is reason to believe that, as students move from the elementary school on to middle and secondary education, tracking may accelerate the process of "polarizing students into pro- and anti-school camps (Gamoran and Berends, 1987, 426)." Less successful students, after experiencing years of failure, may decide that their search for success and self-esteem may be more successful in the opposition to everything the school stands for. If success in high track classes means exhibiting pro-school behavior, then in the low track situation it may seem logical to some students to adopt anti-school behavior.

All this results, in some schools, in pro-school, high track students achieving success by following school rules, and for anti-school students, success comes from flaunting those rules. High track students find success in the classrooms, and low track students find success in the hallways and playgrounds. Even more unfortunately, such attitudes may tend to follow class and ethnic lines, hardening into peer group norms which may make it very difficult for individual minority students to be both successful in school and accepted by their peers. Expecting these students to sacrifice their friendships for school success turns out to be fairly unrealistic. As Maerhoff (1988) writes:

> At school and after school, the peer pressure against academic achievement is strong, especially on black males...fear of being accused of "acting white"

created a social and psychological pressure against exerting academic effort (636–36[sic]).

In sum, the practice of tracking appears to create school situations where students may or may not be placed accurately. Students will be in learning situations where only the top ability groups in the school profit from the arrangement and where the other ninety-percent of the students suffer from the stigma attached to their placement, from the loss of peer group leadership and models of success which have been "skimmed off" to the gifted or high track classes. Under these circumstances, students tend to polarize into pro-school and anti-school groups where teachers jockey for positions which permit them to teach high track students as often as possible. To the degree that this description is accurate, it is a dismal situation, indeed.

WHY TRACKING DOESN'T WORK

Between-class ability grouping, or tracking, is supposed to reduce student heterogeneity so that teachers can plan and deliver lessons which more nearly match the needs of each class group in terms of the pace and the level of the lesson. Educators hope that the practice improves student achievement and self-esteem, but apparently it does not do so, except perhaps for the top ten percent in the lower and middle grades, and for the college bound students in the high school.

First: Stigma

The act of grouping students by prior achievement tends to create a sort of educational "caste system" with the Brahmins and the Untouchables clearly identified. For the latter, self-esteem suffers immeasurably; for the former, an unrealistic elitism may result.

Second: Expectations

Placement into high and low groups may create student expectations which influence their achievement by adding to or subtracting from their motivation. High or low student expectations may also follow from being exposed to good models in high classes and poor models in the low track classes (Berliner and Rosenshine, 1987).

When students are tracked for most or all of the day, the power of expectations acts on teachers and students in ways which lead both to settle for less for low track students. Tracking sets in motion a vicious cycle in which teachers hold low expectations for low-track classes. Then the students, bringing the negative experiences of prior years, and encountering the lowered expectations of the new teacher, react in ways that "confirms and further reduces the expectations held by teachers" (Gamoran and Berends, 1987).

> Teachers tend to behave differently toward low-track students. They tend to slow down the pace of learning.

When teachers face high and low track classes, especially in the upper grades, they may have real reasons to expect different motivations and varying quality in the effort and work they receive. Nevertheless, it seems that teachers make far fewer academic demands on low track students, perhaps much less than they should. When the teacher expects less, this message can be communicated very subtly to the students, who then produce less and confirm the teacher's self-fulfilling prophecy. This becomes a difficult cycle to interrupt. As Maerhoff (1988) writes:

> Teachers in urban schools are confronted by a dilemma, especially in the upper grades, where the lack of earlier preparation leaves a mark of destruction on young people who are academically unprepared. A teacher who asks too much of student[s]... may not only be unrealistic, but may also be setting students up for frustration and failure (636).

Third: Different Teachers

Teachers are not randomly assigned to some mix of high and low track classes. There is reason to believe that the most experienced and sometimes the most effective teachers prefer to teach high track classes. Because of their experience and status in the school, they often do receive assignments to those high track classes, and jealously guard these assignments when they get them. New, unseasoned teachers, and those who have been identified, rightly or wrongly, as less effective are often assigned to the low track classes.

This should not be taken as an ironclad rule meaning that all teachers of high track classes are the best and all the teachers of low track classes are the worst. There must be thousands of exceptions in hundreds of schools around the nation. What do you think about this issue?

Teachers, of all kinds, do tend to behave differently toward low-track students. They tend to slow down the pace of learning. They prepare for class less vigorously. They may persist less strenuously in the face of student resistance. Students in these classes, consequently, fall further and further behind, and each year they present new evidence, to a new set of teachers, that they have, in fact, learned less and less and are increasingly unable to perform with the high track groups.

Some researchers suggest that prolonged exposure to low track classes hurts teachers, too. Teachers along with students become demoralized by remaining at the bottom of the school status hierarchy. It's possible, then, that students in low track classes may not only be assigned the least effective teachers to begin with, but that the abilities and enthusiasm of these teachers may worsen over time (Gamoran and Berends, 1987, 424). As Maerhoff (1988) points out:

> Uninspired teaching…takes a terrible toll on students who are already unmotivated. Students from advantaged backgrounds will often persevere despite poor teaching because of the rewards they expect by staying the course and earning their credentials. Delayed gratification is seldom enough to hold those who have no experience of reaping rewards… [For low track students] failure is as much a part of many classrooms as the textbooks that the children struggle to read (638).

Fourth: Classroom Climate

Students who need the most time to learn and the most positive models to emulate appear to often receive the exact opposite. For reasons sometimes beyond the control of the teacher, classes for low track students are frequently much more difficult to control, to motivate, and to keep on task, so that much more time is wasted on management issues. The students who do still want to learn get less opportunity to do so.

Some research indicates, too, that students who have experienced less academic success have much more difficulty resisting the influence of peers in their classroom. When they are in the presence of other students with a history of poor achievement, they tend to act like them. When these students are in classes with high-achieving students, they are drawn toward that behavior. High ability students, on the contrary, seem more able to resist the negative influence of their less successful peers. What about average students? It is possible that focusing attention on the high and low track groups "has the effect of making students in the middle 'unspecial' and guaranteeing that they are taught in quite 'unspecial' ways (Oakes, 1988, 43)." Of course, great teachers, good curriculum resources, and diverse methodology can produce high quality learning experiences at all levels. Oakes (1988), however, summarizes the evidence on this point:

> Many school districts persist in tracking students in spite of being informed of what the research says.

> It appears, however, that only the most extraordinary average and low-level classes match the curriculum standards, learning opportunities, and classroom climates of even ordinary high-track classes (43).

Fifth: Segregation and Stereotyping

Even if tracking produced higher academic achievement for most students (which, of course, it does not), and more positive self-esteem for all groups (which it does not), it would still be an undesirable and ineffective educational practice. In many districts tracking causes students to be grouped for instruction in ways that, all too often, result in the over-representation of poor and minority group children in the lower tracks, and majority culture and higher socioeconomic class children in higher tracks. Tracking effectively isolates these groups of children from one another, sometimes resulting in the resegregation of schools inside the building. When this happens, it must be wrong, regardless of the outcomes in instruction and self-esteem.

WHY DO TRACKING PRACTICES PERSIST?
If all of this is true, and tracking is so counterproductive, why do schools continue to track their students? There appear to be at least three good reasons why this is so.

First, tracking seems to make such good common sense that, in the absence of a knowledge of the real outcomes that research informs us about, educators do what seems to be the right thing for their students. Summaries of the research, such as this [one] should help that. The fact of the matter is, however, that many school districts persist in tracking students in spite of being informed of what the research says. Why would this happen?

Second, it is possible that tracking persists so tenaciously, in spite of the results for the great majority of the students, partly because of the parents of the small group of students who sometimes appear to benefit. Parents of the top ten percent of students in American public schools tend to be sophisticated in their understanding of the politics of school district decision-making, and skillful in their ability to influence those decisions.

These parents also tend to be among the most articulate, and the most able and willing to devote time and attention to ensuring the quality of their children's school experience. Their opinions and wishes, therefore, tend to receive a great deal more "air time," and their political weight is formidable when it comes time to elect school board members and to exert pressure on members of the school district central office. Who can blame educators [for] paying attention to what these parents say, especially when their sentiments are reinforced for years from the highest levels of the state and federal governments?

The third reason for the persistence of tracking is that it does, in fact, appear to be easier for many teachers to plan and deliver instruction to homogeneous classes. Certainly, most teachers believe this is so and, given the choice, often argue strenuously in favor of tracking, even when they learn of its effects on students and learning.

Few teachers appear to possess a natural ability to teach classes with great ranges of student achievement; even fewer may have the energy it takes even when the talent is present. Fewer teachers, still, have received effective training in teaching heterogeneous groups while in college preparation programs or on-the-job inservice education. Only the most severe critic would blame career teachers for lobbying against heterogeneous grouping strategies, when teachers believe that they may be unable to implement such techniques or that they may not have the energy and persistence required to teach that way for many years.

> Parents of all students should be informed of the effects of tracking on the quality of the academic and social experiences of their children.

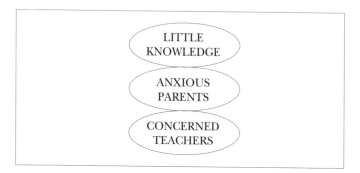

IMPLICATIONS FOR EDUCATORS

Educators are, in the case of tracking, faced with a true moral dilemma. We know that tracking does not produce any permanent benefits for many students, yet powerful members of the community wish to see these practices

continued. And many teachers do not appear willing or
able to implement instructional and classroom management strategies effective with heterogeneous classes. What
should be done?

Clearly, parents of all students should be informed of
the effects of tracking on the quality of the academic and
social experiences of their children. Community members
must also learn about what research says about this form
of ability grouping. Policy-makers must be encouraged to
reexamine the issue in light of the evidence. Share this
[article] with someone like that. In addition to this summary, the work of Oakes and Slavin are very useful.

Whenever possible, students should spend significant
parts of their school day in heterogeneous groups so that
they learn to see themselves as important members of this
diverse group. Regrouping students, within the context of
this larger group, only for skill-based subjects may then
have less undesirable consequences. When students are
regrouped, educators should be certain that the grouping
is a result of actual achievement levels in these subject
areas, rather than as a consequence of general measures of
ability or prior achievement. Frequent regrouping and
assessment of students' placements in groups should help
to make such placement more temporary and less of a
"life sentence."

Active learning should be the key in classes of all
kinds. Teachers should receive meaningful staff development opportunities in learning strategies (e.g., cooperative
learning, mastery learning) which appear to be highly
effective in heterogeneous class settings. Classroom
management strategies which permit teachers to maximize
instructional effectiveness in all kinds of classes should
have a high staff development priority. Strategies for
effectively teaching heterogeneous classes should be at the
top of future inservice education.

For various reasons, elementary and middle schools
might be expected to make the initial attempts, in school
district plans for reducing tracking. It is likely that teachers
at these levels might be persuaded to participate in pilot
projects more readily. Student differences at these grade

levels are, in reality, less pronounced than they are at the high school level.

At the high school level, there may be less flexibility until changes are made at the elementary, middle and junior high school levels. There are, nevertheless, some avenues high schools might explore. Oakes (1988) recommends that: low tracks might become "prep" courses for participating in high track classes; some one year college preparation courses might be offered over a two year period for students with less background. The number of tracks can be reduced.

High school classes composed of combined tracks might, Oakes suggests, be team-taught. Counselors could actively recruit students for inclusion in academic programs rather than only instituting screening programs which keep them out. Students who are considered reasonable "risks" could be arbitrarily placed in tracks higher than they otherwise might merit, and then supported toward success.

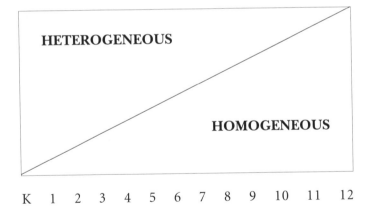

CONCLUSION

Tracking has a tremendous hold in the public schools; it is unlikely that tracking will wither tomorrow or next year, in spite of the overwhelming amount of evidence against its use. Educators and community members must become familiar with the "case against tracking." Alternatives which do not raise impossible expectations for teachers must be developed. Staff development opportunities for teachers must be more available and more effective. Realistic conceptions of equal opportunity for learning must emerge.

What's the Truth About Tracking...Really?

Tracking is an idea whose time has passed. But only the timely arrival of effective alternatives will permit educators to "untrack" the schools.

REFERENCES

Berliner, D., & Rosenshine, B. (1987). *Talks to teachers.* New York: Random House.

Brophy, J. E., & Good, T. L. (1986). Teacher behavior and student achievement. In M. C. Wittrock (Ed.), *Handbook of research of teaching* (third edition), 328–375.

Coldiron, J. R., Braddock, J. H., & McPartland, J. M. (1987). A description of school structures and classroom practices in elementary, middle, and secondary school (Report 14). Center for Research on Elementary and Middle Schools, The Johns Hopkins University.

Evertson, C. (1982). Differences in instructional activities in average and low-achieving junior high English and math classes. *Elementary School Journal, 82,* 329–350.

Felmlee, D. E., & Eder, D. (1983). Contextual effects in the classroom: The impact of ability groups on student attention. *Sociology of Education, 56,* 77–87.

Gamoran, A., & Berends, M. (1987). The effects of stratification in secondary schools: Synthesis of survey and ethnographic research. *Review of Educational Research, 57,* 415–435.**

Good, T., & Brophy, J. (1987). *Looking in classrooms,* 4th Edition. New York: Harper and Row.

Kerckhoff, A. C. (1986). Effects of ability grouping in British secondary schools. *American Sociological Review, 51,* 842–858.

Kulik, J. A., & Kulik, C. L. (1984). Effects of ability grouping on secondary school students: A meta-analysis of evaluation findings. *American Educational Research Journal, 19,* 415–428.

Maerhoff, G. I. (1988). Withered hopes, stillborn dreams: The dismal panorama of urban schools. *Phi Delta Kappan, 69,* 632–38.

**Especially useful resources!

Metz, M. H. (1978). *Classrooms and corridors: The crisis of authority in desegregated secondary schools.* Berkeley: University of California Press.

Oakes, J. (1985). *Keeping track: How schools structure inequality.* New Haven, CT: Yale University Press.**

Oakes, J. (1988). Tracking: Can schools take a different route? *NEA Today, 6,* 41–47.**

Powell, A., Farrar, E., & Cohen, D. K. (1985). *The shopping mall high school.* Boston: Houghton-Mifflin.

Slavin, R. E. (1987). Ability grouping and student achievement in elementary schools: A best evidence synthesis. *Review of Educational Research, 57,* 293–336.**

Sorenson, A. B., & Hallinan, M. T. (1986). Effects of ability grouping on growth in academic achievement. *American Educational Research Journal, 23,* 519–542.

Vanfossen, B. E., Jones, J. D., & Spade, J. Z. (1987). Curriculum tracking and status maintenance. *Sociology of Education, 60,* 104–122.

**Especially useful resources!

Authors

Jomills Henry Braddock, II is Professor and Chair of Sociology at the University of Miami in Florida.

Paul S. George is Professor of Educational Leadership at the University of Florida in Gainesville, Florida.

Daniel Gursky is Communications Associate in the Educational Issues Department of the American Federation of Teachers in Washington, D.C. He is formerly a writer and editor with *Teacher Magazine* and *Education Week*.

David W. Johnson is Professor of Educational Psychology with an emphasis in Social Psychology at the University of Minnesota in Minneapolis.

Roger T. Johnson is Professor of Curriculum and Instruction with an emphasis in Science Education at the University of Minnesota in Minneapolis.

Martin Lipton teaches English at Calabasas High School in Calabasas, California.

Jeannie Oakes, formerly a researcher at the RAND Corporation, is a professor in the Graduate School of Education at the University of California, Los Angeles. She was a senior staff member working on John Goodlad's massive study of schools and is the author of *Keeping Track: How Schools Structure Inequality*.

Robert E. Slavin is Director of the Elementary School Program, Center for Research on Effective Schooling for Disadvantaged Students, The Johns Hopkins University, 3505 N. Charles St., Baltimore, MD 21218.

Adria Steinberg is Editor of *The Harvard Education Letter.*

Anne Wheelock is co-author, with Emily Dentzer, of *Locked In/Locked Out: Tracking and Placement Practices in Boston Public Schools* (Boston: Massachusetts Advocacy Center, 1990).

Acknowledgments

Grateful acknowledgment is made to the following authors and agents for their permission to reprint copyrighted material:

Section 1
College Entrance Examination Board for "Tracking and Ability Grouping: A Structural Barrier to Access and Achievement" by Jeannie Oakes and Martin Lipton. Reprinted with permission from *Access to Knowledge*, copyright © 1990 by College Examination Board, 45 Columbus Avenue, New York 10023. All rights reserved.

The Harvard Education Letter for "The Tracking Wars: Is Anyone Winning?" by Adria Steinberg. Vol. VIII, no. 3, p. 1–4, May/June 1992. Reprinted with permission from *The Harvard Education Letter*, Gutman Library 301, 6 Appian Way, Cambridge, MA 02138. Copyright President and Fellows of Harvard College. All rights reserved.

Phi Delta Kappa for "Keeping Track, Part 1: The Policy and Practices of Curriculum Inequality" by Jeannie Oakes. From *Phi Delta Kappan* vol. 68, no. 1, p. 12–17, September 1986. Reprinted with permission of *Phi Delta Kappan*, P.O. Box 789, Bloomington, IN 47402. All rights reserved.

Phi Delta Kappa for "Keeping Track, Part 2: Curriculum Inequality and School Reform" by Jeannie Oakes. From *Phi Delta Kappan* vol. 68, no. 2, p. 148–154, October 1986.

Reprinted with permission of *Phi Delta Kappan*, P.O. Box 789, Bloomington, IN 47402. All rights reserved.

Section 2

The Center on Organization and Restructuring of Schools for "Achievement Effects of Ability Grouping in Secondary Schools: A Best-Evidence Synthesis" by Robert E. Slavin. From The Center on Organization and Restructuring of Schools, University of Wisconsin-Madison, 1025 W. Johnson Street, Madison, WI 53706. All rights reserved.

The Center for Research on Effective Schooling for "Tracking: Implications for Student Race-Ethnic Subgroups" by Jomills Henry Braddock II. From Report No. 1, Center for Research on Effective Schooling of Disadvantaged Students, The Johns Hopkins University, supported as a national research and development center by funds from the Office of Educational Research and Improvement, U.S. Department of Education.

The RAND Corporation for "Classroom Opportunities: Curriculum Goals and Instruction," excerpted from *Multiplying Inequalities: The Effects of Race, Social Class, and Tracking on Opportunities to Learn Mathematics and Science* by Jeannie Oakes with Tor Ormseth, Robert Bell, and Patricia Camp, R-3928-NSF, p. 80–101. Reprinted with permission of The RAND Corporation, 1700 Main Street, P.O. Box 2138, Santa Monica, CA 90406-2138. All rights reserved.

Teacher Magazine for "On the Wrong Track?" by Daniel Gursky, May 1990, p. 42–51. Reprinted with permission of *Teacher Magazine*, Suite 250, 4301 Connecticut Avenue, N.W., Washington, DC 20008. All rights reserved.

Section 3

The Association for Supervision and Curriculum Development for "Are Cooperative Learning and 'Untracking' Harmful to the Gifted?" by Robert E. Slavin. From *Educational Leadership*, vol. 48, no. 6, p. 68–71, March 1991. Reprinted with permission of the Association for Supervision and Curriculum Development, 1250 N. Pitt Street, Alexandria, VA 22314. Copyright © 1991 by the Association for Supervision and Curriculum Development. All rights reserved.

D.W. Johnson and R.T. Johnson for "What to Say to People Concerned with the Education of High-Ability and Gifted Students." From an unpublished report, Cooperative Learning Center, University of Minnesota, Minneapolis, MN. All rights reserved.

Section 4

The Harvard Education Letter for "After Tracking—What?: Middle Schools Find New Answers" by Adria Steinberg and Anne Wheelock. Vol. VIII, no. 5, p. 1–5, September/October 1992. Reprinted with permission from *The Harvard Education Letter*, Gutman Library 301, 6 Appian Way, Cambridge, MA 02138. All rights reserved.

Phi Delta Kappa for "Detracking Schools: Early Lessons From the Field" by Jeannie Oakes and Martin Lipton. From *Phi Delta Kappan* vol. 73, no. 6, 448–454, February 1992. Reprinted with permission of *Phi Delta Kappan*, P.O. Box 789, Bloomington, IN 47402. All rights reserved.

The Center for Research on Elementary and Middle Schools for "Research Identifies Effective Programs for Students At Risk of School Failure." Reprinted with permission of The Center for Research on Elementary and Middle Schools, The Johns Hopkins University, Baltimore, MD 21218. All rights reserved.

Paul S. George for "What's the Truth about Tracking and Ability Grouping Really?" © 1988, Paul S. George, University of Florida, Gainesville, FL 32611. All rights reserved.

Index

ADDITIONAL RESOURCES TO INCREASE YOUR TEACHING EXPERTISE . . .

The Skylight Catalog

The Skylight Catalog presents a selection of the best publications from nationally recognized authorities on cooperative learning, thinking, assessment, multiple intelligences, and school restructuring. IRI/Skylight offers several other services too!

Training of Trainers

IRI/Skylight provides comprehensive inservice training for experienced educators who are qualified to train other staff members. IRI/Skylight presenters possess years of experience at all levels of education and include authors, field experts, and administrators. IRI/Skylight's training of trainers program is the most powerful and cost-effective way to build the skills of your entire staff.

Training Programs

IRI/Skylight training is available in your district or intermediate agency. Gain practical techniques and strategies for implementing the latest findings from educational research. No matter the topic, IRI/Skylight has an experienced consultant who can design and specially tailor an inservice to meet the needs of your school or organization.

Network

An IRI/Phi Delta Kappa partnership, *The Network of Mindful Schools* is a program of site-based systemic change, built on the core values advocated by Arthur L. Costa. Each member school is committed to restructuring itself to become a "home for the mind." The network is built on three elements: a site leader, a faculty that functions as a team, and an external support system to aid in school transformation.

To receive a free copy of the IRI/Skylight Catalog, find out more about The Network of Mindful Schools, or for more information about trainings offered by IRI/Skylight, contact:

IRI/Skylight Publishing, Inc.
200 E. Wood Street, Suite 274, Palatine, Illinois 60067
800-348-4474
FAX 708-991-6420

There are

one-story intellects,

two-story intellects, and three-story

intellects with skylights. All fact collectors, who have

no aim beyond their facts, are one-story men. Two-story men compare,

reason, generalize, using the labors of the fact collectors as well as their

own. Three-story men idealize, imagine, predict—

their best illumination comes from

above, through the skylight.

—Oliver Wendell

Holmes